Power and Knowledge in Southeast Asia

Examining two state-sponsored history-writing projects in Indonesia and the Philippines in the 1970s, this book illuminates the contents and contexts of the two projects and, more importantly, provides a nuanced characterization of the relationship between embodiments of power (state, dictators, government officials) and knowledge (intellectuals, historians, history).

Known respectively as Sejarah Nasional Indonesia (SNI) and Tadhana project, these projects were initiated by the Suharto and Marcos authoritarian regimes against the backdrop of rising and competing nationalisms, as well as the regimes' efforts at political consolidation. The dialectics between actors and the politico-academic contexts determine whether scholarship and politics would clash, mutually support, or co-exist parallel with one another. Rather than one side manipulating or co-opting the other, this study shows the mutual need or partnership between scholars and political actors in these projects. It proposes the need to embrace rather than deny or transcend the entwined power/knowledge if the idea is for scholarship to realize its truly progressive visions.

Analyzing the dynamics of state–scholar relations in the two countries, the book will be of interest to academics in the fields of Southeast Asian history and politics, nationalism, historiography, intellectual history, postcolonial studies, cultural studies and the sociology of knowledge.

Rommel A. Curaming is Senior Assistant Professor at the Universiti Brunei Darussalam (UBD). His areas of research include comparative historiography, history and memory of violence, historical theory, and knowledge politics in Southeast Asia, mainly Indonesia and the Philippines.

Rethinking Southeast Asia
Edited by Duncan McCargo, University of Leeds, UK

Southeast Asia is a dynamic and rapidly changing region which continues to defy predictions and challenge formulaic understandings. This series publishes cutting-edge work on the region, providing a venue for books that are readable, topical, interdisciplinary and critical of conventional views. It aims to communicate the energy, contestations, and ambiguities that make Southeast Asia both consistently fascinating and sometimes potentially disturbing.

Some titles in the series address the needs of students and teachers, published simultaneously in hardback and paperback, including:

Rethinking Vietnam
Duncan McCargo

Rethinking Southeast Asia is also a forum for innovative new research intended for a more specialist readership. Titles are published initially in hardback.

15 **The Army and the Indonesian Genocide***
   Mechanics of Mass Murder
   Jess Melvin

16 **Political Representation in Indonesia**
   The Emergence of the Innovative Technocrats
   Michael Hatherell

17 **Power and Knowledge in Southeast Asia**
   State and Scholars in Indonesia and the Philippines
   Rommel A. Curaming

*available in paperback
For more information on this series, please visit: www.routledge.com/Rethinking-Southeast-Asia/book-series/RSEA

Power and Knowledge in Southeast Asia

State and Scholars in Indonesia and the Philippines

Rommel A. Curaming

LONDON AND NEW YORK

First published 2020
by Routledge
2 Park Square, Milton Park, Abingdon, Oxon OX14 4RN

and by Routledge
52 Vanderbilt Avenue, New York, NY 10017

Routledge is an imprint of the Taylor & Francis Group, an informa business

First issued in paperback 2021

© 2020 Rommel A. Curaming

The right of Rommel A. Curaming to be identified as author of this work has been asserted by him in accordance with sections 77 and 78 of the Copyright, Designs and Patents Act 1988.

All rights reserved. No part of this book may be reprinted or reproduced or utilised in any form or by any electronic, mechanical, or other means, now known or hereafter invented, including photocopying and recording, or in any information storage or retrieval system, without permission in writing from the publishers.

Trademark notice: Product or corporate names may be trademarks or registered trademarks, and are used only for identification and explanation without intent to infringe.

All interviewees have agreed to be quoted directly for Rommel A. Curaming's PhD thesis, titled *When Clio Meets the Titans: Rethinking State-Historian Relations in Indonesia and the Philippines* submitted to Faculty of Asian Studies, Australian National University, December 2006, on which this publication is based. Please advise the publisher of any errors or omissions, and these will be corrected in subsequent editions.

British Library Cataloguing-in-Publication Data
A catalogue record for this book is available from the British Library

Library of Congress Cataloging-in-Publication Data
Names: Curaming, Rommel Argamosa 1970– author.
Title: Power and knowledge in Southeast Asia : state and scholars in Indonesia and the Philippines / Rommel A. Curaming.
Description: Abingdon, Oxon ; New York, NY : Routledge, 2019. | Series: Rethinking Southeast Asia | Includes bibliographical references and index. |
Identifiers: LCCN 2019032538 (print) | LCCN 2019032539 (ebook) | ISBN 9781138344945 (hardback) | ISBN 9780429438196 (ebook) | ISBN 9780429796319 (adobe pdf) | ISBN 9780429796296 (mobi) | ISBN 9780429796302 (epub)
Subjects: LCSH: Historiography—Political aspects—Indonesia. | Historiography—Political aspects—Philippines. | History—Political aspects—Indonesia. | History—Political aspects—Philippines. | Indonesia—Historiography—Political aspects. | Philippines—Historiography—Political aspects. | Indonesia—History. | Philippines—History.
Classification: LCC DS633.5 .C87 2019 (print) | LCC DS633.5 (ebook) | DDC 959.80072—dc23
LC record available at https://lccn.loc.gov/2019032538
LC ebook record available at https://lccn.loc.gov/2019032539

ISBN: 978-1-138-34494-5 (hbk)
ISBN: 978-1-03-208740-5 (pbk)
ISBN: 978-0-429-43819-6 (ebk)

Typeset in Times New Roman
by codeMantra

For my partner in life, Leah; our children, Wynona Eurj and Liam Roj; my parents; and Craig Reynolds.

Contents

List of tables ix
Preface xi
Acknowledgments xix
List of abbreviations xxv

   Introduction: power and knowledge   1

1 Indonesia and the Philippines: a contextual comparison   23

2 Genesis of Tadhana project   43

3 Tadhana in political and historiographic contexts   67

4 The making of Sejarah Nasional Indonesia (SNI)   99

5 SNI: contents and contexts   125

6 The calculus of power–knowledge relations   165

   Conclusion   184

Glossary 193
Index 197

Tables

1.1	Selected Filipino and Indonesian historians	34
3.1	Coverage of the Pre-Spanish Period in Some Philippine History Textbooks	68
3.2	Outline of Tadhana	74
4.1	Outline of SNI 1975 and Members of the Team	105
5.1	Comparison of Outlines and Political Contents of Vol. 6, SNI 1975 and SNI 1984	144

Preface

The multi-volume *National History of Indonesia* (*Sejarah Nasional Indonesia*; henceforth, SNI) has not been taken seriously by scholars. It is often dismissed offhand as dubious, crude, boring, and utterly predictable. Informed that I was about to do research on SNI and Indonesian historiography, an American Indonesianist wryly told me sometime in 2003, perhaps in an unintended but unmistakably patronizing tone, "Well, one can write on one or two pages what SNI and Indonesian nationalist historiography are all about, can't he?"

Hard as I tried then to convince myself otherwise, I was gripped by fear that he might be right. At an early stage of my interest in Indonesian historiography, I gathered from commentaries, by both Indonesian and foreign scholars and journalists alike, a singular picture of the SNI project as a showcase of how the New Order regime had used history for its purpose. Just like everyone else, I held in my mind a view of SNI as exemplar of what is often perceived as an unreliable, manipulated, and self-serving kind of history, the official history.

I set out to read the original 1975 edition of SNI for the first time with this preconception. It didn't come to me as a surprise, therefore, that the military in Indonesia was showered with panegyric commentaries, while the communists and Sukarno were demonized. When I reached the narrative leading up to the pivotal event on 1 October 1965, the September 30 Movement (*Gerakan Tigapuluh September*; henceforth, G30S) 'coup' or 'counter-coup,' things flowed as expected. The economy was badly managed, politics was sharply contentious, and Indonesian society was being torn apart. Then, it came. A few pages after the narrative involving the kidnapping and killing of seven military officers by the G30S, the coverage suddenly stopped, and with it, the six-volume project ended. What happened beyond 1 October 1965 was cast in the dark. No mention of the alleged mutilation of the body parts of the generals or the supposed role of the Communist Party of Indonesia (*Partai Komunis Indonesia*; PKI, henceforth) as the mastermind of the gruesome killings. No mention either of the peaceful and purportedly legitimate transfer of power from Sukarno to Suharto or, more importantly, of the fairly remarkable economic achievements of the New Order. For a history book that practically everyone, including Suharto, regarded as the regime's official history, it struck me as truly odd that it was silent about the events or period that mattered most to its legitimacy.

Even worse for the interest of the regime, there was a key passage in Vol. 6 of SNI (1975) that ran directly against the official explanation of the G30S event, as painstakingly laid out in the publication *The Coup Attempt of the 'September 30 Movement' in Indonesia* (Notosusanto and Saleh 1968). Written by the New Order regime's interlocutors, one of whom was widely regarded as its official historian, Nugroho Notosusanto, *The Coup Attempt of the 'September 30 Movement' in Indonesia* flatly denied dissension or conflict within the armed forces as the key contributory factor. Instead, it laid the blame squarely on the supposed PKI's plan for a power-grab. This publication was produced precisely to counter the so-called Cornell Paper, a scholarly work entitled *A Preliminary Analysis of the October 1, 1965 Coup in Indonesia* (Anderson and McVey 1971). This piece constituted the earliest and the most thorough analysis of the G30S and the killings of the generals. Given that Nugroho Notosusanto himself spearheaded the group of military-employed historians who wrote Vol. 6 of SNI, it baffled me how there could be such a significant contradiction in the two official publications. What kind of official history was SNI?

Intrigued, I tried hard to look for clues. The proceedings of the planning workshop held in Bogor in 1972 clearly indicated the intent of Nugroho and his team to discuss what happened after October 1965 all the way up to the early 1970s. They also planned to exult the achievements of the New Order in contradistinction to the supposed lapses of Sukarno's Old Order. So, why did they not in fact do so in SNI? The possible reasons for this, and what they did to compensate for it, make for a rather surprising story that reveals a complex interplay between the power of scholars and the political interests of the state, as will be discussed in the subsequent chapters. In a state-sponsored project like this, one tends to expect history and historians to be manipulated or co-opted as state operatives hold the upper hand. This expectation is particularly strong in the case of Indonesia's New Order regime. Before it unraveled and collapsed in 1998, in the wake of the financial crisis, it appeared to be all dominant and powerful. It seemed to be not the case here as scholars or historical scholarship managed, to an extent, to assert their own power. It was then that I felt relieved, knowing that rather than a mere page or two, as claimed by the American scholar I mentioned above, the SNI and Indonesian historiography were worth a serious, full-length study with potentially important theoretical and political implications.

Observers have opined that the underdevelopment of local historical scholarship in Indonesia was among the key reasons for history's vulnerability to manipulation, as was rampant during the New Order era (e.g. Purwanto 2000, 2001). This idea operates within the widely held liberal assumption that 'good' scholarship and politics stand in oppositional relations. Juxtaposed with the case of Tadhana project, a very ambitious history-writing project initiated personally by the president of the Philippines and a dictator, Ferdinand Marcos, the need to re-examine SNI became, in my view, all the more pressing. Among other notable things about Tadhana project, the participation of Filipino scholars in it was underpinned by the relative strength of historical scholarship in the Philippines at that time. Such strength was manifest in the participants' ambitious scholarly agenda as well as in the confidence in their ability to withstand or deflect political manipulation. For Marcos's political purpose, the usefulness of the scholars precisely lay in their high level of expertise. Contrary, therefore, to the common idea that weak scholarship is prone to political manipulation, the case of Tadhana suggests that things were more complicated as the strength of historical scholarship made Tadhana attractive for Marcos's political purpose. Given the different socio-political and historical contexts, the contrasting position of the scholars vis-à-vis the state, the varying level of development of scholarly traditions in the two countries, and the rather unexpected outcome and dynamics of the state–scholar interaction, comparing the two history-writing projects promises to offer a more nuanced characterization of the relationship between power and knowledge.

In contemporary academic culture, particularly in area studies and social sciences, any reference to the power-knowledge nexus may be met with a polite but jaded response. Many have moved on, or at the outset stayed away, perhaps thinking that the idea that knowledge is a function (in the mathematical sense) of power is simply wrong or counter-productive, or, in a theoretical and analytic sense, already exhausted. Others who earlier on had opted to coast along this analytic flow have adopted different approaches, theories, or vocabularies, perhaps to reflect conceptual refinement or to cross new intellectual frontiers. Possibly, it was also to keep up with the intellectual fashion. On the opposite extreme, others think that the idea has long been a self-evident truth, so, there is no need for further investigation. "What else do we not know?" they may sardonically ask.

In my view, at least two reasons drive the need to examine further the analytics of power–knowledge relations. First is the persistence of analytic constipation. This refers to the tendency among scholars (and other analysts who apply scholarly conventions) to stay safe within the well-accepted boundary and to downplay, ignore, hide, or hold back certain key aspects of analysis due to unconscious or conscious effort to uphold certain analytic, political, moral, ethical, or whatever predispositions. In the case of the analysis of power-knowledge, it points to the acknowledgment of the very close, even mutually constituting, relationship between the two, but this recognition only goes to a certain point, well off the logical conclusion (For more details, see Curaming 2015). That is, that power, in a broad sense of ability to make a difference, enables, influences, or shapes knowledge, and vice versa. In short, power/knowledge. Analytic constipation is analytically convenient, but it is politically and ethically problematic because it prevents the full accounting or mapping out of all forms of power that enable knowledge production and consumption. It diverts attention away from the question of power and full accountability of agents (e.g. scholars) in knowledge production and reverts towards debates on empirical accuracy and methodological or theoretical soundness. These debates are ultimately unresolvable outside the ambit of another layer of power relations, but it is precisely this denial of the fundamental question of power that renders knowledge the power of 'truth' or appearance of facticity which makes it useful for whatever ideological shades of political use and misuse. Analytic constipation dogs even the most politically progressive, knowledge-focused critical scholars, who employ approaches like postcolonial theory, poststructuralism, cultural studies, and decoloniality movement. While they acknowledge the deeply political nature of knowledge, they hesitate to cross the line and confront and carry out the logical conclusion of power/knowledge. Following Bourdieu (Bourdieu 1990; Bourdieu and Wacquant 1989), I will try to show in this study that a possible reason for this hesitance lies in the self-interest of the scholarly class, whose power largely depends on the continued concealment or mystification of the nature and source of their power.

Second, I suspect that the partial admission of the deeply political nature of scholarship is sustained by the lack of attention to exemplary cases which typify the subtle and nuanced intermeshing between power and knowledge. I shall demonstrate that the state-sponsored history-writing projects in Indonesia and in the Philippines that are analyzed here are two such exemplary cases. The analysis of these projects draws attention to the context, mechanics, and dynamics of the relationship between embodiments of power and knowledge. It highlights the need to undertake critical analysis that foregrounds rather than downplays the collective self-interest of the scholarly class in accounting for power relations that enable knowledge production.

The main impetus for this book lies in a deep-seated anxiety about the ambivalent ethical and political implications of the well-intentioned scholarly practice, including those by the progressive or liberal strands of academia. On the one hand, the ideal of impartial scholarship is seen as an altruistic pursuit of truth for the common good, while self-identified committed or partisan scholars explicitly fight for the protection and interests of various marginalized groups. On the other, and this is often underemphasized, the same types of scholarship may also be appropriated by groups, institutions, or individuals for their selfish interests, sometimes to the detriment of the unsuspecting public. Rather than fulfill its avowed aim to help redress inequality and injustice, the patently well-intentioned scholarship could end up reinforcing or intensifying the problems (Chomsky 1997; Oreskes and Conway 2010; Rabin-Havt 2016). One is left soberly wondering, if progressive and impartial scholarship can, and often enough they do, serve the selfish interests of the unscrupulous and powerful groups and individuals, what hope is left for the marginalized? (See Curaming (2017) for a more detailed discussion.)

There are scholars, of the more conservative bent, who believe they ought not to worry about the consequence of their work. Their obligation, so this view goes, is to describe and analyze phenomenon as accurately and impartially as possible. What happens afterwards is neither their concern nor their responsibility. Such a view is, I argue, ethically untenable as it is precisely this claim to neutrality or impartiality that renders even well-meaning scholarship prone to political misuse. By its very nature, scholarship serves the interests of groups or individuals of whatever ideological shades: the rightists, leftists, centrists, or politically oblivious, each of them believe in the truthfulness and political rightfulness of their position. The salience and potency of politics from any ideological standpoint is enabled by the very idea of the existence and knowability of factual or objective truth, regardless of whether in fact such objectivity can be attained. No entity can better signify this aspiration than modern scholarship. Unwilling or not, aware or otherwise, accurate or distorted, any scholarship, just because it cannot exist in a social vacuum, can hardly escape lending a hand to a range of ideological positions. Constantly in need of self-reassurance, sophisticated political agents who care to be liked or loved, not just feared, 'shop' in the scholarly marketplace of ideas for whatever is compatible with the justificatory requirements of their political interests. They ignore or dismiss as untrue or, in contemporary parlance, as "fake news", those that are incompatible with their interests. As knowledge circulates in a social space, it assumes a life of its own. Regardless of truthfulness or falsity of knowledge claims, and whatever the intent upheld by their authors, they can give way to uses and meanings contrary to the original intent. The question of greater importance, therefore, is not whether or not knowledge is a function of power or politics, but which or whose politics enables a knowledge claim, and whose politics is supported by such knowledge claim.

The instances in which a strictly neutral position is attained mislead us into thinking that good scholarship is truly an antidote to the political. The idea is that it is just a matter of getting things empirically, methodologically and theoretically right to transcend political 'contamination.' Easily missed is the point that neutrality or impartiality (or at least the claim to, or the appearance of it) constitutes scholarship's own politics. It is what makes scholarship credible, respectable, and influential. In other words, it is what makes scholarship powerful and, in the same breath, political. It is a sort of politics of the third space. Neither leftist nor rightist, not liberal or conservative. It is a political act—a purposive exercise of power, albeit not acknowledged as such—in between, above, below, or beyond the fray. By missing this insight, well-intentioned progressive scholarship could inadvertently undermine its progressive aspirations by ending up complicit in keeping the academic-political system stacked up against the marginalized groups whom it expressly seeks to protect or fight for (Curaming 2017).

Scholars who self-identified as progressive or pro-marginalized groups purposefully offer well-intentioned counter-analysis to neutralize pro-conservative or elite-serving scholarship. This aspiration underpins the development of various strands of critical approaches—postcolonial theory, poststructuralism, postmodernism, feminism, cultural studies, decoloniality movement, etc. The efforts and the good intentions that drive these approaches are praiseworthy. However, one challenge is that political positioning—liberal, conservative, centrist, etc.—is far from being fixed. It is relational, perhaps like all other power relations. It shifts depending on the contexts of actual knowledge use, and depending on the current positions of the subject (the knower) and the object of knowledge claims (the known).

Over the course of undertaking this study, there have been three big puzzles that consumed my wonderment. First, why the urge to elide, obscure, avoid, downplay, manage, or deny the inescapability of power/knowledge despite power relations being evident, perhaps it is even a fundamental ingredient, in every stage of knowledge production and consumption? From the moment we define words; create concepts; formulate theories; gather and interpret data; write books; and let them circulate for public consumption, all these require decision to interpret and select one option over another, which means exercise of power and entering into a power relation. And, second, when power/knowledge is acknowledged, why is it only acknowledged half-way? Why the refusal to push it to its logical conclusion? Finally, if we take the logic of power/knowledge to its conclusion, what are its far-reaching implications, on both scholarly and political practice? These questions are far bigger than what this study can address. What it hopes to achieve is modest: to help keep the conversation going.

The rise of the so-called post-truth condition in the past several years has given me much to think about the questions I have noted above. Post-truth, according to Lee McIntyre, refers to "the idea that feelings sometimes matter more than facts," and "facts are subordinate to our political point of view" (2018, 11, 13). An indicator on this condition is the diminishing or loss of faith in experts and scholarly knowledge. Perhaps nothing exemplifies the post-truth condition more clearly than US President Donald Trump's disregard for the science behind climate change, calling key elements of it "fake news" and at the same time winning the support of a surprising number of people in the United States and elsewhere. Critics are quick to assume the intellectual and moral high-ground, dismissing Trump and his supporters as deplorably ignorant and offering fact-checking and sophisticated analysis as a mechanism to address the situation. They were probably thinking that with 'right' or accurate knowledge and understanding, people would come to their senses and no longer be 'misled' or 'brainwashed.' But after some time, it became clear that for people who have grown skeptical of the long-established authorities—political, intellectual, religious, etc.—no amount of fact-checking or rigorous scholarship would suffice to convince them. Hence, the idea of post-truth came about to identify the period or situation in which it has become easy for many people to accept the so-called 'manipulated,' 'distorted,' or 'alternative' facts, or even 'downright lies,' as truth in blatant disregard of the established protocols for knowledge verification used by experts or scholars (Fuller 2018).

One important point that is often missed in critiques of the post-truth condition is that the contempt for experts and scholarly knowledge espoused by the likes of Trump and his supporters applies not to all but only to certain kind of experts or scholarship: those with whose views or findings they do not agree. Experts whose findings are compatible with their views are sought, welcomed, and even eagerly promoted (Oreskes and Conway 2010). In other words, the truth referred to in 'post-truth' is not the transcendental truth (or the God-knows-it kind of reality), as often implied in critiques, but a particular kind of truth. It is from a specific standpoint (modern, scientific, and liberal) preferred and upheld by certain groups with, of course, their own interests (Poovey 1998). This brand of truth has over time been accepted and became so 'normalized,' we no longer notice the network of power that allow such truth to be upheld and sustained. When alternative sources of power arise—like the populism of Trump and the 'true feeling' (Berlant 1999) of the mass of people who believe in him—what critics obsess about are the supposed lies and deceptions and the ostensive continuous decline in people's morality and rationality (Ball 2017). As Steve Fuller argues in his compelling and aptly titled book *Post-truth: Knowledge as Power Game,* many critics had missed a very crucial point: that the extent of success by Trump and his supporters in negating the normalized truth brings to light the amount and types of alternative powers needed to create and establish alternative truth (Fuller 2018, 2016).

Therein lies the crux of the matter. Nietzsche and Foucault, among others, had long critiqued the notion of truth that was equated to factuality or transcendental truth, which was conceived in opposition to the idea of power. For them, truth is a function of power relations. Given the knee-jerk reactions to blame the 'liberal left's' postmodernism or poststructuralism for the post-truth condition (Calcutt 2016), it seems rather ironic that a possible solution lies in poststructuralists' admonition to pay serious attention to the question of power. Each truth claim needs a corresponding network and types of power to be considered by many as truth, and the power of the scholarly class is but one of the possibilities. The centuries old dominance of science as the legitimate way of knowing has conditioned scholars to normalize this way of truth-determination. But things appear to be changing. With science's objectivity-based authority being usurped by the "fake newsmakers," the solution lies not exclusively in doing more fact-checking simply because the authority of scholars has already been undermined by alternative powers. In my view, there is a need to push the logic of power-knowledge to its conclusion, to power/knowledge, to re-focus our analytic attention on the network of power relations that made knowledge claims, including science and fake news, possible and acceptable to many. Mapping out such a network of power relations will render transparent the interests that prop up, and are supported by, each body of knowledge. Arguably, this is the way to help common people to decide more rationally which claim they would believe in. Since the hesitance of the scholarly community to acknowledge fully the power-driven or political nature of scholarship is a key hindrance to power/knowledge, the task is to demonstrate in what specific ways scholarly practice may be political. It is as a part of this effort that the comparative analysis of the two state-sponsored history projects—SNI and Tadhana—has been pursued in this book.

References

Anderson, Benedict, and Ruth T. McVey. 1971. *A Preliminary Analysis of the October 1, 1965, Coup in Indonesia*. Ithaca, NY: Modern Indonesia Project, Cornell University.

Berlant, Lauren. 1999. "The Subject of True Feeling: Pain, Privacy, and Politics." In *Cultural Pluralism, Identity Politics, and the Law*, edited by Austin Sarat and Kearns Thomas, 49–84. Ann Arbor: University of Michigan Press.

Ball, James. 2017. *Post-Truth*. La Vergne, TN: Biteback Publishing.

Bourdieu, Pierre. 1990. "The Scholastic Point of View." *Cultural Anthropology* 5 (4): 380–91. https://doi.org/10.1525/can.1990.5.4.02a00030.

Bourdieu, Pierre, and Loic Wacquant. 1989. "For a Socio-Analysis of Intellectuals: On Homo Academicus: An Interview with Pierre Bourdieu." *Berkeley Journal of Sociology* 34: 1–29.

Calcutt, Andrew. 2016. "The Surprising Origins of 'Post-Truth' – and How It Was Spawned by the Liberal Left." *The Conversation*, November 18. http://theconversation.com/the-surprising-origins-of-post-truth-and-how-it-was-spawned-by-the-liberal-left-68929, accessed on 12 August 2017.

Chomsky, Noam. 1997. *Objectivity and Liberal Scholarship*. Detroit: Black and Red.

Curaming, Rommel. 2015. "Postcolonial Criticism and Southeast Asian Studies: Pitfalls, Retreat, and Unfulfilled Promises." *Suvannabhumi: Multidisciplinary Journal of Southeast Asian* 7 (2): 3–25.

Curaming, Rommel A. 2017. "Beyond Knowledge Decolonization: Rethinking the Internalist Perspective and 'Progressive' Scholarship in/on Southeast Asia." *Situations: Cultural Studies in the Asian Context* 10 (2): 65–90.

Fuller, Steve. 2016. "Embrace the Inner Fox: Post-Truth as the STS Symmetry Principle Universalized." *Social Epistemology Review and Reply Collective*, December 25. https://social-epistemology.com/2016/12/25/embrace-the-inner-fox-post-truth-as-the-sts-symmetry-principle-universalized-steve-fuller/#comments, accessed on 14 August 2017.

———. 2018. *Post-Truth: Knowledge as a Power Game*. New York: Anthem Press.

McIntyre, Lee C. 2018. *Post-Truth*. Cambridge, MA: MIT Press.

Notosusanto, Nugroho, and Ismail Saleh. 1968. *The Coup Attempt of the "September 30 Movement" in Indonesia*. Djakarta: Pembimbing Masa.

Oreskes, Naomi, and Erik M. Conway. 2010. *Merchants of Doubt: How a Handful of Scientists Obscured the Truth on Issues from Tobacco Smoke to Global Warming*. New York: Bloomsbury Press.

Poovey, Mary. 1998. *A History of the Modern Fact: Problems of Knowledge in the Sciences of Wealth and Society*. Chicago: University of Chicago Press.

Purwanto, Bambang. 2000. "Ketika Sejarah Menjadi Sekedar Alat Legitimasi." An unpublished paper.

———. 2001. "Mencari Format Baru Historiografi Indonesiasentris: Sebuah Kajian Awal." Paper presented at the 7th National History Conference, Jakarta, October 28–31.

Rabin-Havt, Ari. 2016. *Lies, Incorporated: The World of Post-Truth Politics*. New York: Anchor Books.

Acknowledgments

A work of this magnitude can only be a product of multiple efforts. The greatest debt I owe is to God, who has bestowed upon me and my family an unending stream of blessings all through these years. Given the heavy psychological inertia that had to be overcome over the past dozen years to complete this project, only through God's grace and mercy its publication became possible.

Remiss I would be if, next to God, I did not thank my wife and partner in life, Leah, without whose unconditional love and support, not to mention untold sacrifices, this project would not have seen the day. Thank you very much, Sweetie! To our adorable children, Wynona Eurj and Liam Roj, who have shared the burden of my prolonged absence, both physically and mentally, while working on this project, I am also indebted. To my parents, Loreto (deceased) and Flora, who right from the beginning instilled in me the value of learning, I will forever be very grateful. The support of my siblings and other relatives is also deeply appreciated.

I cannot thank enough the Australian National University (ANU), particularly the now defunct Faculty of Asian Studies, for the full scholarship grant in 2002–2006 that afforded me a chance to complete the PhD thesis upon which this book is based. I will always be grateful to the ANU for the four most intellectually exhilarating years of my life thus far. Indispensable was my panel of supervisors, described by an Australian scholar with the words "Wah! Hebat ya?! Pasukan berat!" (Wow! Great! A formidable force!) when I informed him who my supervisors were. Despite the differences in our scholarly orientations, or theoretical and methodological preferences, they gave me full freedom to explore, for which I was (and still am) immensely grateful. First is Prof. Ann Kumar, whose obviously irate reactions to my mixed, melodramatic, and extravagant metaphors, as well as to the grammatical, semantic, and stylistic murder that often I committed, shook the complacent in me. Not only did she instill a Spartan discipline in writing, but she also gave face to the cold-blooded brutality of the scholarly world that a novice like me cannot but cope with if I opt to stay in academia. It was discouraging and unnerving at first, but with God's and friends' help, I managed to emerge from the experience a stronger and better, not bitter, person.

xx *Acknowledgments*

I certainly did not enjoy the experience, but it served as a major turning-point in my intellectual development, for which I am honestly grateful.

To Prof. Robert Cribb, whose penetrating comments, critical questions, and painstaking attention to detail, I owe enormous debt. Along with Craig Reynolds, he has elevated criticism to a fine art: he rebukes with gentleness, castigates with concern, lambastes without palpable hostility and condescension. He sets a standard of scholarship that inspires, challenges, and ennobles at the same time.

To Craig Reynolds, God knows I cannot be thankful enough. His genuine interest in the topic right from the beginning and his faith in my capability inspired me to rise above the mediocrity that otherwise I would have easily settled in. One of my pillars of strength all through the years of doing a PhD and beyond, he made me believe that I could do things. Through the right combination of exacting scholarship, openness to new ideas, theoretical savviness, gentle encouragement, exemplary work ethic, huge reservoir of patience, emotional sensitivity, and adept administrative skills, he nurtures in a way that only a truly great supervisor can. By allowing himself to stay in the panel when the situation made him feel the urge to let go, and by doing much more than what was called for by his duty as a co-, not a main supervisor, I have earned a lifetime of debt to him that can be repaid only by doing the same thing for my current and future students. It is a very tall order, indeed. Together, my three supervisors have provided a composite of an exemplary definition of what a scholarly community is. Whatever good things in the field of scholarship and in life in general I might achieve, they certainly are a huge part of it.

To good friends and former fellow PhD students at the ANU who made my life in Canberra really worth remembering, I will always be grateful. Mary Kilcline-Cody, in more ways and to a much greater extent than she could ever imagine, had helped me through some of the most difficult months of my PhD journey. The friendship, encouragement, and companionship of the gang at the Annex of Baldessin Precint and beyond all made a lot of difference in my effort to survive the most critical months. I should also express my appreciation to John Monfries for taking on the task of proofreading and editing the draft of the thesis before submission. In this vein, I should also mention Jeanine Furino and her team at Codemantra, Angel de Asis-Tomintz, Leah Curaming, and Wynona Eurj Curaming, who kindly assisted me in the past several months in editing and proof reading this book manuscript.

I should also not forget the research fellowship grant from the Endeavour Award Australia 2008 which I fruitfully spent at La Trobe University's Philippines Australia Studies Centre (PASC). It was under the leadership of Dr. Hogan Trevor. Among other things, my brief stint there enabled me to break the psychological barriers that held me back from embarking on the challenging task of revising the thesis. It was quickly followed by a postdoctoral fellowship (2008–2010) at the Department of Malay Studies of the National University of Singapore (NUS), then under the helm of

Prof. Syed Farid Alatas. The conducive atmosphere at the NUS enabled me to jumpstart the long process of revising the thesis for publication. Had I stayed a year longer, this book could have come out as early as 2011 or 2012. I appreciate the warmth and friendship of colleagues at the Department of Malay Studies. I am particularly indebted to the inspirations, and support of Dr. Syed Muhd Khairudin Aljunied over the years. His phenomenal scholarly productivity can only inspire, and torment psychologically (wink), struggling mortals like me. The library fellowship grant from the Center for Southeast Asian Studies of the University of Michigan in 2015 also helped me gather relevant materials, and it gave me precious time to think through a number of crucial points. Also, the Critical Theory Workshop organized by Gabriel Rockhill and which I attended in July 2019 in Paris, at the École des Haute Études en Sciences Sociales (EHESS), gave me much to think about the arguments I propose in this book vis-à-vis the ongoing debates in critical theory.

I appreciate the University of Brunei Darussalam (UBD) for, among many other things, the time off in the past two years from administrative duty that allowed me almost undivided time and attention to complete this project. To colleagues and students who served as a springboard for testing a number of the not-so-conventional ideas that form part of the arguments of this book, I appreciate their feedback, nurturance and tolerance of my self-indulgent intellectual explorations. Mention I must make of Dr. Khondker Iftekhar Iqbal and Prof. Phan Le-ha who have been among my intellectual sparring partners at UBD.

For initiating me into the world of postcolonial theory, from which the seed of ideas in this study germinated, I am thankful to Dr. Goh Beng Lan's MA-level module called Postcolonial Perspectives on Southeast Asia, which I took at the NUS sometime in AY 2000–2001. It was her rhetorical question, striking for moral confidence, "Why should I feel guilty for being a scholar?" during our email exchanges in 2001 that probably led me deep into the roots of scholarly politics. In hindsight, that question struck me: how well-meaning scholars could be so blissfully oblivious to the possible dark sides of an honest-to-goodness scholarship, including ones that are avowedly progressive. It has dawned on me that the arguments in this book have developed from the extended engagement with that rhetorical question.

I am also grateful to the Ford Foundation-funded and Bangkok-based Asian Scholarship Foundation (ASF), then under the inspired leadership of Dr. Lourdes Salvador, for a research fellowship grant in 2001–2002 that enabled me to continue studying Bahasa Indonesia and do research on Indonesian historiography at University of Gadjah Mada (UGM). The University's Center for Southeast Asian and Social Studies under the directorship of Prof. Bambang Purwanto hosted my stay in Indonesia in 2001–2002. At that early stage, it was Prof. Bambang Purwanto's ideas on Indonesian historiography that fascinated me and nurtured my nascent interest in Indonesia. That was a formative experience for which I am grateful to him as it laid the groundwork for this study.

During my fieldwork that took place in Jakarta, Yogyakarta and Manila in 2004–2005, and beyond, I have earned debts of gratitude to so many people and institutions whose names cannot all be mentioned here. I am particularly thankful to scholars who took part in the two projects and who graciously shared their time and stories with me. Some of them have since passed on. Without their cooperation, this project would not have been possible. A call out to the University of Indonesia's History Department for hosting my stay there in 2005. They were all welcoming and helpful. I would like to specifically mention Mas Kresno Brahmantyo and Ibu Titi (Tri Wahyuning Irsyam), whose assistance was particularly valuable. I am very appreciative as well of all friends and colleagues at UGM's History Department. The list is lengthy, and I can only mention some here. Other than Prof. Bambang Purwanto, I must not fail to mention the late Profs. Sartono Kartodirdjo, and Adrian Lapian, as well as Prof. Djoko Suryo, among several others, who were so kind and generous with their time. They were genuinely interested in this project. It is my regret that I did not manage to provide Prof. Sartono a copy of my thesis (he requested for it), or a copy of this book before he passed on.

In the Philippines, I also incurred a debt of gratitude to many individuals and institutions, only some of whom I can mention here. First, the participants in Tadhana project who agreed to be interviewed, particularly the members of the core group, Profs. Zeus Salazar, Samuel Tan and Serafin Quiason. I am so grateful for their time and support. Second, the Center for International Studies of the University of the Philippines-Diliman (UPD), under the leadership in 2004–2005 of Dr. Cynthia Zayas, and the History Department of the De La Salle University, under the then Department Chair Dr. Ronaldo Mactal, accommodated me as a visiting fellow during my fieldwork in Manila. Finally, to the helpful staff at the libraries of the Asian Center (UPD), the Main Library (UPD), the Ateneo de Manila University, the De La Salle University, the Lopez Museum, the Ayala Museum, and the National Library, I am also very thankful.

To very good friends Dr. Michael Montesano and Prof. Patricio Abinales, who have been unwavering, in their encouragement and support all through these years, my appreciation is deeply heartfelt. I cherish the valuable comments of Profs. Caroline Hau, Ben Anderson and Joel Kahn on parts of the earlier version of the manuscript. I regret my inability to complete and get this book out soon enough before Profs. Anderson and Kahn passed on. To Prof. Henk Maier, erstwhile a colleague at UBD, I owe enormous debt for his encouragement, genuine interest, and the valuable feedback he gave me after reading each chapter of an early version of the manuscript. I cannot thank him enough. I also owe Prof. Duncan McCargo a great deal for his interest in this long-delayed book project, for his valuable editorial assistance, and for being instrumental in having it published at long last. Without his patience, support and gentle push, I would have not succeeded in overcoming my inner demons that for so long have obstructed this book's publication.

I must also acknowledge the comments and suggestions for improvement of the two peer reviewers (they know who they are) who recommended the publication of this manuscript under the Asian Studies Association of Australia (ASAA) Southeast Asia Series in 2009–2010. The subsequent turn of events prevented the publication of this book under that series, but the fact remains that I owe them as well as its former editor, Dr. Howard Dick, an enormous debt for their contributions in improving the early version of the manuscript.

A mention should also be made of the support, assistance, and friendship of Dr. Freddy Kalidjernih, whose struggle as a budding academic paralleled mine.

For all other friends and institutions that I inadvertently missed, my sincere apologies and appreciation for your contributions in making this project possible.

All these go without saying that, for all remaining errors and shortcomings, the responsibility is solely mine.

Abbreviations

ABRI	*Angkatan Bersenjata Republik Indonesia* (Armed Forces of the Republic of Indonesia)
ADHIKA	*Asosasyon ng mga Dalubhasa at may Hilig sa Kasaysayan* (Association of Scholars and History Enthusiasts);
BAKAS	Bagong Kasaysayan/Bahay-Saliksikan ng Kasaysayan (New History/History Research House)
BTI	*Barisan Tani Indonesia* (Peasants' Front of Indonesia)
DPR-GR	*Dewan Perwakilan Rakyat-Gotong Royong* (House of Representatives-Mutual Support)
EDSA	Epifanio de los Santos Avenue, one of the major avenues in Metro Manila
FH	*Filipino Heritage*
Gerwani	Gerakan Wanita Indonesia (Indonesian Women's Movement)
G30S	*Gerakan Tigapuluh September*, The September 30 Movement
IAHA	International Association of Historians of Asia
Lekra	*Lembaga Kebudayaan Rakyat*, Institute for the Peoples' Culture
LIPI	*Lembaga Ilmu Pengetahuan Indonesia* (Indonesian Institute of Sciences)
MPRS	*Majelis Permusyawaratan Rakyat Sementara* (Provisional People's Consultative Assembly)
MSI	*Masyarakat Sejarawan Indonesia* (Association of Historians of Indonesia)
Nasakom	Nasionalisme, agama dan komunisme (Nationalism, religion and communism)
NHC	National Historical Committee
NHI	National Historical Institute
NMPC	National Media Production Center
PHA	Philippine Historical Association
PHC	Philippine Historical Committee
PHRMC	Philippine Historical Research and Markers Committee
PKI	*Partai Komunis Indonesia*, Communist Party of Indonesia

PNHS	Philippine National Historical Society
PMP	*Pendidikan Moral Pancasila* (Pancasila Moral Education)
PPPP (P4)	*Pedoman Penghayatan dan Pengamalan Pancasila* (Guidelines for the Realization and Implementation of Pancasila)
PSPB	*Pendidikan Sejarah Perjuangan Bangsa* (National Struggle History Education)
PSSC	Philippine Social Science Council
Pusjarah	Pusat Sejarah ABRI, Armed Forces History Center
SNI	*Sejarah Nasional Indonesia* (National History of Indonesia), title of the six-volume history of Indonesia
SNI-SMP	*Sejarah Nasional Indonesia untuk Sekolah Menengah Pertama* (National History of Indonesia for Junior High School)
SNI-SMA	*Sejarah Nasional Indonesia untuk Sekolah Menengah Atas* (National History of Indonesia for Senior High School)
SOAS	School of Oriental and African Studies
SSK	Sociology of Scientific Knowledge, one of the branches of sociology of knowledge
SSN2	*Seminar Sejarah Nasional II,* the Second National History Seminar held in Yogyakarta in August 1970
Supersemar	Abbreviation for *Surat Perintah Sebelas Maret,* 'Instruction Letter of 11 March';
Tritura	Abbreviation for *Tri Tuntutan Rakyat*, 'Three Demands of the People'
TRD	*Today's Revolution: Democracy*
UC	University of California
UI	Universitas Indonesia, University of Indonesia
UGM	Universitas Gadjah Mada, Gadjah Mada University
UPD	University of the Philippines Diliman Campus
VOC	*Vereenigde Oostindische Compagnie* or Dutch East-India Company

Introduction
Power and knowledge

The oppositional relationship between the scholarly and the political is a widely held supposition. At its most assertive, this idea posits the ideal form of scholarship (*the* 'good' scholarship) as that which is above, insulated, or free from politics. The knowledge that it produces is assumed to be truthful, impartial, or objective. That which is tainted by politics is presumed to be manipulated, distorted and false or inaccurate. It ceases to be knowledge; at best, it is mere ideology. This supposition also asserts that scholarship transcends or neutralizes politics via rigorous application of data-gathering and analytic techniques that ensure empirical accuracy, methodological efficacy, and theoretical sophistication. In the path-breaking but apparently under-appreciated book *Politics of Knowledge,* the volume editors Fernando Domínguez Rubio and Patrick Baert call this formulation the "liberal view" of scholarship–politics relations (2012, 2). This idea has deep roots in the optimism of the late seventeenth- and eighteenth-century Enlightenment, when scientific reason and knowledge were invoked as the solution to the many problems supposedly wrought by superstitions, ignorance, and backwardness in the past. The Enlightenment notion of rationality has been doubted or critiqued since the era of Romanticism in the eighteenth and nineteenth centuries. These critiques persisted, re-echoed, and refined in contemporary social epistemology, sociology of knowledge, and critical theories of feminist, postcolonial, or poststructuralist bent. Be that as it may, the liberalist view of knowledge as a container of truth, rather than a reflection of power relations, remains widely shared by many, including both progressive and conservative scholars.

The tendency among many scholars to normalize or naturalize the supposed conflictual relationship between scholarship and politics made it easy to forget its fairly recent origins. In much of the history of civilizations across the world, political leaders usually struck a mutually beneficial if not also harmonious relationship with the class of 'knowledge workers,' such as scribes, chroniclers, priestly groups, technocrats, and scholars (Bauman 1987). The maturation in the nineteenth and twentieth centuries of the forces unleashed by the intellectual, scientific, religious, and industrial revolutions in Europe had found expression in the Dreyfus Affair in France and the strident critiques by the Polish and Russian intelligentsia, which helped pave the way for the strengthening of the notion of the autonomy of the intellectuals (Jennings and Kemp-Welch 1997). In the turbulent post-war decades characterized by the anti-imperialist and Cold War sentiments, the expectation was heightened for scholar-intellectuals particularly in the West and the rest of the non-communist world to "speak truth to power" (Said 1993). Those who are silent, consort with, or work for the powers-that-be or the 'Establishment' were seen with suspicion, if not also derision.

Against this backdrop, several scholars from the bastion of the anti-state and left-leaning activism, the University of the Philippines at Diliman campus (UPD) in Quezon City, agreed sometime in the early 1970s to participate in the ambitious history-writing project that Ferdinand Marcos, the president of the Philippines and a dictator at that time, was mulling over. This undertaking would be known as Tadhana project. Hearing about the project through the grapevine, many fellow Filipino and foreign scholars were scandalized and deeply suspicious, even livid. "How could have they sold their souls to, of all people, Marcos?!" they rhetorically asked. At about the same time, thousands of miles to the south in Indonesia, a comparable project was being pursued. Through the initiative of its 'official historian,' Nugroho Notosusanto, Suharto's New Order regime was eager to produce a 'standard' national history. It was to be called simply *Sejarah Nasional Indonesia* (*National History of Indonesia*; SNI hereafter). The initial reactions to this initiative differed from those to Tadhana project. The Indonesian public welcomed the news with anticipation, while the Indonesian scholars were rather skeptical of Indonesian scholars' readiness to undertake the task.

The contrasting initial reactions to the two projects attested to the different and complex political and academic contexts in the two countries at that time, which I shall clarify below and in the next chapter. Not long after, however, observers viewed both projects plain and simple as political tools. Undertaken at a crucial juncture of the two regimes' political consolidation, suspicions mounted that they were none other than vehicles for regime-justification or self-glorification. Echoing Julien Benda (1969), critics viewed these projects in line with the idea of the 'treason of intellectuals.'

Embedded in the idea of the 'treason of intellectuals' is the expectation for scholars to remain autonomous and to avoid serving the interests of political leaders. There is no denying that both projects may be criticized for these sorts of reasons. Katharine McGregor's (2007) *History in Uniform* constitutes by far the most thorough documentation and analysis of the military's role in shaping the history of Indonesia. It demonstrates the ways and the extent to which academic historians like Nugroho Notosusanto willfully served the interests of the regime. It also shows how the military and New Order regime used official textbooks, museums, and the monuments to justify and promote themselves. Michael Wood's (2005) *Official History in Modern Indonesia* also examines how the New Order regime sought to legitimize its rule through the use of history, focusing mainly on books and textbooks. In addition, it looks into non-official historiography, that which emanates from the Islamic community, and dubs it "history in waiting" (2005, 150). Both books depict almost a perfect congruence between the interests of the regime and the contours of Indonesia's official historiography. Similarly, the two books were silent about the agency or active role of the scholars who wrote these histories. Implicit in their analysis is the widely held supposition that in official history projects like these, historians and history are powerless, that they are co-opted or manipulated. As for Tadhana, there has so far been no detailed and serious study done of it, aside from the PhD thesis (Curaming 2006) upon which this book is based. Whenever it is talked about in private conversations or mentioned in passing in published discussion of intellectual developments in the Philippines, the tenor of analysis is in line with McGregor's and Wood's, as noted above.

This book takes a different tack. Comparing the state–scholar relations in the Philippines and Indonesia, as evidenced in Tadhana project and SNI, this book demonstrates the supposedly oppositional connection between scholarship and politics as only one of the possible permutations of this relationship. Scholarship and politics may also be complementary or mutually reinforcing. They may run parallel or ignore one another. At their strongest link, they may be mutually constitutive. It is the context of knowledge production and consumption that decides. By identifying and explicating the particular contexts, as well as the mechanism that allowed the scholars and scholarship to hold their own in the face of politically motivated pressures, and by elucidating the actual manners by which the two sides clash, reinforce, restrict, or constitute one another, this study seeks to foreground the power and agency of scholars and scholarship as well as the shifting contexts that enable the exercise of such power. Doing so shifts attention away from the long-drawn-out and ultimately sterile debates on whether knowledge is driven by power or not. Arguably, the more productive task is to address empirical questions. Whose and/or what kind of powers drive which form/s of knowledge, how, under what contexts, and why? Whose and/or what knowledge frames the exercise of whose power, in what context, and how? By addressing these questions, this book yields insights that suggest the rather illusory aspirations of the 'liberal' approach for a non- or an apolitical scholarship. By underscoring the deeply concealed political nature of scholarly practice, this book hopes to help re-orient liberal or progressive scholarship to make it more honest about its own politics and thus make it less prone to misuse. Only then can it realize its avowed promise of emancipation and empowerment of the marginalized though the use of knowledge.

Background

The two history-writing projects compared in this book, Tadhana and SNI, were carried out in two archipelagic countries in Southeast Asia: Indonesia and the Philippines. On the map, the over 20,000 combined islands and islets of these countries form a porous boundary between the Indian and Pacific Oceans. Along with Malaysia, these countries constitute perhaps the most comparable subset in the region. Together, they comprise much of what is often called the Insular Southeast Asia or, to use a more poetic and ambiguous term, the Malay World. Sharing the same geographical zone, their similar tropical climates nurture broadly similar vegetation, topography, and base culture. Linguistically, people mostly belong to the Malayo-Polynesian language family that branches into hundreds of distinct but related languages. Were it not for the colonization that saw the Philippines falling under the control of the Spaniards and later the Americans, Indonesia under the Dutch, and Malaysia under the British, a number of nationalities or polities with boundaries conforming more closely to the logic of geography might have taken shape. Sumatra and Malay Peninsula, for instance, could have formed together or each developed as independent entities; Mindanao and Borneo or Mindanao, Borneo, and Sulawesi could have done the same thing. The fact that different Western countries—with contrasting policies, length of presence and depth of impact—colonized these countries sets one of the grounds for a potentially fruitful comparison.

Both Indonesia and the Philippines underwent long periods of colonization and fought bitter anti-colonial revolutions against Euro-American colonizers. The memories of these revolutions serve as a keystone for the master narrative of their nationalist imaginations. World War II played important roles in the two countries' nation- and state-building efforts. The experience under the Japanese occupation inflamed or radicalized the two countries' nationalisms and cast a shadow over the political developments in succeeding decades (Agoncillo 1965; Friend 1988; Mark 2018). Of greater importance, both countries nurtured communist movements that were among the most developed and most active in the Third World (Hindley 1964; McVey 1965; Saulo 1990; Weekley 2001). In addition, they underwent periods of 'democratic experiments' and long spells of authoritarian rule. They expelled their dictators and had to negotiate challenging periods of democratic transitions. There were differences of course in the timing, extent, modalities, impact, and dynamics of how these features or events actually played out. As will be discussed in the next chapter, such differences make a comparison between the two cases all the more potentially insightful.

The regimes that gave rise to the two history-writing projects under consideration here emerged at about the same time in the mid-1960s, and both flourished in the 1970s. Against the backdrop of intensifying decolonization and the Cold War, this period proved conducive for the growth of authoritarianism and nationalism, not just in the Southeast Asian region but also in other parts of the Third World. This period also saw the bourgeoning interest in writing nationalist histories among post-colonial societies in Asia, Africa, and elsewhere. Given the prevailing *zeitgeist*, state-sponsored projects like Tadhana and SNI seemed not unusual nor unexpected (Bevernage and Wouters 2018). What lent these projects some distinction was the dynamic, proximate and rather intimate interaction between the state or state operatives and the scholars, making the analysis of state–scholar and power–knowledge relations potentially insightful and productive. By the mid-1980s, the Marcos regime collapsed, while the Suharto government grew even more in strength. It lingered until its unexpected demise in 1998. The contrasting longevity of the two regimes, among other factors, set different frames for public responses to the projects. It did not significantly affect, however, the logic that underpins dynamic relationship between the embodiments of power and knowledge that characterized the two projects. The next chapter provides a more detailed analysis of the contextual factors that affected the contents and structure as well as public responses to two projects.

Analytics of power-knowledge

The analytic tack adopted by McGregor (2007) and Wood (2005) follows a long tradition in the sociology of knowledge that is anchored on the dominant ideology thesis. This thesis posits the interests of the ruling classes (the state, political leaders and the elites they represent) as the paramount factor in shaping ideology (or knowledge) that is propagated through the schools, media and other apparatuses. This ideology influences subordinated classes to think and behave in ways that are compatible with the interests of the ruling classes (Abercrombie, Hill, and Turner 1980, 1–2). Called here *statism-elitism* for lack of better term, this approach appears to be the most common mode of analysis of the power-knowledge nexus.

In Asia, the long-standing controversies surrounding the Japanese textbooks, which have lingered since the 1960s, stand as examples of a statist-elitist approach (for example, Ienaga 1970, 1992; Nishino 2008; Saito 1995). A notable feature of the case of Japan is the emphasis on the strength of, in Althusser's terms, the ideological state apparatus. The focus of analysis is the state's control of knowledge production and transmission channels as well as the responses of the foreign governments and domestic civil society groups to this censorship (Hein and Selden 2000; Reedy 1999). In the Philippines, the writings of the very influential scholar Renato Constantino, such as 'Miseducation of the Filipinos' (Constantino 1966) and the two-volume synthesis of the Philippine history, *The Philippines: A Past Revisited* (Constantino 1975) and *The Philippines: The Continuing Past* (Constantino 1978), represent a Marxist line of analysis that locates the state and the elites as the fountainhead of the dominant influence on education and the mentality of the people. The highly regarded *Limits of Educational Change* by Luisa Doronila (1989) follows a similar line of analysis. With pedagogical (teaching-related) factors ruled out after finding that teachers hardly deviate from the prescribed textbooks and other curricular requirements, it shows that despite the government rhetoric pointing to national identity formation as a key aim of public education, the goal was not achieved due to the less-than-nationalistic contents of the textbooks. Doronila attributed such a lack of nationalism to the economic and political interest of the dominant class in collusion with international agencies such as the World Bank. The textbooks she analyzed were products of the project funded by the World Bank, which is an institution that "we can hardly expect to be interested in helping Filipinos acquire education relevant to their own needs," according to Letizia Constantino (1982, 21). Doronila's book demonstrates clearly how the public school system reproduces the interests of the dominant class.

Studies of Indonesia likewise offer some notable examples. Lyn Parker's (1992) 'The Creation of Indonesian Citizens in Balinese Primary School' is noteworthy for providing empirical evidence of the success of the state educational apparatus in creating citizens according to the definition set by the state. Barbara Leigh's two articles 'Making the Indonesian State' (Leigh 1991) and 'Learning and Knowing Boundaries' (Leigh 1999) reinforce Parker's arguments. By looking into the contents of the textbooks and how questions in the national examinations are formulated, she shows not only how the school system transmits knowledge that is favorable for justifying the regime but also how educational practices create among the students a mindset amenable to ideological conditioning and make them subservient to the interests of the state.

The centrality of the state also informs the analysis of textbooks in David Bourchier's (1994) 'The 1950s in New Order Ideology and Politics' as well as in Daniel Dhakidae's (2003) analysis of the state–intellectual relations in the New Order. In the same vein, the edited volume *Social Science and Power in Indonesia* argues that "the development of Indonesian social science—its very nature and character—is inextricably linked to the shifting requirements of power over time," in which the state was the most important locus (Hadiz and Dhakidae 2005, 2). This point is most starkly shown in the analysis of the role of the state in shaping history (Adam 2005) and professional social sciences associations (Laksono 2005) in Indonesia.

The transparent source of authority that is explicit in the statist-elitist approach gives off the impression that the interests of the politically powerful are determinate of the shape of knowledge. By simplifying power–knowledge relations into power=knowledge, this approach renders static, lopsided, unequivocal, and unidimensional the possibly dynamic, complex, and multi-layered interactions. While the notion of official history or military history is paradigmatic of this approach, we would be negligent if we ignored the possibility that official histories may offer a more textured approach to power–knowledge relations. Tim Cook's (2006) *Clio's Warriors: Canadian Historian and Writing of the World Wars* shows that notwithstanding the constraints under which military historians operated, their professional training enabled them to make use of historical sources in a more nuanced and balanced manner than is widely supposed. The same thing may be said of Sir Edward Edmonds, who led the writing of the monumental 28-volume official history of World War I. While this work was critiqued for being a propaganda, raising eyebrows and eliciting witty but loaded question as to whether it was "Official but not history?" (French 1986), Andrew Green (2003) reassessed the magnum opus and has argued that Edmonds was more impartial and nuanced than many had believed.

Aware of the limitations of the statist-elitist approach, other scholars have developed a more pluralistic approach. Called here *pluralism*, for lack of a more elegant and precise term, this approach gives more emphasis to the conflicting roles or interests of various stakeholders, the state and the elites being just two of them. Rather than seeing the school system or historical knowledge as a mere reproducer of, or a vehicle to advance the interests of, the dominant class, this approach sees it as a battlefield where power is contested and power relations constituted. Exemplifying this approach, Thaveeporn Vasavakul's (1994) *Schools and Politics in South and North Viet Nam: A Comparative Study of State Apparatus, State Policy and State Power (1945–1965)* demonstrates a textured relationship between politics and schooling in the former North and South Vietnam, and looks into the 'processes by which the two school apparatuses were formed and expanded in order to ascertain how they reflected and effected ideological and economic changes' (1). The author highlights a major problem with the state-focused approach discussed above when she forcefully argues that it cannot be assumed *a priori* that all "school apparatuses are state apparatuses—a premise that precludes any systematic discussion of the process by which statism took over the school system and of how the degree and form of statism changed over time" (9–10).

Lee Kam Hing's (1995) book *Education and Politics in Indonesia* dovetails well with Thaveeporn's approach. A historical study, it describes the contested character of education in Indonesia during the formative period from 1945 to 1965 when several competing forces—the state, communists, nationalists, the teachers' union, and several Islamic groups—struggled to influence the shape of educational policies. The expanding literature on 'history wars' in countries like the United States (Linenthal and Engelhardt 1996; Nash, Crabtree, and Dunn 1997), East Asia (Lewis 2017; Nozaki 2001; Wang 2008), and Australia (Clark 2008; Macintyre and Clark 2003; Sammut 2017) foreground the various centers or sources of power that compete for their preferred interpretation of historical knowledge. Several studies on the Japanese textbooks carry similar line of analysis (e.g., Nozaki 2008; Nozaki and Selden 2009).

What differentiates the first (*statism-elitism*) from the second approach (*pluralism*) is the extent to which recognition is accorded to the influence of the state and the non-state groups in shaping educational policies or historical knowledge. *Statism-elitism* emphasizes more heavily the role of the state or the dominant class, whereas the latter focuses on the multiple sources of influences. In both approaches, the roles of individuals seem ignored. What is emphasized is the process of knowledge production at the top or middle level, and it is assumed that what gets transmitted to or consumed by the general public is largely similar to what was produced at the upper-middle level. These approaches have their own usefulness. No doubt there are cases when the roles of the state and groups in civil society are dominant. However, these could also be problematic for downplaying the power of individuals to make a difference, particularly in less restricted political contexts.

The third approach, which I call *personalism*, draws particular attention to how knowledge is actually consumed publicly or privately. It recognizes the important roles of individuals in the analysis of knowledge production. A notable illustrative example of this approach is Lyn Parker's 'The Subjectification of Citizenship: Student Interpretations of School Teachings in Bali' (Parker 2002). By using various anthropological techniques, Parker demonstrates that "the process of creating national citizens in schools was, despite the homogeneous and authoritarian nature of the school system, an open-ended and potentially transforming one" (3). Studies like this stand as a corrective to the common tendency to deny individual students' agency in the face of the seemingly overpowering and monolithic school system in an authoritarian state like Indonesia's New Order. That it is possible, even likely, to 'subjectify' citizenship in a fairly controlled environment indicates that individuals should not be neglected in the analysis of knowledge production and consumption.

A certain type of memory studies that locate memory as a counterweight to history and have emphasized more the individual rather than the social aspect of remembering also exemplifies the personalist approach. This approach acknowledges the importance of the actual consumption of knowledge in the analysis of knowledge production. It also shifts the locus of power from the visibly powerful—such as the state, the elite, or various interest groups—to the individual knower. Recognizing the agency of the knower renders the act of knowledge consumption simultaneously as knowledge production. There has been an expansive literature on memory-history interface (e.g., Cubitt 2014; Hutton 1993; Olick and Robbins 1998). Much of this literature deals with social or collective memory, but that which focuses on individual memory and personal narrative is also sizable. Notable examples from Southeast Asia include several chapters in the edited volumes *Oral History in Southeast Asia: Memories and Fragments* (Loh, Dobbs, and Koh 2013), *Southeast Asian Lives: Personal Narratives and Historical Experience Personal Lives* (Waterson 2007), *Contested Memories in Southeast Asia* (Waterson and Kwok 2012) and *Beginning to Remember: The Past in the Indonesian Present* (Zurbuchen 2005).

The first three approaches identified above address the question of who or what has the power to determine or influence the shape of knowledge. In these approaches, it is taken for granted that knowledge is a handmaiden of power—something that the powerful creates, uses, or shapes in accord with their own interests. I should note that 'powerful' here refers not just to the conventionally and visibly powerful, such as the state, elites, various interest groups, and institutions, but also to individuals who assert their right to remember or know. In these approaches, the possible autonomy of knowledge as itself having power is ignored. This lack of recognition limits the range of power-knowledge interaction that may be scrutinized. Another approach, therefore, should also be noted here.

Maybe called *mutualism,* this approach draws primarily from Michel Foucault, in whose formulation power and knowledge are reciprocal constructs whose relationship is that they presuppose and constitute each other. In his words, "There is no power relation without the correlative constitution of a field of knowledge, nor any knowledge that does not presuppose and constitute at the same time, power relations" (Foucault 1979, 27). Two things set the mutualist approach apart from the three others. First, the recognition of knowledge as not just dependent on power but having its own power. Second, the role of the agents or subjects in the knowing process. The first three approaches are clear about this. The state or elite, the various interest groups, and the individuals are agents or subjects who use and produce knowledge. Foucault's concept of power/knowledge, on the other hand, is non-subject, or non-actor based. As he told us, the subject is not the one who has power; it is power that makes the subject (Foucault 1980, 98). This non-humanist stance of Foucault's power-knowledge analytics poses a challenge. Once 'applied' in analyzing empirical data, what we shall have is an untenable situation where power is exercised without an exerciser or a knowing process (or knowledge) without a knower. For instance, he described genealogy as "a form of history which can account for the constitution of knowledge... without having to make reference to a subject" (117). Since this study deals with specific subjects, such as scholars and political power holders—subjects who appear to 'have' power and to know willfully—Foucault's notion of subject–power relations can only be of limited use.

Vis-à-vis the three other approaches, the relative strength of the mutualist approach for the purpose of this study is the weakness of the others, and vice versa. Whereas mutualism is inclusive in the sense that it focuses on both knowledge and power as equally important loci of analysis, the three others put a premium on power to the neglect of knowledge. Likewise, whereas the sites of power that the mutualist approach aims to deal with are expansive, the three other approaches focus on their respective domains, which are restricted. On the other hand, in its inclusivity, the mutualist approach seems hard-pressed in dealing with differentiation— a differentiation that can only be achieved and accounted for if the subjects or agents are recognized, as is the case in the three approaches. An attempt to synthesize the two—inclusivity and differentiation—gave rise to yet another approach.

The fifth approach may have been best exemplified by Edward Said's (1978) *Orientalism*. He drew inspiration from Foucault's power analytics but rejected its non-humanist tenets. Rather than rejecting agents and subjects, Said emphasized their essential role in a political act, including knowledge production. In the case of Indonesia and the Philippines, the respective works of Simon Philpott (2000), *Rethinking Indonesia: Postcolonial Theory, Authoritarianism and Identity*, and Reynaldo Ileto (1999/2001) "Orientalism and the

Study of Philippine Politics" are notable. Inspired by Said and Foucault, these studies recognize the broader political context in which knowledge production was undertaken. At the same time, they focus on how knowledge itself, as autonomously powerful, influences the behavior or perceptions—or power—of the people. In other words, knowledge is shaped by, and at the same time it shapes, power relations between subjects or agents.

This study builds on the foundation set by the five approaches discussed above. Being a story and analysis of two state-sponsored history-writing projects, it recognizes at the outset the paramount power of the state or elites (first approach, *statism-elitism*). The two projects compared here may also be considered as sites of power struggle, as the battlefield of 'history wars' (second approach, *pluralism*), for they constitute a partnership with scholars who had different interests. They also elicited in varying degrees discordant responses from various civil society groups and individuals. Moreover, having been done through a collective effort under varying degrees of restriction, the contradictions or slippages—in the forms of fluid, inconsistent or even contradictory interpretations—in these projects indicate the agency of individual members of the team (third approach, *personalism*). On the other hand, an aspect of the Foucauldian approach, the fourth approach, constitutes a fundamental starting point of this study: the mutuality of the relationship between power and knowledge as manifest in partnership between scholars and political leaders and the mutual need for each other. Finally, the fifth approach, the Saidian approach, will inform the analysis of how power relations played out between or among actors, groups, and institutions.

Wide as the reach of the five approaches may be, there are reasons to believe that taken together they remain inadequate as tools for mapping out fully all the important sites of power play. Strikingly missing are the scholars and scholarship itself. Considering their central role in knowledge production and adjudication—being, in Bauman's (1987) words, the 'legislators' and 'interpreters' of knowledge—any analysis would be incomplete without them in the equation. Ileto, Philpott and others who traverse the postcolonial, poststructuralist analytic stream came close with their emphasis on the political act that seems inherent in scholarly institutions and scholarly practice. They seem to be not close enough, however. One proof of this is that while they expose and bewail the political character of scholarship, and while they were far from oblivious to the political character of their own critique, they did not account for their own power or political interests and factor them into their analysis. The result is that like many others before them, they stopped short of the logical conclusion of the power-knowledge relations, power/knowledge.

By underscoring the power of scholars and scholarship in the face of political power, this study seeks to demonstrate the need to break this analytic deadlock, with a view towards raising issues with possibly far-reaching theoretical, methodological and ethical implications.

Philpott's and Ileto's cases are not idiosyncratic. Their ambivalence dogs even Michel Foucault himself and Pierre Bourdieu, both of whom are undoubtedly among those who have pushed the farthest the frontiers of power-knowledge analytics. For instance, notwithstanding the fame (or notoriety) Foucault gained for explicating power/knowledge, he excluded the hard or natural sciences among knowledge that are the focus of this analysis. This smacks of setting the limits to certain forms of knowledge which may be examined as a function of power. That is, power/knowledge only to a point.

Bourdieu's stance seems even more illustrative. More deeply than Foucault, he has explored the disguised political character of knowledge and scholarship, as discussed more explicitly in his books *Pascalian Meditations* (Bourdieu 2000) and *Homo Academicus* (Bourdieu 1988). His field theory of science provides an illuminating explanation for the behavior of the scholars. As paraphrased by Frederic Vandenberghe (1999, 58), Bourdieu's theory posits that:

> The struggle that scientists wage within the field is always a struggle for the power to define the definition of science which is best suited to their specific interests which, if accepted as the legitimate definition would allow them to occupy with legitimacy the dominant position in the field. And given that there is no external and impartial arbiter, the scientific-cum-political legitimacy claims are always a function of the relative power of the competing groups.

Categorically, Bourdieu (1976, 94) has noted that it is in scholars' interest to be seen as disinterested; it is in their politics to appear to be anti-political. However, rather than conceding the possibility that all scholarly acts, including his own and science itself, may be political acts, and thus ought to be analyzed as a function of power relations, he insists on the possibility of 'trans-historical truths,' which implies that it is just a matter of employing the right scholarly approach to transcend the political. In the end, he re-inscribes the opposition between politics and 'good' scholarship. Essentially, his call for a reflexive sociology (Bourdieu 1990) signifies and entails the need for more science as an antidote to what Pels (1995) calls 'knowledge-politics.' In Bourdieu's view, "science is one way of constructing alternative categories of being that can serve as an exemplar of transgressive practices both inside and outside academia" (Schubert 1995, 1010). It is not difficult to see the merit of such a position. If science (or knowledge in general) has been instrumental in setting restrictive and oppressive limits to the freedom of individuals (what Bourdieu call symbolic violence), then it is also the way to neutralize these restrictions and regain freedom.

Ultimately, however, I think his proposal is misleading and unsatisfactory. By holding on to the assumption that the political can be transcended through a more accurate science (or knowledge), he disregards his own analysis of science (or knowledge in general) as a field governed by power relations. Rather than thinking that power relations evaporate at the moment accurate science is attained, it ought to be taken as precisely one of the enabling factors for establishing the judgment of the accuracy of science. Knowledge is a human creation; it is a representation of reality that we create to understand the real. It is not reality itself. By removing humans (or the agency of scholars or the power relations that enables such agency) in knowledge production, we are bound to overlook the power of the scholars and scholarship that serves as the glue that creates the potentially insidious partnership between power and knowledge. What makes the partnership between the two potentially dangerous and liable to misuse by individuals and groups of any ideological orientation, is the aura of credibility and the supposed neutrality or apoliticality that the undisclosed power of the scholars and scholarship lends to knowledge claims. As Bauman (1987, 13–20; 1992) has noted, the scholars and scholarship, as embodiments of objectivity or impartiality of knowledge, are often unwitting accomplices in reproducing and maintaining an unjust social order. It may be constituted and justified through authoritative knowledge, regardless of whether it is true or false. I believe that this insidious partnership between power and knowledge may be neutralized by pushing power-knowledge analysis to its conclusion: power/knowledge. This entails recognition of the power of scholars and scholarship as an autonomous field, as its own politics that ought to be factored in mapping out the unequal power relations that enable knowledge production. This is the direction to which this study points.

Conceptual issues

The whole exercise entails conceptual readjustments to the key concepts of knowledge and power. Among philosophers, there are many complex epistemological issues involved in the quest for an acceptable definition of knowledge. These are closely tied to how 'true proposition' may be identified or established, which unfortunately cannot be addressed here in detail. Suffice to note that in much of these efforts, knowledge is restricted to those ideas and/or information that have undergone or 'survived' a test of truth justification. It is in this sense that Longino (2002, 10) is justified in regarding knowledge as one of those 'success terms.' Depending on the type or hierarchy of knowledge, the requirements of such a test vary, with the scholarly and scientific knowledge being the most rigorous and thus occupying the top of the hierarchy. For knowledge to be considered acceptable, it must undergo strict processing: documentation, verification, analysis, synthesis, peer review, and continual inter-subjective assessment. Those that cannot satisfy designated requirements are relegated to the lower positions in the hierarchy. They are called by various names, such as hypothesis, opinion, belief, ideology, myth, memory, superstition, hearsay, gossip, rumor, old wives' tale, folklore, and legend. These are labels that can only imply the extent of their distance from the ideal: knowledge in the scholarly or scientific sense. In other words, as Longino (2002) argues, knowledge is a normative concept, not just a descriptive one.

To analyze the full range of the power-knowledge nexus, the conception of knowledge noted above appears to be too restricted. By limiting knowledge mainly to those that have undergone the processing machine called scholarship, we take for granted that the scholarship machine, and its scholar-operators, is a neutral instrument, with no interest (or power) to promote or pursue. Since this is not the case, as already noted above, the claim to neutrality of the scholars and scholarship and the privileged position of the knowledge they sanction should not be *a priori* accepted. The reason is simple: they are included among the sites of power that need to be examined. How scholarship has been able for so long to maintain the veneer of neutrality upon which its authority is based is in itself an interesting and crucial question. Interpreting Bourdieu, Brubaker (1985, 755) claims that "the logic of... self-interest underlying certain practices... [including scholarship] is misperceived as a logic of disinterest... (T)his misperception is what legitimates these practices and thereby contributes to the reproduction of the social order in which they are imbedded."

One consequence of the restricted definition of knowledge is the tendency to divert our focus to the methodologies or technicalities of knowledge production, downplaying, if not eliding altogether, its social and political character as well as the ethical responsibility that goes with knowledge production and consumption. Not only does this situation enable scholars to affirm and naturalize easily their claim to disinterestedness and impartiality, thus effectively concealing the sources of their power, as mentioned above—it also allows them to escape the question of accountability.

To forestall these problems, knowledge must be defined using a clean, neutral slate which can accommodate all possible attempts to represent or understand reality, regardless of whether they are in fact true or not. By doing this, I follow a long tradition in sociology of knowledge that goes back to Karl Mannheim, if not earlier, who posited that the truth-value of a statement is secondary to understanding the social context in which knowledge has come to be considered as knowledge (1936, 339). As defined, thus, knowledge simply refers to ideas or information (or a set thereof) that are believed to be true. Believed by whom? By individuals or groups who willfully exercise power to believe or to know, including scholars. This definition is very close to the idea of Peter Berger and Thomas Luckmann, who declared in their book *Social Construction of Reality: A Treatise on Sociology of Knowledge* that "the sociology of knowledge must concern itself with whatever passes for 'knowledge' in a society, regardless of the ultimate validity or invalidity (by whatever criteria) of such 'knowledge'" (Berger and Luckmann 1966, 15). However, I diverge from their too much emphasis on the sociality of knowledge. While I recognize the enormous influence of social elements, I also recognize the capacity of individuals to think and decide for themselves. In this instance, I find useful Bruno Latour's aversion towards the over-socialized conceptualization of human in the social sciences. His Action-Network Theory posits a basic premise that "society is not what holds us together, it is what is held together. Social scientists," he further declares, "have mistaken the effect for the cause" (Latour 1986, 276).

Two things should be underscored in adopting this definition of knowledge. First, I do not *a priori* assume that the social or the groups take precedent over the individual, or vice versa. Skirting around the long-standing debates on methodological holism versus methodological individualism, this move is an analytic strategy that allows a space for each circumstance—the so-called context—to determine which power, or which particular combination thereof, carries more weight. Second, whether the belief will prove to be true or not is secondary here. Just as in the case above, the imperative for the leveling of the analytic field requires that the presumption of veracity of competing beliefs, for whatever reason, and by whoever, should be made the default mode. This will allow the 'seeing' of the configuration of power relations obtained in a given situation as a determinant for deciding whether a particular claim or proposition is knowledge or not.

Power also needs to be broadly and more neutrally conceptualized. In the conventional sense, power is associated with the influential political institutions and individuals or the interest groups that operate within or against them. This is the state-centered conception of power, and this restricts the domain of the political within and around the activities of the state institutions and actors or groups who oppose or support them. Betrand de Joevenel's (1949) *On Power: Its Nature and the History of Its Growth* is a paradigmatic example of this conception. Power is considered as a sort of 'thing' possessed and exercised by actors and groups with the view to acquire and maintain or enhance it further. It is likened to an instrument that enables the few to coerce, control or limit the thoughts or behavior of the many. This conception of power is often referred to as 'power-over.'

Another approach focuses on the legitimate capacity to act, that is, 'power to.' Barry Hindess (1996, 1) notes that while this concept of power is often seen as idiosyncratic in power theorizing, it is, in fact, central to much of Western social and political theory. This notion of power is more useful for the purpose of this study, as will be clarified below.

Following Steven Lukes (1974), Barry Barnes (1988), Thomas Wartenberg (1990) and Michel Foucault (1980), among others, this study operates on the proposition that it is not sufficient to regard the 'powerful' as only those highly visible political institutions, interest groups or individuals who occupy vital positions in society. As far as power-knowledge interplay is concerned, a narrow conception of power misleads us into assuming that the state or the elite, or certain key individuals, as the only or the primary key to understanding the shape of knowledge. Since, as already noted, it is often the case that the interests of the visibly powerful do not coincide neatly with the shapes of knowledge, observers have a *prima facie* reason for dismissing offhand the power-knowledge nexus. The key is to expand the notion of power to encompass generalized capacities not only of individuals or groups but also of other agents, not all of them are easily identifiable. The operational definition of power in this study simply refers to the capacity or ability to make a difference. As an ability, power is at once a cause and an effect of a confluence of social interactions. It is circular in structure, as Dyrberg shows in his book *The Circular Structure of Power: Politics, Identity, Community* (1997), and it is knowledge, as Barnes (1988) argues, that serves as one of the nodal points that make such circularity possible.

Such a definition of power carries far-reaching implications on the concept of the political. Traditionally, the domain of the political has been confined to activities of the state and the responses of the non-state actors to these activities, which in short means it is state-centric. Carl Schmitt's (1996, 26–36) well-known booklet *The Concept of the Political* defines the political based on the distinction between friends and enemies. Effectively, it broadens the domains of the political, but it has also been criticized for not being broad and inclusionary enough. Agnes Heller (1991, 340), for one, offers an alternative: "The practical realization of the universal value of freedom in the public domain is the modern concept of the political." In my view, Schmitt's stress on conflict and Heller's emphasis on freedom (or any interest for that matter) may be combined to produce a more adequate conceptualization, such that the attainment of freedom (or any interest) may be achieved in the context of a struggle between two or more opposing groups. Both Heller and Schmitt, however, give premium to the public as the domain where the political is operative. If power is simply the ability to make a difference, it thus permeates society, and everyone has the potential to have this attribute. It follows that the private or personal sphere is equally liable to politicization. As feminists happily proclaim, 'the personal is political.' In short, the field of the political encompasses practically all facets of human interactions, but it does not mean that everything is political. It only means that everything may be politicized, and this is contingent on the configurations of various forces in a given context.

Foucault's (1980, 121) declaration that "We need to cut the King's head: in political theory that has still to be done" has no doubt contributed significantly to the broadening of the sphere of the political. By rescuing the concept of power from the confines of the question of sovereign power, he not only destroyed the walls that for so long restricted the sphere of the political as separate from the social, economic, and other fields—he also set power analytics that allow analysis of wide-ranging phenomena that were previously thought to be inherently non-political, including knowledge itself. One of Foucault's provocative points is that the political is in the social (Dyrberg 1997, 112). He did not mean to say that the state is not important, but "for all the omnipotence of its apparatuses, (it) is far from being able to occupy the whole field of actual power relations, and further because (it) can only operate on the basis of other, already existing power relations"

(Foucault 1980, 122). This is far from saying that knowledge was never an object of social and political analysis before Foucault. As early as Greek philosophers, perhaps even earlier, social and political influences on knowledge production have been mulled over. The importance of Foucault rests, among other things, on making it possible to push the effort to understand the power-knowledge nexus to its logical conclusion.

Structure of the book

The two state-sponsored history-writing projects that are objects of this study took shape in two Southeast Asian countries that are comparable: Indonesia and the Philippines. The projects germinated at about the same time in the 1970s and under the auspices of two authoritarian regimes that shared some fundamental similarities. Despite basic similarities, however, there were also essential differences in the context within which the two projects emerged. As Chapter 1 shows, the contrasting patterns of colonial experience in the two countries prefigured forms of nationalism that were more fluid in the Philippines and more hegemonic in Indonesia, a situation that informs the parameters and shapes of nationalist historiography in the two countries. It also underscores the less constrained relationship between the state and civil society in the Philippines than that which exists in Indonesia. This relationship influenced how different interest groups, including the scholars, operated or interacted with the state and with other civil society groups. Furthermore, the chapter narrates and compares the development of the historical profession in the two countries and argues that the contrasting timing or trajectory of such development has had an impact on the ways in which the scholars who took part in the two projects dealt with the state. These points are crucial in the analysis of the two projects that will be done in the subsequent chapters.

The succeeding four chapters focus on the formation and contents of the two projects and the public responses to them. Chapter 2 recounts the story of how Tadhana came about. It looks into the circumstances leading to the inception of the project. It also explicates motivational forces that led Marcos and the scholars to forge a partnership to realize the project. The main argument is that the partnership was made possible by mutual needs occasioned by the rise of competing nationalisms in the Philippines in the 1960s and 1970s. The chapter also provides snapshots of the dynamics of the relationship among the scholar-participants, and between them and the state actors who ran the project.

Contrary to the commonly held view of Tadhana as nothing more than a tool for Marcos's self-aggrandizement, Chapter 3 argues that the better way to understand it is to take it simultaneously as a political and a scholarly project, both by Marcos and by the scholars. This chapter demonstrates, first, the sharply contentious historiographic terrain within which Tadhana tried to insert itself. It shows that scholars (the core group in particular) 'perform' a political act as they pursue their own historiographic agenda. This chapter also shows how Marcos tried to appropriate the scholarly contents of Tadhana to advance his own political interests. While it is commonly assumed that the political impinges on the scholarly by distorting truth, this chapter demonstrates that the truth (or scholarly aspiration) is not necessarily antithetical to the political. Rather, truth (or appearance of truth) is enabled by the political and also that it is an important ingredient that makes the political all the more potent, which explains at least in part why history is attractive to many political leaders like Marcos. The chapter, in a nutshell, explains how the interests of the scholars and those of Marcos complemented or reinforced each other, and how they fitted into the broadly defined existing socio-political and academic order of the time.

The case of SNI is discussed in Chapters 4 and 5. Paralleling Chapter 2, Chapter 4 recounts the process that gave birth to SNI from the moment of its inception up to the time of public reactions to its publication. The context and the driving forces for the project are identified and discussed, and certain incidents are described in detail to demonstrate the dynamics among the key players. In contrast to popular accounts that depict SNI as not much more than a manipulated military project, this chapter shows that its scholarly designs managed to restrict the political interests of the regime.

Chapter 5 focuses, like Chapter 3, on the political and historiographic contexts that make the structure and contents of the project intelligible. It shows the ways and the extent to which SNI reflected the political interests of the New Order regime. More importantly, contrary to what has become by now a standard, uncomplicated, or unambiguous understanding of SNI as the New Order's official history, this chapter offers a close re-reading of the various editions of SNI. The result is a much more complex interpretation of the past as portrayed in SNI. Whereas the general perception portrays the scholars as manipulated by the New Order regime, this chapter demonstrates that scholarship-related factors, such as the use of the multi-dimensional-structural approach, the pressure emanating from the community of scholars, and the stature of Sartono Kartodirdjo, have, taken together, made a dent in the political designs of Nugroho Notosusanto. There are even passages in the 1975 and 1984 editions that directly go against the official explanation of the event involving the September 30 Movement (G30S). In short, rather than treating SNI as exemplar of the New Order regime's effort at thought control, Chapter 3 and this chapter suggest that it may better serve the function of highlighting its limits, in effect demonstrating the often unrecognized power of the scholars

Chapter 6 puts the pieces together in a comparative platform. It highlights the similarities and the differences of the features of the two projects. By showing the ways in which various actors and factors interacted, this chapter helps to map out the range of contexts and modalities by which embodiments of knowledge and power interacted in these projects. It argues that a similar logic of power relations underpins the interaction;

it is in the logistics of power—distribution and combination—that they differ. More specifically, this chapter shows that there is no inherent opposition between politics and 'good' scholarship. It cannot also be assumed, for instance, that weak scholarship is necessarily vulnerable to political manipulation, as exemplified by SNI. Conversely, a more scholarly or 'scientific' historical work is not necessarily less liable to political interests, as the case of Tadhana shows. The dynamic configuration of the individual, group, and institutional interests as they interact with the broader social forces at a particular moment set a frame within which the relationship may be defined. This chapter also offers an alternative interpretation of the state–scholar relations, as exemplified by the cases of prime movers of the projects, Nugroho Notosusanto and Zeus Salazar. Rather than dismissing them as morally flawed for allowing themselves to be manipulated or co-opted by the regime, they may instead be seen as potent agents, with their own interests to pursue and power to dispense with. Rather than condemning their partnership with the state as idiosyncratic, this chapter suggests that the logic of power-knowledge relations that undergirds such a partnership may in fact be the norm, and what makes it (and other similar cases) appear as an aberration is the well-meaning but deeply concealed political interests that promote and naturalize the 'liberal' aspirations for the presumed autonomy of the scholars. It is an act that invites morally framed attacks, so the chapter suggests, because, among other possibilities, it endangers the collective interest of the scholarly class whose power depends on the claim to being apolitical, impartial or objective. The idea behind this point is not to absolve them of moral responsibility for whatever negative consequences brought about by their partnership with the state. Critics can go on pontificating on their supposed sins or moral depravity, but the more important task for analytic purpose is to demonstrate that both sides—the critics and the critiqued—were politically interested. By rendering their political stance transparent, the public would be in better position to decide which side they take, if any.

The final chapter concludes by teasing out the implications of the suggested alternative analytic approach. It suggests in particular a more serious pursuit of the ethics of accountability in scholarly practice. That is, by claiming to be outside or above the ambit of power relations, the scholarly community as a whole (not on the level of individual scholars) in effect removes itself from responsibility for whatever consequences the knowledge it produces might have. By doing this, it unwittingly becomes an accomplice in causing, maintaining or justifying social injustice, inequality, and violence, both physical and symbolic. As this is a situation that the community of scholars often expresses that they wish to remedy, one step along this line is to recognize the hidden politics that underlies scholarly practice. What goes with power is responsibility, and to the extent that the scholars are cognizant of their power and its potentialities, they are in better position to avoid doing harm in their effort to do good.

References

Abercrombie, Nicholas, Stephen Hill, and Bryan Turner. 1980. *The Dominant Ideology Thesis*. London and Boston, MA: G. Allen & Unwin.

Adam, Asvi Warman. 2005. "History, Nationalism, and Power." In *Social Science and Power in Indonesia*, edited by Vedi Hadiz and Daniel Dhakidae, 247–273. Jakarta and Singapore: Equinox Publishing and ISEAS.

Agoncillo, Teodoro A. 1965. *The Fateful Years: Japan's Adventure in the Philippines, 1941–45*. 2 vols. Quezon City: R. P. Garcia Pub. Co.

Barnes, Barry. 1988. *The Nature of Power*. Urbana: University of Illinois Press.

Bauman, Zygmunt. 1987. *Legislators and Interpreters: On Modernity, Post-Modernity, and Intellectuals*. Ithaca, NY: Cornell University Press.

———. 1992. "Love in Adversity: On the State and the Intellectuals, and the State of the Intellectuals." *Thesis Eleven* 31 (1): 81–104. doi:10.1177/072551369203100107.

Benda, Julien. 1969. *The Treason of the Intellectuals (La Trahison des Clercs)*. Translated by Richard Aldington. New York: Norton.

Berger, Peter L., and Thomas Luckmann. 1966. *The Social Construction of Reality; A Treatise in the Sociology of Knowledge*. 1st ed. Garden City, NY: Doubleday.

Bevernage, Berber, and Nico Wouters, eds. 2018. *The Palgrave Handbook of State-Sponsored History after 1945*. London: Palgrave Macmillan.

Bourchier, David. 1994. "The 1950s in the New Order Ideology and Politics." In *Democracy in Indonesia, 1950s and 1990s*, edited by David Bourchier and John Legge, 50–62. Clayton, VIC: Centre of Southeast Asian Studies, Monash University.

Bourdieu, Pierre. 1976. "Le Champ Scientifique." *Actes de la Recherche en Sciences Sociales* 2–3: 88–104.

———. 1988. *Homo Academicus*. Translated by Peter Collier. Cambridge: Polity Press in Association with Basil Blackwell.

———. 1990. *In Other Words: Essays towards a Reflexive Sociology*. Translated by Matthew Adamson. Cambridge: Polity Press.

———. 2000. *Pascalian Meditations*. Translated by Richard Nice. Stanford, CA: Stanford University Press.

Brubaker, Roger. 1985. "Rethinking Classical Theory: The Sociological Vision of Pierre Bourdieu." *Theory and Society* 14 (6): 745–775.

Clark, Anna. 2008. *History's Children: History Wars in the Classroom*. Sydney: University of New South Wales Press.

Cook, Tim. 2006. *Clio's Warriors: Canadian Historians and the Writing of the World Wars*. Vancouver: UBC Press.

Constantino, Renato. 1966. *The Miseducation of the Filipino*. Quezon City: Malaya Books.

———. 1975. *The Philippines: A Past Revisited*. Quezon City: Tala Pub. Services.

———. 1978. *The Philippines: The Continuing Past*. Quezon City: Foundation for Nationalist Studies.

Constantino, Letizia R. 1982. *World Bank Textbooks: Scenario for Deception*. Quezon City: Foundation for Nationalist Studies.

Cubitt, Geoffrey. 2014. *History and Memory*. Oxford: Manchester University Press.

Curaming, Rommel. 2006. "When Clio Meets the Titans: Towards Rethinking State-Scholar Relations in Indonesia and the Philippines." PhD Thesis, Canberra: Australian National University.

Dhakidae, Daniel. 2003. *Cendekiawan dan Kekuasaan dalam Negara Orde Baru (Intellectuals and Power in the New Order Regime)*. Jakarta: Gramedia Pustaka Utama.

Doronila, Luisa. 1989. *The Limits of Educational Change: National Identity Formation in a Philippine Public Elementary School*. Quezon City: University of the Philippines Press.

Dyrberg, Torben Bech. 1997. *The Circular Structure of Power: Politics, Identity, Community*. London: Verso.

Foucault, Michel. 1979. *Discipline and Punish: The Birth of the Prison*. Translated by Alan Sheridan. New York: Vintage Books.

———. 1980. *Power/Knowledge: Selected Interviews and Other Writings, 1972–1977*. Edited by Colin Gordon. New York: Pantheon Books.

French, David. 1986. "'Official but Not History'? Sir James Edmonds and the Official History of the Great War." *The RUSI Journal* 131 (1): 58–63. doi:10.1080/03071848608522793.

Friend, Theodore. 1988. *The Blue-Eyed Enemy: Japan against the West in Java and Luzon, 1942–1945*. Princeton, NJ: Princeton University Press.

Green, Andrew. 2003. *Writing the Great War: Sir James Edmonds and the Official Histories 1915–1948*. London: Frank Cass.

Hadiz, Vedi, and Daniel Dhakidae, eds. 2005. *Social Science and Power in Indonesia*. Jakarta: Equinox Publishing.

Hein, Laura Elizabeth, and Mark Selden. 2000. *Censoring History: Citizenship and Memory in Japan, Germany, and the United States*. Armonk: M.E. Sharpe.

Heller, Agnes. 1991. "The Concept of the Political Revisited." In *Political Theory Today*, edited by David Held, 330–343. Oxford: Polity Press.

Hindess, Barry. 1996. *Discourses of Power: From Hobbes to Foucault*. Oxford: Blackwell Publishers.

Hindley, Donald. 1964. *The Communist Party of Indonesia, 1951–1963*. Berkeley: University of California Press.

Hutton, Patrick. 1993. *History as an Art of Memory*. Burlington: University of Vermont.

Ienaga, Saburo. 1970. "The Historical Significance of Japan's Textbook Lawsuit." *The Bulletin Concerned of Asian Scholars* 2 (4): 3–12.

———. 1992. *Truth in Textbooks, Freedom in Education, Peace for Children*. Tokyo: NSLTS.

Ileto, Reynaldo. 2001. "Orientalism and the Study of Philippine Politics." *Philippine Political Science Journal* 22 (45): 1–32. https://doi.org/10.1080/01154451.2001.9754223.

Jennings, Jeremy, and Tony Kemp-Welch, eds. 1997. *Intellectuals in Politics: From the Dreyfus Affair to Salman Rushdie*. London: Routledge.

Joevenel, Bertrand de. 1949. *On Power: Its Nature and the History of Its Growth*. Translated by J.F Hungtington. New York: The Viking Press.

Laksono, Paschalis Maria. 2005. "Social Sciences Associations." In *Social Science and Power in Indonesia*, edited by Vedi Hadiz and Daniel Dhakidae, 221–246. Jakarta: Equinox Publishing & ISEAS.

Latour, Bruno. 1986. "The Powers of Association." In *Power, Action and Belief: A New Sociology of Knowledge?*, edited by John Law. London: Routledge & Kegan Paul.

Lee, Kam Hing. 1995. *Education and Politics in Indonesia: 1945–1965*. Kuala Lumpur: University of Malaya Press.

Leigh, Barbara. 1991. "Making the Indonesian State: The Role of School Texts." *Review of Indonesian and Malaysian Affairs* 25 (1): 17–43.
———. 1999. "Learning and Knowing Boundaries: Schooling in New Order Indonesia." *Sojourn: Journal of Social Issues in Southeast Asia* 14 (1): 34–56.
Lewis, Michael, ed. 2017. *"History Wars" and Reconciliation in Japan and Korea: The Roles of Historians, Artists and Activists*. New York: Palgrave Macmillan.
Linenthal, Edward, and Tom Engelhardt, eds. 1996. *History Wars: The Enola Gay and Other Battles for the American Past*. New York: Metropolitan Books.
Loh Kah Seng, Stephen Dobbs, and Ernest Koh, eds. 2013. *Oral History in Southeast Asia: Memories and Fragments*. Basingstoke: Palgrave Macmillan.
Longino, Helen. 2002. *The Fate of Knowledge*. Princeton, NJ: Princeton University Press.
Lukes, Steven. 1974. *Power: A Radical View*. London: Macmillan.
Macintyre, Stuart, and Anna Clark. 2003. *The History Wars*. Carlton, VIC: Melbourne University Press.
Mannheim, Karl. 1936. *Ideology and Utopia: An Introduction to the Sociology of Knowledge*. Translated by Louis Wirth and Edward Shils. London and Henley: Routledge & Kegan Paul.
Mark, Ethan. 2018. *Japan's Occupation of Java in the Second World War: A Transnational History*. London: Bloomsbury Academic.
McCarthy, E. Doyle. 1996. *Knowledge as Culture: The New Sociology of Knowledge*. New York: Routledge.
McGregor, Katharine. 2007. *History in Uniform: Military Ideology and the Construction of Indonesia's Past*. Southeast Asia Publications Series. Singapore: NUS Press.
McVey, Ruth. 1965. *The Rise of Indonesian Communism*. Ithaca, NY: Cornell University Press.
Nash, Gary, Charlotte Crabtree, and Ross Dunn. 1997. *History on Trial: Culture Wars and the Teaching of the Past*. New York: A.A. Knopf.
Nishino, Ryota. 2008. "The Political Economy of the Textbook in Japan, with Particular Focus on Middle-School History Textbooks, Ca. 1945–1995." *Internationale Schulbuchforschung* 30 (1): 487–514. https://www.jstor.org/stable/43057356
Nozaki, Yoshiko. 2001. "Japanese Politics and History Textbooks Controversy, 1982–2001." *International Journal of Educational Research* 37 (6–7): 603–622.
———. 2008. *War Memory, Nationalism and Education in Post-War Japan, 1945–2007: The Japanese History Textbook Controversy and Ienaga Saburo's Court Challenges*. London/New York: Routledge.
Nozaki, Yoshiko, and Mark Selden. 2009. "Japanese Textbook Controversies, Nationalism, and Historical Memory: Intra- and Inter-National Conflicts." *The Asia-Pacific Journal* 24 (5). www.japanfocus.org/site/make_pdf/3173.
Olick, Jeffrey, and Joyce Robbins. 1998. "Social Memory Studies: From 'Collective Memory' to the Historical Sociology of Mnemonic Practices." *Annual Review of Sociology* 24: 105–140.
Parker, Lyn. 1992. "The Creation of Indonesian Citizens in Balinese Primary Schools." *Review of Indonesian and Malaysian Affairs*, 26: 42–70.
———. 2002. "The Subjectification of Citizenship: Student Interpretations of School Teachings in Bali." *Asian Studies Review* 26 (1): 3–37. doi:10.1080/10357820208713329.

Pels, Dick. 1995. "Knowledge Politics and Anti-Politics: Toward a Critical Appraisal of Bourdieu's Concept of Intellectual Autonomy." *Theory and Society* 24 (1): 79–104. doi:10.1007/BF00993323.

Philpott, Simon. 2000. *Rethinking Indonesia: Postcolonial Theory, Authoritarianism and Identity.* New York: Macmillan.

Reedy, Sean Matthew. 1999. "Mechanisms of State Control: An Historical Study of the Treatment of the Pacific War in Japanese High School History Textbooks from 1945 to 1995." PhD diss., University of San Francisco.

Rubio, Fernando Domínguez, and Patrick Baert. 2012. "Politics of Knowledge: An Introduction." In *The Politics of Knowledge*, edited by Fernando Domínguez Rubio and Patrick Baert, 1–10. London and New York: Routledge.

Said, Edward. 1978. *Orientalism.* London: Routledge and Kegan Paul.

———. 1993. "The Reith Lectures: Speaking Truth to Power." *Independent*, July 22. www.independent.co.uk/life-style/the-reith-lectures-speaking-truth-to-power-in-his-penultimate-reith-lecture-edward-said-considers-1486359.html

Saito, Yutaka. 1995. "The History and Function of Textbook Regulation in Japan." *Japanese Studies* 15 (3): 10–20. doi:10.1080/10371399508521826.

Sammut, Jeremy. 2017. *The History Wars Matter.* CIS Occasional Paper 159. Sydney, NSW: The Centre for Independent Studies.

Schmitt, Carl. 1996. *The Concept of the Political.* Chicago: University of Chicago Press.

Schubert, Daniel. 1995. "From a Politics of Transgression toward an Ethics of Reflexivity: Foucault, Bourdieu and Academic Practice." *American Behavioral Scientist* 38 (7): 1003–1017.

Saulo, Alfredo B. 1990. *Communism in the Philippines: An Introduction.* Quezon City: Ateneo de Manila University Press.

Thaveeporn, Vasavakul. 1994. "Schools and Politics in South and North Vietnam: A Comparative Study of State Apparatus, State Policy and State Power: 1945–1965." PhD diss., Cornell University.

Vandenberghe, Frederic. 1999. "'The Real Is Relational': An Epistemological Analysis of Pierre Bourdieu's Generative Structuralism." *Sociological Theory* 17 (1): 32–67.

Wang, Zheng. 2008. "National Humiliation, History Education, and the Politics of Historical Memory: Patriotic Education Campaign in China." *International Studies Quarterly* 52 (4): 783–806. doi:10.1111/j.1468-2478.2008.00526.x.

Wartenberg, Thomas. 1990. *The Forms of Power: From Domination to Transformation.* Philadelphia, PA: Temple University Press.

Waterson, Roxana, ed. 2007. *Southeast Asian Lives: Personal Narratives and Historical Experience.* Singapore: NUS Press.

Waterson, Roxana, and Kian Woon Kwok, eds. 2012. *Contestations of Memory in Southeast Asia.* Singapore: NUS Press.

Weekley, Kathleen. 2001. *The Communist Party of the Philippines, 1968–1993: A Story of Its Theory and Practice.* Quezon City: University of the Philippines Press.

Wood, Michael. 2005. *Official History in Modern Indonesia: New Order Perceptions and Counterviews.* Social, Economic, and Political Studies of the Middle East and Asia, v. 99. Leiden: Brill.

Zurbuchen, Mary Sabina, ed. 2005. *Beginning to Remember: The Past in the Indonesian Present.* Seattle: University of Washington Press.

1 Indonesia and the Philippines
A contextual comparison[1]

As a Filipino, I had a shock of recognition when I stayed in Indonesia for the first time in 2001. Indonesians did not just look the same as many of my compatriots. They also seemed to behave and think in similar ways: laughed at the same styles of jokes; slighted by comparable types of insults; and enjoyed or hated, depending mainly on class, comparable tacky ghost stories and mushy telenovelas. Filipinos also seem to share Indonesians' propensity for religiosity and fatalism, as well as a laid-back lifestyle. They appeared to me as strikingly tolerant of, or resilient to, inefficiency, poverty, injustice and inequality. Apart from within the religious sphere (I am a Catholic), I hardly felt far from 'home.'

Impressions of difference also stood out. Growing up in a country where nationalism was at best confused or ambivalent, I felt Indonesians were generally more at ease with their nationalism. It seemed as natural and clear-cut to them as it was contrived and ambivalent to me. Despite the much greater geographic and demographic challenges and ethnic diversity, nation-building in Indonesia seemed to me had been more successfully accomplished than it had been in the Philippines. The complex set of explanations for these similarities and differences deserves some scrutiny. "Indonesia and the Philippines are the same enough to be put together, but different enough to make comparison interesting," as Pringle perceptively observed (1980, 1).

The reference I have made here to my admittedly subjective and personal experience in and of Indonesia is strategic. It flags my subject-position as analyst: a Tagalog Filipino of middle-class background; a Catholic of liberal spirituality; rurally born and raised, but now urban- and overseas-based. I am a transnationally-oriented academic contract worker and a family man of libertarian personal aspirations and liberal public–political orientation. As an academic, I acknowledge the deeply concealed political nature of scholars' aspiration for autonomy or impartiality. Such disclosures are meant to serve the purpose of full transparency, not to excuse or justify my own partialities. My intellectual, political, and personal background are among the sources of my biases. They bear on my analytic proclivities in general, and on my views of Indonesia and the Philippines in particular. Of equal importance, I explicitly waive the right to absolve myself of any responsibility for whatever possible adverse consequences my analysis might have. I undertake this study with full awareness that, despite all my good intentions as a scholar, my interpretations and the empirical supporting data presented here may be appropriated by anyone or any group for their own interests, both self-serving and altruistic.

This chapter seeks to compare the contextual factors—historical, political, institutional and academic—that are most relevant to the narrative and analysis carried out in this book. No attempt at a comprehensive comparison between Indonesia and the Philippines is offered here. The focus is limited to areas that have a direct bearing on the analyses and arguments being developed in this book. First is the pattern of colonization and the nationalist responses to it; second, the state-formation, state–society relations and the contrasting fate of the anti-state actors, the communist and other left-leaning parties in the two countries; and finally, the patterns of development of the two countries' nationalist historiography and historical professions. The main task is to demonstrate that the contrasting colonial experience, processes of state-formation and roles of the left in the two countries reflected or paved the way for a less hegemonic nationalism and less restrictive state–civil society relations in the Philippines than in Indonesia in the 1970s and 1980s, the period when the two projects analyzed here took shape. These factors have had important repercussions on the development of historical scholarship and the relationship between state and scholars in the two countries during the period under consideration, and perhaps even beyond.

Patterns of colonization and nationalist responses

While the idea of 300 years of Dutch colonization of Indonesia has long been debunked as a myth (Resink 1968), it is true that parts of what came to be called the Philippines and Indonesia were under the control of Westerners for about three centuries. The first Spanish expedition reached the area in the 1520s, and starting from the 1560s the Spanish presence gradually began to expand and eventually took root in the lowland areas of the Philippines. The Dutch, on the other hand, established themselves in Indonesia on a piecemeal basis, depending initially on the Dutch East India Company's economic interests: Maluku and Batavia (Jakarta) regions from the early seventeenth century, the whole of Java in the eighteenth century, a large part of Sumatra in the nineteenth century and the rest of the country by the early twentieth century.

The enormous size of Indonesia, spread out as it is across three time zones, made it so much less manageable or penetrable than the Philippines. With a land area less than one-sixth of Indonesia's, the Philippine archipelago was not only considerably smaller but also much more compact. Additionally, Dutch colonial activities, being primarily focused on commerce, at least in the first two centuries, proved less intrusive to the core cultures of the indigenous population. The socio-cultural life of a significant portion of the population in Indonesia began to be more deeply affected only in the late eighteenth and early nineteenth centuries, with the intensification of economic activity, and the implementation of the Ethical Policy in the early 1900s. The Ethical Policy was an ambitious socio-economic program designed to promote the welfare of the indigenous population. On the other hand, the missionary zeal of the Spaniards resulted early on in the conversion of the natives in the Philippines, the indigenous lowland cultures being penetrated to their core (Phelan 1959). It must be noted though that the process of conversion cannot be assumed to be straightforward (Rafael 1988). The brand of Christianity that developed in the Philippines had been significantly infused with indigenous elements, as captured by the term "folk Christianity," but the foreign contributions, particularly in providing a code of ethics, were truly significant (Macdonald 2004).

Another important difference lies in the number of principal colonizers. The Dutch were the only principal colonizer of Indonesia; whereas the Philippines, along with a few other countries, has experienced being under the rule of two very different colonizers. The length of the period of colonization, as well as the depth and contrasting impacts of these colonizers, made the case of the Philippines quite distinctive. African countries, such as Tanzania, may have changed hands from one colonizer (Germany) to another (Britain), but the impact was nowhere near as sharp or unsettling as it was in the case of the Philippines when it passed from three centuries of Spanish rule into a new era of American control, which then spanned over four decades. An important consequence of this experience was the ambivalent attitude among Filipinos towards colonization and the ambiguous sense of nationalism it spawned. Whereas nationalism in Indonesia were clearly anti-colonial, dominated as they were by negative attitudes towards the Dutch, the anti-colonial nationalism that came out of the 'womb' of the 1896 Philippine Revolution were 'aborted' (Quibuyen 1999) by the mixed blessings, both perceived and real, brought by the new colonizers, the Americans. Called "bi-nationalism" by Alfred McCoy (1981) and "colonial nationalism" by Patricio Abinales (2002), the ambiguous character of Filipino nationalism was clearly displayed in the intensification of the radical anti-colonial nationalism in the 1960s and 1970s, while the movement for the Philippines to become the 51st state of the USA—the Philippine Statehood USA—was also gaining ground. It was reported as recently as December 2016 that this movement continues to gather signatures for the petition for statehood (Bustos and Cabacungan 2014).

The timing of the two countries' national revolutions may have also contributed to such ambivalence. Whereas Indonesia gained full independence after the National Revolution (or War of Independence) of 1945–1949, the Philippines had to contend with the co-opting and disarming policies of yet another colonizer, the United States, soon after declaring independence from Spain in 1898. If, after 50 years, Indonesian scholars talked about the "heartbeat of Indonesian revolution" (Abdullah 1997), their Filipino counterparts grieved over an 'aborted nation' (Quibuyen 1999).

Mass education programs served as one of the Americans' disarming policies (Francisco 2015; Suzuki 1991). Figures show that by the 1920s, nearly one million children in the Philippines received their education in English. By 1938, it was twice as many (Steinberg 1987, 264–265). While such programs created generations of Filipinos forever grateful to the Americans, in stark contrast with the supposedly painful memories of colonial experience under Spain, it also served as a breeding ground for nationalisms of varying shades, such as colonial vs. anti-colonial nationalism. The emergence, for instance, of homegrown historians who were educated during the American period and who had very different nationalist temperaments, as exemplified by Gregorio Zaide and Nicholas Zafra, on the one hand, and Teodoro Agoncillo and Renato Constantino, on the other. They illustrate the ambivalent impact of US-sponsored education in the Philippines. The distinction between the two sets of scholars shall be further discussed later in this book.

Indonesian nationalism was by no means monolithic and no less contentious. Just as in the Philippines, competing 'nations-of-intent,' borrowing Sani's (1976) and Shamsul's (1998) terminology, existed in Indonesia, as evidenced, for example, in the regional revolts in the 1950s; the persistence of the Islamist groups who wished to establish the Islamic state; the rise of communism; as well as the separatism of Papua, Aceh and Timor-Leste. Robert Cribb has identified four competing nations-of-intent: the Islamist; the communist; the developmental nationalist; and that of the indigenous aristocracies and the *mestizos*, which he calls the "multi-ethnic nation-of-intent" (Cribb 2004). The primary difference between the cases of Indonesia and the Philippines lies in the distribution of power among the promoters of the competing visions of the nation. While the coalescing of forces in Indonesia allowed the emergence of dominant elites, particularly upon the mass killings of the communists in 1965–1966, in the Philippines no episodes of comparable nature and scale happened. Various powerful groups of elites struggled for dominance, precluding the formation of an unassailable 'exemplary center' of nationalism as well as politics. Stalemated, competing nations-of-intent are perpetually locked in a state of conflict, both actual and potential.

In the case of Indonesia's nationalist movement, the "idea of unity has quickly acquired crucial symbolic value" (Cribb 1999, 16), and "cultural, social and ideological differences" did not hinder "enthusiasm for national unity" (Cribb and Brown 1995, 9). On the other hand, persistent discord has rocked its Philippine counterpart from the 1880s up to the present. In both cases, the need for unity was certainly recognized, but such recognition did not, in the Philippines, translate into a largely unified front against common enemies (such as colonialism), as was the case in Indonesia. No sooner had the Americans taken control of parts of Philippines, for instance, than a number of Filipino elites and erstwhile very high-ranking officials in the turn of the century revolutionary government switched sides. In the succeeding decades, a number of contentious questions arose: who should be the national hero, Rizal or Bonifacio? What should be the medium of instruction, Filipino or English? And should Rizal's novels be made required reading in Philippine schools and universities? These are just a few examples that illustrate the persistent divisiveness of nationalism in the country. During their formative decades, Indonesian nationalisms were also deeply divided, as seen in the struggle in the decades before the war among various groups to define the future of the nation, with the Islamists pushing to enshrine Islamic law (*Syariah*) as obligatory for all Muslims, while the nationalists opposed it (Kahin 1952; Shiraishi 1990). In the 1950s and 1960s, the political divide among Islamist, communist, nationalist, and other groups was deepening and sharpening (Feith 1962). Amid these divisions, there emerged a locus of power capable of balancing, neutralizing, or overpowering divisiveness, at least for a period. Examples include Sukarno's adept, if ultimately failed, attempt to synthesize the competing ideologies of nationalism, religion and communism into *Nasakom*; the installation of *Pancasila* as the national ideology; and the decisive wiping-out of the communists in 1965–1968, which smothered opposition. These ideological moves were not replicated in the Philippines, where the competing interests co-existed in a stalemate, held in tenuous equilibrium by a shifting balance of power among alliances of elite families. The title of an edited volume, *An Anarchy of Families (McCoy 1993)* evocatively captures the situation. Despite the earlier beginnings of Philippine nationalism, there was nothing comparable to the material and symbolic significance of *Sumpah Pemuda* ('Youth Pledge'), or the national ideology, *Pancasila*, two important markers of intent to achieve unity in Indonesia (Darmaputera 1988; Foulcher 2000). Ferdinand Marcos made an attempt to propose what amounted to an ideology for the Filipino nation (see Marcos 1979, 1980), but due to his unpopular actions and policies, it was dismissed by many Filipinos as nothing but a self-serving ploy.

Megan Thomas, in her book *Orientalists, Propagandists, and* Ilustrados: *Filipino Scholarship and the End of Spanish Colonialism* (Thomas 2012), noted the 'peculiar' character of the earliest period in the development of Philippine nationalism. She observes that right at its very inception, Philippine nationalism was infused with a high level of cosmopolitanism that was difficult to find in many other colonial societies. Whereas in many other colonial societies, the 'middle class' that led the nationalist movement were in between two poles, the colony and the metropole, Filipino nationalist leaders were in between multiple centers, which included Hong Kong, Japan, Germany, Belgium, and France. This was made possible, according to Thomas, by the fairly extensive travelling of these early nationalists (Thomas 2012). This travel exposed them to stimuli beyond Spanish colonialism, and afforded them multiple viewpoints that tamed the parochial tendencies of various anti-colonial nationalisms, including that of Indonesia. The idea of cosmopolitan nationalism highlights the more than superficial roots of the fluid and multiple characters of Philippine nationalism.

Viewed from the perspective of the development of Philippine nationalism, the degree of unity evoked among early Indonesian nationalists by the notion of 'Indonesia' was quite remarkable (Elson 2008). As observers have noted, 'Indonesia,' at least to the educated, was to the modern and the future what regional ethnic groups were to the feudal and the past (McVey 1996, 14). Subsuming the local or regional by the national in the Indonesian nationalist imagination did not, ultimately, prove as difficult to attain as it did in the Philippines. This was the case despite the real threats posed by regional rebellions in Indonesia in the 1950s, in addition to the secessionist aspirations in Aceh as well as Papua; the latter persists up to now. Regionalism remains robust, and is even intensifying in the Philippines, as exemplified by Cebuanos, who would rather use English than Filipino (which has its roots in Tagalog) and would rather sing the national anthem in Cebuano than in the national language (Avila 2009). Likewise, while the project of modernity in the Philippines was initially identified with the nationalism that accompanied the 1896 revolution, in a way functionally similar to that in Indonesia, the US colonization of the Philippines promised and, to an extent, delivered the more tangible and more readily attainable fruits of the modern. This was realized in the form of schools, roads and bridges, and at least the trappings of democracy. Thus, the strength of the promise of modernity that accompanied the Filipino nationalist project that culminated in the 1896 revolution was diminished by the American colonial project. This is one of the results of having had two different colonial experiences. The cosmopolitan, the national, and the regional elements competed and/or co-existed in shaping nationalisms in the Philippines, in contrast to the case of Indonesia, where the unifying elements proved more dominant than the competing ones.

State-formation and state–society relations

As postcolonial states, the state-formation in Indonesia and the Philippines was significantly influenced by their colonial experiences. The extent to which the Indonesian postcolonial state built upon its predecessor was considerable (McVey 1996), but this is perhaps more true in the Philippines, where governmental and other political ideals, practices, and structures (such as constitutions, political party system, and a system of checks and balances) were clearly legacies of the United States (Hedman and Sidel, 2000, 7–8). The supposed 'training' in the 'art of democratic governance' that the Filipino leaders underwent within the colonial framework ensured close ties with the Americans (Owen 1971). The contrasting fashion by which independence was declared in Indonesia and the Philippines after World

War II speaks volume to this contrast. As described by Ruth McVey (1996, 14), "Indonesia's declaration of independence, instead of the high ceremony and ringing statement of goals that we might expect of a revolutionary state, was a bare announcement read before a few people, under the reluctant gaze of the Japanese." On the other hand, a highly anticipated and festive inauguration among a massive crowd was staged in the Philippines in 1946: Filipino leaders took the mantle of leadership after being 'prepared' for it for decades.

Another fundamental difference between the two countries lay in the decolonization process. Whereas Indonesia succeeded in divesting itself of many tangible and intangible legacies of the colonial era—Dutch property ownership, political use of the native aristocracies, and the Dutch language, among others—the neo-colonial relationship between the United States and the Philippines lingered (Benda 1965; Shalom 1981). As aptly described by McCoy (1981), the case of the Philippines was "independence without decolonisation." English continued to be used in schools, education remained patterned after the Americans and American pop culture has permeated the Philippine society up to now. The Americans maintained control of the vast plantations, military bases, mines, and businesses, while the Filipino elites enjoyed preferential access to the American market, among other perks. This set the enabling conditions for the character of the Philippine government's relationship with its American counterpart in the succeeding decades (Shalom 1981). The persistent close ties between the two governments served as one of the fulcrums of the anti-colonial nationalist backlash. To the consternation of his critics, Marcos was able to surf on the wave of such a backlash and had utilized nationalist rhetoric to justify his authoritarian rule. As will be discussed in Chapter 4, a clear example of this effort is *Tadhana* project, one of the two projects that are the subject of this study.

The roads to authoritarianism were different in the two countries. While both underwent 'democratic experimentation,' the crucial difference lay in the length of time they spent on it. Whereas parliamentary democracy was crushed a few years after it was tried in Indonesia in 1950–1957, the Philippines had more time to develop democratic practices and institutions. These included the municipal and provincial elections (1901 and 1902), the establishment of the Philippine Assembly in 1907, the Filipinization or appointment of Filipinos in government positions, and the establishment of the Filipino-led Commonwealth government in 1935. These marked a gradual and progressive pattern of increased Filipino role in the democratic experiment. Within 25 years after independence in 1946, the experiment seemed to be working, notwithstanding the 'fiesta' and elitist character of the democracy that had emerged. 'Fiesta' refers to the ephemeral, skin-deep, or just for a show, atmosphere of fun and conviviality that accompanies democratic practices in the Philippines. As one scholar puts it, referring to EDSA uprising, "Filipinos moved from dictatorship to democracy with characteristic spectacle—color, music, emotion, and drama" (Boudreau 1999, 11).

In other words, by the time an authoritarian regime was installed upon the declaration of Martial Law in 1972 (Brillantes 1987), the Philippines had already undergone seven decades of (at least nominal) democratic practice. This makes it easy for the dictatorial period between 1972 and 1986 to appear an anomaly in the otherwise continuous evolution of the experiment.

The authoritarianism of the New Order regime, on the other hand, hardly appeared to be an anomaly. In many respects, it was a continuation of Sukarno's Guided Democracy and the feudal character of the traditional political culture as well as the autocratic features of the Dutch colonial government (Anderson 1983). If anything, the brief parliamentary experiment in the 1950s was the one that appeared anomalous within the broader historical scheme (Benda 1982). Such a view is reinforced by the tendency of many Indonesian politicians since the Guided Democracy period to use this period as a metaphor for political chaos and ineptitude (Bourchier 1994).

Given the wider democratic latitude the Philippines had enjoyed for a longer period of time, it is no surprise that state–civil society relations in the Philippines were more dynamic and confrontational in the 1970s and 1980s than they were in Indonesia. The structure of power relations within the society was more fluid and polyvalent or polycentric in the Philippines than it was in Indonesia (Hedman 2001). Different interest groups such as labor unions, church organizations, political parties, and professional associations had ample time to grow, acquire power, and exert influence on the process, if not the outcome, of political struggles within the public sphere. Indonesia had similar experiences from the 1950s up to the mid-1960s, but its trajectory was dramatically altered by the cataclysmic events in 1965–1966 that saw the mass killings of real and suspected communists and sympathizers. This episode effectively installed what Ariel Heryanto calls "state terrorism" (Heryanto 2005). By state terrorism, it refers to the reign of terror that put in place a resilient anti-communist 'master narrative' that psychologically coerced the public and legitimated the use of "repressive measures geared to intimidate the citizenry" for an indefinite period of time (Heryanto and Hadiz 2005, 267). This period coincided with years of systematic mass indoctrination most clearly evident in programs such as *Pedoman Penghayatan dan Pengamalan Pancasila*, or in popular parlance P4 (a course on the Guidelines for the Realization and Implementation of Pancasila), *Pendidikan Moral Pancasila* (PMP, Pancasila Moral Education), and *Pendidikan Sejarah Perjuangan Bangsa* (PSPB, History of National Struggle Education) (Bourchier 1996, 227–263; McGregor 2007, 156–160). Dissent did exist, but it could only to a limited extent flourish in such an environment (Heryanto 2005).

Some observers opined that the New Order regime was more firmly grounded in authoritarianism than the Marcos dictatorship (Boudreau 1999). That the Marcos regime tottered in the early 1980s and eventually collapsed in 1986, whereas the New Order persisted until 1998 supports this view. On the whole, this is clearly the case. However, in the first five to seven years of the two regimes' existence, the period particularly relevant to this study, this was not the case. The considerable strength or durability of the New Order regime rested significantly on a sudden reversal of fortune associated with the 1965–1966 events. That the communists were decimated hardly owed to the enormous power of the military or the emerging New Order regime. Perhaps the reverse was truer: the military and the Suharto regime became dominant because the communists were wiped out in such a gruesome fashion. As Ariel Heryanto (2005) perceptively argues, the strength of the New Order significantly derived from the hyper-reality effect of its actual (and limited) power, grossly amplified by the overriding state of fear among the people propagated by the events of 1965–1966.

Marcos, on the other hand, was able to establish (in 1972) and maintain dictatorship (*de jure* until 1981 but *de facto* until 1986) on the basis of accumulated strength of will- and fire-power (Boudreau 1999, 4–7). Whereas Sukarno and the communists in Indonesia were emasculated by the sharp turn of public opinion in the weeks and months following 1 October 1965, leaving the incipient New Order regime without strong opposition, Marcos faced, from the 1960s to the 1980s, a formidable array of forces, including the political oppositionists, the armed Muslim secessionists in Mindanao, and the communists across the country.[2] His dictatorship was installed and maintained through arduous, calculated and skillful manipulations of competing and complementary forces and interests. Hardly was luck or serendipity a factor. Whereas the New Order was empowered by the weakness of the opposition, the Marcos regime thrived despite strong and continued resistance. In other words, by the early to mid-1970s when the two history-writing projects were taking off, the Marcos regime appeared more vigorous than, or at least of equal strength to, the New Order. As the 1970s and 1980s wore on, however, Suharto's formidable rise, peaking in the late 1980s, was paralleled by the Marcos regime's continuous decline and eventual ouster by the mid-1980s.

The fate of the communist movement in the Philippines contrasted sharply with that in Indonesia. It grew from strength to strength in the 1970s and 1980s, having learned well from the tragic experience of its counterpart in Indonesia and from the failures of its precursor, the Partido Komunista ng Philippines (PKP) (Fuller 2007; Guillermo 2018). The repressive measures under the Marcos dictatorship also helped facilitate an increase in membership and widen significantly the sympathetic mass base. By the time of the Marcos regime's demise in 1986, the communists had reached a threshold of military power and ideological influence that worried the Philippine government and the Americans (Fuller 2007; Weekley 2001). In other words, by the time the two history-writing projects were underway, ideological struggles were intensifying in the Philippines, while these had been flattened in Indonesia. One of the significant repercussions of this situation on the course of intellectual or scholarly development in the Philippines was the popularity of the class or Marxist line of analysis, which competed well with other long-established scholarly traditions. As will be discussed in Chapter 4, *Tadhana*'s emphasis on the indigenous was in line with Marcos's desire

32 *Indonesia and the Philippines*

to offer an alternative to Marxist and other foreign-originated analytic approaches. By contrast, class analysis was visibly absent in the Indonesian social sciences (Farid 2005).

Historiography and history profession

The early development of nationalist historiography closely followed that of the nationalist movement in general. It is not surprising, therefore, that the nationalist historiography in the Philippines took shape earlier than in Indonesia for it was there that Southeast Asia saw the rise of the earliest anti-colonial nationalist movement. By nationalist historiography, I mean the body of ideas and practices employed by professional and non-professional historians in writing history with an outcome, intended or not, of recognizing or justifying a nation or a nation-state, as well as the identity that creates or reinforces such an entity.

As early as the 1880s, intellectuals like Pedro Paterno (1857–1911), Trinidad H. Pardo de Tavera (1857–1925), Isabelo de los Reyes (1864–1938), and more notably, Jose Rizal (1861–1896) produced pioneering works which constituted the earliest formulation of the nationalist interpretation of Philippine history (Mojares 2006; Quibuyen 1998; Schumacher 1979). Some of their works were notable for the sophisticated methods, by the standard of the time, employed in the synthesis and/or analysis of data. Rizal's *Annotations of Morga's Sucesos de las Islas Filipinas* and Isabelo de los Reyes's *El Folk-Lore Filipino* are good examples (Ocampo 1998; Anderson 2000). Palma's *Historia de Filipinas* (1935), which may be regarded as the best one-volume survey of the history of the Philippines in the first half of the twentieth century, was another (Agoncillo 2003, 26). While none of these authors was a professionally trained historian, they laid the foundations upon which future efforts at 'modern' nationalist scholarship would be built. A comparative advantage of the Philippines was that, in the words of Anderson, it "was the only colony in the nineteenth-century Southeast Asia to have a real university" (Anderson 2000, 61), referring to the Pontifical University of Santo Tomas (UST). Run by the Dominican order, this institution was founded in 1611, conferred degrees starting in 1624 and became a university in 1645.

Indonesia would have to wait decades for at least nominally similar developments. Starting from the 1920s or 1930s, the fictional writings or speeches of Mohammad Yamin (1903–1962), Sukarno (1901–1970), Sanusi Pane (1905–1968) and other nationalists planted the germ of nationalist historiography (Klooster 1982, 54). The succeeding decades of the 1940s and 1950s saw the publication of historical works such as Mohammad Yamin's *6000 Years Red and White* (*6000 Tahun Sang Merah-Putih*) (Yamin 1951), whose hagiographic overly nationalistic character prompted some observers to regard these as pre-scientific in methods and interpretations (Klooster 1982; Notosusanto 1965). Perhaps Achmad Djajadiningrat's (1877–1943) thesis in 1913, which critically reassessed the sources on the history of Banten, stands alone in the period prior to World War II for observing 'modern' historical methods (Kartodirdjo 2001). The theme of Djajadiningrat's thesis, however, was at best tangential to nationalist historiography. In other words, whereas Filipino historians as early as the pre-Second War years already had a foundation to build upon, their Indonesian counterparts had almost nothing (Kumar 2015). They had to "start from scratch," as Nugroho Notosusanto reported (1965, 2).

Historical studies following standard methods done by professionally trained Indonesian historians did not appear until after the establishment of history departments at the University of Indonesia (UI) and University of Gadjah Mada (UGM) in 1950 and 1951, respectively. It happened only after a number of Indonesian scholars, such as Sartono Kartodirdjo (Amsterdam), Taufik Abdullah (Cornell), Ong Hok Ham (Yale), and Kuntowijoyo (Columbia), went abroad for graduate studies. In contrast, formal institutionalization of historical studies in the Philippines was accomplished much earlier, with the establishment of the Department of History at the University of the Philippines (UP) in 1910 (Apilado 1993, 90). Despite being the initial seat of colonial historiography, it was also there that nationalist historiography bloomed later on. For instance, two of the most important products of the UP History Department during the American period, Gregorio Zaide (1907–1988) and Teodoro Agoncillo (1912–1985), are known, respectively, for their colonial nationalist and radical nationalist tendencies. This is emblematic of the range of ideological orientations that Filipino historians of this period assumed. The presence in the department of an American historian who had sympathies with the nationalist cause, Austin Craig (1872–1949), may have provided an impetus for the growth of nationalist historiography within the strictures of the colonial framework.

Indonesia produced its first professional historian only in 1956, in the person of Sartono Kartodirdjo. Widely believed among Indonesian scholars to be the first PhD in history, Sartono obtained his PhD in 1966 from the University of Amsterdam. An Indonesian Chinese named Lie Tek Tjeng graduated from Harvard in 1962 with specialization in Japanese history. Perhaps because his BA and MA were not on Indonesian history but in Sinology, he was often forgotten in surveys of Indonesian historians. In the list drawn up by Sartono in 1963, for instance, Lie Tek Tjeng was visibly absent (Kartodirdjo 1963). By the time SNI history-writing project was underway in the early 1970s, there were only four PhDs of history in Indonesia, but only two were of consequence in so far as Indonesian history-writing was concerned. Aside from Sartono, the other one was Taufik Abdullah (1936–), who obtained a PhD from Cornell University in 1970. The two others were Lie Tek Tjeng and Marwati Djoened Poesponegoro, who specialized in European history and obtained a PhD in 1968 from University of Paris-Sorbonne (Abdullah 1975). The case of the Philippines was vastly different in that even before World War II, several Filipinos had obtained MAs and PhDs abroad, and there were even a few who obtained theirs from a local university, the University of Santo Tomas (see Table 1.1).

Table 1.1 Selected Filipino and Indonesian historians

Filipino historians	Education	Indonesian historians	Education
Agoncillo, Teodoro (1912–1985)	BA UP (1934) MA UP (1939)	Abdullah, Taufik (1936–)	BA UGM (1961) MA Cornell (1967) PhD – Cornell (1970)
Alip, Eufronio (1904–1976)	BA UP (1927) MA Uni. of Manila (1928) PhD UST	Alfian, Ibrahim (1930–2006)	BA UGM (?) PhD UGM (1980)
Alzona, Encarnacion (1895–2001)	MA UP (1918) MA Harvard (1920) PhD Columbia (1922)	Kartodirdjo, Sartono (1921–2007)	BA/Doktorandus – UI (1956) MA – Yale (1962) PhD – Amsterdam (1966)
Benitez, Conrado (1889–1971)	MA Chicago (1911) PhD Chicago (1915 or 1916)	Kuntowijoyo (1943–2005)	BA UGM (1969) MA Connecticut (1974) PhD (1980) Columbia
de la Costa, Horacio (1916–1977)	BA Ateneo (1935) MA (Sacred Heart College) (?) PhD Harvard (1951)	Lapian, Adrian (1929–2011)	BA/Doktorandus– UI (?) PhD UGM (1987)
Fernandez, Leandro (1889–1948)	MA Chicago (1913) – PhD Columbia (1926)	Leirissa, Richard (1938–)	BA UI (1965) MA Hawaii (1974) PhD UI (1990)
Fonacier, Tomas (1898–1981)	MA Stanford (1931) PhD Stanford (1933)	Lie Tek Tjeng (1931– ?)	PhD Harvard (1961 or 1962)
Foronda, Marcelino	BA UST (1950) MA UST (1951) PhD Salamanca (1954)	Notosusanto, Nugroho (1931–1985)	BA & PhD UI (1978)
Ganzon, Guadalupe (1908–1985)	BSE UP (1929) MA UP (1940) PhD Stanford (1949)	Onghokham (1933–2006)	BA/Dokt UI (1968) PhD Yale (1975)
Salazar, Zeus (1934–)	BA History, UP (1955) PhD Ethnology, Sorbonne (1968)	Poesponegoro, Merwati Djoened (1910–?)	BA Stanford (?) MA Connecticut (?) PhD Sorbonne (1968)
Zafra, Nicolas (1892–1981)	BA UP (1916) BSE UP (1918) MA UP (1920)	Suryo, Djoko (1939–)	BA UGM (1965) MA UGM (1970) PhD Monash (1983)
Zaide, Gregorio (1907–1986)	BA UP (1929) MA UP (1931) PhD UST (1934)		

Updated version of the table that appeared in Curaming (2008, 134).
Legend: UP—University of the Philippines; UST—University of Santo Tomas; UI—University of Indonesia; UGM—University of Gadjah Mada.

When the Department of History at the University of the Philippines opened in 1910, initially combined with Sociology and Economics, all members of the teaching staff were Americans. Two years later, a Filipino historian, Conrado Benitez, was appointed. By 1920, all teachers in the department were Filipinos, invariably with advanced degrees (or studying for them) from the department or abroad (Apilado 1993).

One indicator of the seriousness of the professionalization effort was the opening of the MA in History program in 1916, after this was approved by university authorities in 1915. By 1918, it had produced graduates who would become important historians, such as Encarnacion Alzona and Nicolas Zafra (Apilado 1993). Teodoro Agoncillo and Gregorio Zaide, two of the biggest names in the Philippine history profession, were also products of this program (see Table 1.1). Alzona went to the United States to pursue a PhD at Columbia University. She earned in 1922 the distinction for being the first Filipino woman with a PhD in history. She was well known for writing the acclaimed *A History of Education in the Philippines* (Alzona 1932), among other works. She and Leandro Fernandez, who also completed a PhD in Columbia and who wrote *The Philippine Republic* (Fernandez 1926), may be considered as pioneers in 'scientific' history-writing methods in the Philippines (Agoncillo 2003). The three others were homegrown scholars—that is, they did not pursue further studies overseas—but they nevertheless emerged among the most well-known historians for the period of 1940–1980s. They even overshadowed some of the foreign-trained historians in the country. This suggests the quality or strength of training they received from local history programs.

Again, the same thing cannot be said in the case of Indonesia. The first generation of Indonesian historians were all trained overseas, excluding Adrian Lapian, if he may be considered part of that generation (see Table 1.1). Nugroho Notosusanto was in a grey area as he studied for two years at the SOAS, but without obtaining a degree. As will be clarified further below, he obtained a PhD in a local university, University of Indonesia. The local departments of history encountered difficulties at the early stages of their professionalization effort. A severe shortage of teachers plagued the two departments of history during the first decade of their existence. Furthermore, the teachers were mostly philologists and lawyers, not historians (Abdullah 1975, 123). As Nugroho Notosusanto (1965, 3) reported, both these departments were "(o)n the brink of being closed (for) lack of teachers." Students complained about the lack of courses offered due to acute staff shortages. Some students who were initially interested in History moved to Archaeology and other courses because of this problem. One of my interviewees recalled that the department was almost a non-entity then. Only by accident did he learn of the 'existence' of the history program, when he read in a newspaper that Sartono Kartodirdjo would graduate as the first history major.[3] While it was not as bad in the following decade, it was still bad enough to prompt Nugroho Notosusanto to complain in 1965 that the lack of professionally trained historians remained an acute and basic problem. He put the problem this way:

> It has been a vicious circle: we want to train a great number of historians because we now have too few; and because we have too few... we cannot train new historians as quickly as we should (sic) like to do.
> (Notosusanto 1965, 2–3)

In Sartono's article surveying the state of history profession in Indonesia in the 1960s, he described it as "still in (its) infancy" (Kartodirdjo 1963, 26). The purge of leftist scholars in the wake of the 1965–1966 events further shrank the pool of already limited intellectual resources. Local universities did not produce their first PhD in history until 1977, in the person of Nugroho Notosusanto himself. Progress was slow from that point on. By Nugroho's count, as noted in a news item in *Kompas* on January 7, 1980, there were only six PhDs in history in Indonesia.[4]

Professional organizations for historians were also established much earlier in the Philippines than in Indonesia. The Philippine National Historical Society (PNHS) was founded in 1941. Smaller, less known organizations preceded the PNHS, such as the one founded by Felipe G. Calderon in 1905, the *Asociación Histórica de Filipinas* (History Association of the Philippines), and the one established in 1916 or 1917 by Carlos Sobral and his group, the *Sociedad Histórico-Geográfica* de Filipinas (Historico-Geographic Society of the Philippines) (Bauzon 1993). A breakaway group in 1955 formed another organization called the Philippine Historical Association (PHA). There has been both tacit and open competition between the two groups since then. For instance, when the Philippine Social Science Council (PSSC) initiated the Philippine Encyclopedia of the Social Sciences Project, it was quite odd that history was allotted two volumes, whereas other disciplines had one each. One volume was prepared by the members of the PHA (Volume 1), and the other was prepared by the members of PNHS (Volume 2). Another group was formed in 1989 from among the members of the Department of History, University of the Philippines. It is called Asosasyon ng mga Dalubhasa, May Hilig, at Interes sa Kasaysayan ng Pilipinas, Inc. (ADHIKA) (Association of History Scholars and Enthusiasts). Another group that is noteworthy is BAKAS or Bagong Kasaysayan/Bahay-Saliksikan ng Kasaysayan (New History/History Research House). Unlike the three others that have a broad-based membership, BAKAS is a small group of professional historians, originally from the University of the Philippines, who seek to pursue and promote *Pantayong Pananaw* (From Us-For Us Perspective). This approach will be further discussed in Chapter 3. There were other groups, but these are the largest or the most active and impactful.

In Indonesia, their lone counterpart, *Masyarakat Sejarawan Indonesia* (MSI) (Association of Historians of Indonesia), was founded in August 1970. Another group is ASPENSI (Asosiasi Sarjana Pendidikan Sejarah

Indonesia or Association of Indonesian Scholars of History Education), but it is mainly for history teachers and teacher educators.

A number of contrasts between these organizations should be noted. Whereas its Philippine counterparts were either less dependent on or practically independent of the government, the MSI relied on the government for its sustenance. The Philippine Historical Association may have had a fairly close relationship with the government. Since its inception in 1955, the President of the Republic was invited as an honorary president of the organization (de Ocampo 1975; Fabella 1963). However, the extent of its ties with the state was much less than that of the MSI.

Whereas the MSI held national conferences, funded by the state, only occasionally (1957, 1970, 1981, 1985, 1991, 1996, 2001, 2008, etc.), in the Philippines almost every year, the PNHS, PHA, and ADHIKA hold their own national conferences in addition to a number of regional ones (de Ocampo 1975). Most of these conferences were held with minimum financial support, if any, from the government. The bulk of the funding usually came from the registration, sponsorship and membership fees.

In both countries, the government established institutional infrastructures specifically for promoting historical consciousness. In the Philippines, the National Historical Institute (NHI) was founded in 1972. It traces its historical roots to the Philippine Historical Research and Markers Committee established in 1933, which in 1936 was superseded by the Philippine Historical Committee. The basic function of these committees focused on the identifying, marking and safe-keeping of historic sites and antiquities. In 1967, this committee was replaced by the National Historical Commission. Another reorganization took place in 1972 to form the NHI, whose function was not just the marking and preservation of historic sites but also the active promotion of history through education, public campaigns and research (Gealogo 1993).

In Indonesia, the *Direktorat Sejarah dan Nilai Tradisional* (Directorate for History and Traditional Values) serves a similar function to the NHI. Unlike in the Philippines, however, there are other government agencies in Indonesia, aside from the Ministry of Education and Culture, that promote historical research and public awareness. These include the Armed Forces History Center, which does not have a parallel in the Philippines, and certain sections of the Indonesian Institute of Sciences or LIPI (Abdullah 1975, 139). The Armed Forces History Center, founded in 1964, is by far the most active and most productive history-related institution in Indonesia, having published about 50 books by 1972 (Ibid.). Since then, it has been even more prolific (McGregor 2007, 55–59).

To sum up, the cases of the Philippines and Indonesia share some broad similarities, but there have also been significant differences. The contrasts are pronounced in the impact of the colonial experience, state–civil society relations, and the timing and tenor of the development of historical profession. In preparation for analysis in the succeeding chapters, the following points need to be highlighted.

First, the contrasting patterns of colonial experience in the two countries prefigured forms of nationalism that were more fluid in the Philippines and hegemonic in Indonesia. Such forms of nationalism simultaneously influenced and were reinforced or affected by the shapes of nationalist history-writing in the two countries.

Second, the relationship between the state and civil society was far less constrained in the Philippines than in Indonesia. The polyvalent character of power relations in the Philippines allowed a greater space for different interest groups to operate or compete. While the centralization of power in few individuals or institutions was largely the norm in postcolonial Indonesia before 1998, the opposite, to a significant extent, was the case in the Philippines. Marcos's dictatorship appears anomalous within the Philippine political matrix. The longer tradition of political contestations in the Philippines made opposition comparatively easier to mobilize, as was reflected in the persistent critiques of Marcos and his legacies.

Third, the historical profession in the Philippines developed much earlier and under a freer environment than that in Indonesia. By the time a strong, manipulative state emerged in the early 1970s with Marcos's declaration of martial law, the profession was already institutionalized. Their Indonesian counterparts, on the other hand, had to develop under the aegis of a restrictive state from the Guided Democracy era up to the New Order. Even up until the end of the New Order, Indonesian historians still struggled for professional respectability, something that their Philippine counterparts had achieved decades back and which by the 1970s several Filipino historians took for granted.

Finally, while the New Order was, on the whole, more authoritarian than the Marcos regime, and thus was in a stronger position to impose what it wanted, this was not to be the case in the early to mid-1970s, when the two history-writing projects were undertaken. The two regimes were more or less on an equal footing.

The last two points are particularly salient for the analysis in subsequent chapters. It is commonly assumed that there is an inverse relationship between the strength of the scholarship and the extent to which scholars may be influenced by political power. To the extent that scholarship is 'scientific,' it is less vulnerable to political manipulations. Observers of Indonesian historiography, for instance, usually attribute the weaknesses of the historical profession to the strength of state manipulation. Historians were seen as powerless in the face of societal and political pressures. As noted above, the strength of the two states was more or less comparable; it was in the level of advancement attained by the history profession that the two cases significantly differed. One might have expected, therefore, that Filipino historians, given the level of their scholarly achievement, would fare significantly 'better' in their encounter with an authoritarian regime. We shall see in the succeeding chapters if, or to what extent and in what ways, this view might be correct.

Notes

1. A version of this chapter previously appeared in *Philippine Studies*, 56 (2): 123–150 (2008) under the title "Contextual Factors in the Analysis of State-historian Relations in Indonesia and the Philippines." Permission granted by *Philippine Studies*.
2. The Marcos Diary contains passages, specifically entries for early January 1970, that show how worried Marcos was about the coalition of these forces. By 1972, the rebellion in Mindanao exploded, and the intensity of fighting in 1974–1975 drained the resources of the Marcos regime.
3. Interview with an anonymized informant, 8 June 2005, Jakarta.
4. It seems that Nugroho did not include Lie Tek Tjeng and Merwati Poesponegoro. I can identify eight: Sartono Kartodirdjo (Amsterdam, 1966), Taufik Abdullah (Cornell, 1970), Onghokham (Yale, 1975), Kuntowijoyo (Columbia, 1980), Nugroho (UI, 1977), Poesponegoro (Paris, 1968), Abraham Alfian (UGM, 1980), and Lie Tek Tjeng (Harvard, 1962).

References

Abdullah, Taufik. 1975. "The Study of History." In *The Social Sciences in Indonesia*, edited by Koentjaraningrat, 89–166. Jakarta: Indonesian Institute of Sciences (LIPI).
———. ed. 1997. *The Heartbeat of Indonesian Revolution*. Jakarta: PT Gramedia Pustaka Utama and Program of Southeast Asian Studies, LIPI.
Abinales, Patricio. 2002. "American Rule and the Formation of Filipino 'Colonial Nationalism'." *Southeast Asian Studies* 39 (4): 604–621.
Agoncillo, Teodoro A. 1965. *The Fateful Years: Japan's Adventure in the Philippines, 1941–45*. 2 vols. Quezon City: R. P. Garcia Pub. Co.
———. 2003. "Philippine Historiography in the Age of Kalaw." In *History and Culture, Language and Literature: Selected Essays of Teodoro A. Agoncillo*, edited by Bernardita Churchill, 3–29. Manila: UST Press.
Alzona, Encarnacion. 1932. *A History of Education in the Philippines, 1565–1930*. Manila: University of the Philippines Press.
Anderson, Benedict. 1983. "Old State, New Society: Indonesia's New Order in Comparative Historical Perspective." *The Journal of Asian Studies* 42 (3): 477–496.
———. 2000. "The Rooster's Egg: Pioneering World Folklore in the Philippines." *New Left Review* 2: 47–62.
Apilado, Digna. 1993. "State of the Art: Department of History: University of the Philippines." In *Philippine Encyclopedia of the Social Sciences, Volume 2: History*, edited by Philippine National Historical Society (PNHS), 90–93. Quezon City: Philippine Social Science Council.
Avila, Bobbit. 2009. "About the National Anthem and Our Language." *Philippine Start*, May 12. www.philstar.com/opinion/2009/05/12/466453/about-national-anthem-and-our-language.
Bauzon, Leslie. 1993. "State of the Art: The Philippine National Historical Society." In *Philippine Encyclopedia of the Social Sciences, Volume 2: History*, edited by Philippine National Historical Society (PNHS), 93–94. Quezon City: Philippine Social Science Council.
Benda, Harry J. 1965. "Decolonization in Indonesia: The Problem of Continuity and Change." *The American Historical Review* 70 (4): 1058–1073. doi:10.2307/1846903.

———. 1982. "Democracy in Indonesia." In *Interpreting Indonesian Politics: Thirteen Contributions to the Debate*, edited by Benedict Anderson and Audrey Kahin. Ithaca, NY: Southeast Asian Studies Program, Cornell University.
Boudreau, Vincent. 1999. "Diffusing Democracy? People Power in Indonesia and the Philippines." *Bulletin of Concerned Asian Scholars* 31 (4): 3–18.
Bourchier, David. 1994. "The 1950s in the New Order Ideology and Politics." In *Democracy in Indonesia, 1950s and 1990s*, edited by David Bourchier and John Legge, 50–62. Clayton, VIC: Centre of Southeast Asian Studies, Monash University.
———. 1996. "Lineages of Organicist Political Thought in Indonesia." PhD Thesis, Monash University.
Brillantes, Alex. 1987. *Dictatorship and Martial Law: Philippine Authoritarianism in 1972*. Quezon City: Great Book Publisher.
Bustos, Loren, and Vanessa Cabacungan. 2014. "Timeline: Efforts to Make the Philippines a US State." *Rappler*, April 23. www.rappler.com//newsbreak/iq/56124-timeline-ph-us-state-annexation.
Cribb, Robert. 1999. "Nation: Making Indonesia." In *Indonesia beyond Suharto: Polity, Economy, Society, Transition*, edited by Donald Emerson, 3–38. New York: M.E. Sharpe.
———. 2004. "Nations-of-Intent in Colonial Indonesia." A paper presented in the *18th IAHA Conference*, Academia Sinica, Taipei, Taiwan, December 6–10.
Cribb, Robert, and Colin Brown. 1995. *Modern Indonesia: A History since 1945*. London: Longman.
Curaming, Rommel. 2008. "Contextual Factors in the Analysis of State-Historian Relations in Indonesia and the Philippines." *Philippine Studies* 56 (2): 123–150.
Darmaputera, Eka. 1988. *Pancasila and the Search for Identity and Modernity in Indonesian Society: A Cultural and Ethical Analysis*. Leiden: Brill.
de Ocampo, Esteban. 1975. "A Record of Achievement: The PHA, 1955–1975." *Historical Bulletin* 4 (1–4): 308–339.
Elson, Robert. 2008. *The Idea of Indonesia: A History*. Cambridge: Cambridge University Press.
Fabella, G. 1963. "The First Seven Years." *Historical Bulletin* 3 (1): 73–86.
Farid, Hilmar. 2005. "The Class Question in Indonesian Social Sciences." In *Social Science and Power in Indonesia*, edited by Vedi Hadiz and Daniel Dhakidae, 167–195. Jakarta and Singapore: Equinox Publishing and ISEAS.
Feith, Herbert. 1962. *The Decline of Constitutional Democracy in Indonesia*. Ithaca, NY: Cornell University Press.
Fernandez, Leandro. 1926. *The Philippine Republic*. New York: Columbia University Press.
Foulcher, Keith. 2000. "Sumpah Pemuda: The Making and Meaning of a Symbol of Indonesian Nationhood." *Asian Studies Review* 24 (3): 377–410. doi:10.1080/10357820008713281.
Francisco, Adrianne. 2015. "From Subjects to Citizens: American Colonial Education and Philippine Nation-Making, 1900–1934." PhD diss., Berkeley, CA: University of California Berkeley.
Fuller, Ken. 2007. *Forcing the Pace: The Partido Komunista Ng Pilipinas: From Foundation to Armed Struggle*. Quezon City: University of the Philippines Press.
Gealogo, Francis. 1993. "State of the Art: The National Historical Institute." In *Philippine Encyclopedia of the Social Sciences, Volume 2: History*, edited by Philippine National Historical Society (PNHS), 95. Quezon City: Philippine Social Science Council.

Guillermo, Ramon. 2018. "Blood-Brothers: The Communist Party of the Philippines and the Partai Komunis Indonesia." *Southeast Asian Studies* 7 (1): 13–28.
Hedman, Eva-Lotta. 2001. "Contesting State and Civil Society: Southeast Asian Trajectories." *Modern Asian Studies* 35 (4): 921–951.
Hedman, Eva-Lotta, and John Sidel. 2000. *Philippine Politics and Society in the Twentieth Century: Colonial Legacies, Post-Colonial Trajectories.* London/New York: Routledge.
Heryanto, Ariel. 2005. *State Terrorism and Political Identity in Indonesia: Fatally Belonging.* London: Routledge.
Heryanto, Ariel, and Vedi Hadiz. 2005. "Post-Authoritarian Indonesia." *Critical Asian Studies* 37 (2): 251–275. doi:10.1080/14672710500106341.
Kahin, George McTurnan. 1952. *Nationalism and Revolution in Indonesia.* Ithaca: Cornell University Press.
Kartodirdjo, Sartono. 1963. "Historians in Indonesia Today." *Journal of Southeast Asian History* 4 (1): 23–30.
———. 2001. *Indonesian Historiography.* Yogyakarta: Penerbit Kanisius.
Klooster, H. A. J. 1982. "Some Remarks on Indonesian Nationalist Historiography." In *Papers of the Dutch-Indonesian Historical Conference*, edited by G. J. Schutte and H. Sutherland, H, 47–62. Leiden and Jakarta: Bureau of Indonesian Studies.
Kumar, Ann. 2015. "Indonesian Historical Writing after Independence." In *The Oxford History of Historical Writing: Volume 5: Historical Writing Since 1945*, edited by Daniel Woolf and Axel Schneider, 576–593. Oxford: Oxford University Press.
Macdonald, Charles. 2004. "Folk Catholicism and Pre-Spanish Religions in the Philippines." *Philippine Studies* 52 (1): 78–93.
Marcos, Ferdinand. 1979. *Toward a Filipino Ideology.* Manila: F.E. Marcos.
———. 1980. *An Ideology for Filipinos.* Manila: F. E. Marcos.
McCoy, Alfred. 1981. "The Philippines: Independence without Decolonisation." In *Asia: The Winning of Independence*, edited by Jeffrey Robin, 23–70. London: Macmillan.
———. ed. 1993. *An Anarchy of Families: State and Family in the Philippines.* Madison, WI: University of Wisconsin, Center for Southeast Asian Studies.
McGregor, Katharine. 2007. *History in Uniform: Military Ideology and the Construction of Indonesia's Past.* Singapore: NUS Press.
McVey, Ruth. 1996. "Building a Behemoth: Indonesian Construction of the Nation-State." In *Making Indonesia*, edited by Daniel Lev and Ruth McVey, 11–25. Ithaca, NY: Southeast Asian Studies Program, Cornell University.
Mojares, Resil. 2006. *Brains of the Nation: Pedro Paterno, T.H. Pardo de Tavera, Isabelo de los Reyes, and the Production of Modern Knowledge.* Quezon City: Ateneo de Manila University Press.
Notosusanto, Nugroho. 1965. "Problems in the Study and Teaching of National History in Indonesia." *Journal of Southeast Asian Studies* 6 (1): 1–16.
Ocampo, Ambeth. 1998. "Rotten Beef and Stinking Fish: Rizal and the Writing of Philippine History." *Kinaadman* 20: 141–183.
Owen, Norman, ed. 1971. *Compadre Colonialism: Studies on the Philippines under American Rule.* Ann Arbor: Center for South and Southeast Asian Studies, University of Michigan.
Phelan, John. 1959. *The Hispanization of the Philippines: Spanish Aims and Filipino Responses 1565–1700.* Madison: University of Wisconsin Press.

Pringle, Robert. 1980. *Indonesia and the Philippines: American Interests in Island Southeast Asia*. New York: Columbia University Press.

"Prof. Nugroho Guru Besar Ilmu Sejarah," Kompas. 1980, January 7.

Quibuyen, Floro 1999. *A Nation Aborted: Rizal, American Hegemony, and Philippine Nationalism*. Quezon City: Ateneo de Manila University Press.

Rafael, Vicente. 1988. *Contracting Colonialism: Translation and Christian Conversion in Tagalog Society under Early Spanish Rule*. Quezon City: Ateneo de Manila University Press.

Resink, Gertrudes. 1968. "Between the Myths: From Colonial to National Historiography." In *Indonesia's History between the Myths: Essays in Legal History and Historical Theory*, 15–25. The Hague: W. van Hoeve Publishers, Ltd.

Sani, Rustam. 1976. "Melayu Raya as a Malay Nation of Intent." In *The Nascent Malaysian Society*, edited by H. M. Dahlan, 11–25. Kuala Lumpur: Jabatan Antropologi dan Sosiologi, UKM.

Schumacher, John. 1979. "Propagandists Construction of the Philippine Past." In *Perceptions of the Past in Southeast Asia*, edited by Anthony Reid and David Marr, 264–279. Singapore: Heinemann Asia.

Shalom, Stephen. 1981. *The United States and the Philippines: A Study of Neocolonialism*. Philadelphia, PA: Institute for the Study of Human Issues.

Shamsul, Amri Baharrudin. 1998. "Nations-of-Intent in Malaysia." In *Asian Forms of the Nation*, edited by Stein Tonnesson and Hans Antlov, 323–346. Surrey: Curzon Press.

Shiraishi, Takashi. 1990. *An Age in Motion: Popular Radicalism in Java, 1912–1926*. Ithaca, NY: Cornell University Press.

Steinberg, David Joel, ed. 1987. *In Search of Southeast Asia: A Modern History*. Rev. ed. Sydney: Allen & Unwin.

Suzuki, Mary Bonzo. 1991. "American Education in the Philippines, the Early Years: American Pioneer Teachers and the Filipino Response, 1900–1935." PhD Diss., University of California Berkeley, Berkeley.

Thomas, Megan. 2012. *Orientalists, Propagandists, and Ilustrados Filipino Scholarship and the End of Spanish Colonialism*. Minneapolis: University of Minnesota Press.

Weekley, Kathleen. 2001. *The Communist Party of the Philippines, 1968–1993: A Story of Its Theory and Practice*. Quezon City: University of the Philippines Press.

Yamin, Mohammad. 1951. *6000 Tahun Sang Merah Putih (6000 Years of Red and White)*. Djakarta: Siguntang.

2 Genesis of Tadhana project

In an extemporaneous speech delivered in 1967, Ferdinand Marcos publicly declared, perhaps for the first time, his desire to write a history. Before an audience of historians and history teachers, he fancied the day that he would be able to do so once his stint in politics was over (Marcos 1967). He did not have to wait that long. Inspired by Churchill's multi-volume *A History of the English-Speaking Peoples* (Churchill 1956), he forged a partnership with a group of young Filipino scholars and embarked beginning in 1973–1974 on an ambitious project to write a multi-volume Philippine history. In terms of scope, projected output, and the required financial and intellectual resources, the project was staggering. *Tadhana*, as it became known, stands out in the history of Philippine scholarship as not only the most ambitious, but easily the most controversial history-writing project ever undertaken.

This chapter will, first, reconstruct the story leading to the birth of Tadhana project. Second, it will identify and discuss the possible motivations that drove Marcos to undertake the project, along with those that impelled the scholars to participate in it. Finally, it will provide snapshots of how the project actually operated with the aim of examining the dynamics and power relations between key actors involved.

A caveat is in order before I proceed. Given the secrecy with which the Marcos government had shrouded the project, as well as the stigma (for scholar-participants) attached to being associated with the unpopular Marcos regime, Tadhana project was not openly discussed for many years. Nevertheless, since its inception in the 1970s, Tadhana formed a topic of passionate conversations in private as part of the gossip mills that characterize Philippine academic-political life. Except for brief recollections by a few participants in 1989, nothing has yet been published about Tadhana that can help reconstruct the story, or stories, of its making. This chapter, thus, relies on oral history data gathered from the interviews of the participants in the project—the only ones who could provide relevant information. The nature of such oral sources admittedly makes them vulnerable

44 *Genesis of Tadhana project*

to suspicion of self-serving biases and unreliability. These personal stories will be treated, with caution, as perceptions or recollections of what informants believed to be true, rather than as the truth itself. Despite the limitations of these sources, I believe it is possible to establish at least the broad contours of the features and the overall developmental chronology of the project. It is in areas that require interpretive assessment—of power relations, motivations, and attitudes—that participant recollections pose particular challenges. Power relations in general, and power-knowledge in particular, operate partly in the realm of speculations, rumors, or assumptions. We can, at the very least, take these personal recollections as indicative of how participants position themselves vis-à-vis fellow members of the project and also in relation to those who were critical of the project. Rather than being treated as insurmountable limitations, I take the subjective elements of their testimonies as among the key constituting elements of power relations that shape Tadhana project.

Genesis

Marcos was elected president in late 1965 on the wave of the reformist image he successfully propagated during his campaign. He and his wife, Imelda, cultivated close ties with Filipino artists and intellectuals, including historians. The extemporaneous speech mentioned above was delivered as a keynote address in a conference organized by the Philippine Historical Association (PHA), one of the leading professional associations of historians in the country. Amid heightened awareness of the problems in Philippine historiography in the 1960s, an idea was floated to establish a commission to write Philippine history (Nakpil 1971). This idea attracted Marcos's attention. Initially, he sought the participation of the two biggest names in Philippine history at the time, Teodoro Agoncillo and Horacio de la Costa, to spearhead the project. The choice of these scholars with contrasting characteristics was instructive about Marcos' evolving interest in history-writing. Agoncillo was a homegrown historian; he did not undertake graduate studies overseas and apparently he did not care to pursue them, unlike many of his contemporaries. He gained fame through his books *Revolts of the Masses* (1956), *Malolos: The Crisis of the Republic* (1960), and the very popular textbook *A Short History of the Filipino People* (Agoncillo and Alfonso 1960). The latter was reprinted and revised several times (with the slightly different title *History of the Filipino People*) even after Agoncillo passed away in 1985. As will be discussed below, these books occupied a seminal position in promoting an anti-colonial form of nationalism that was brewing in the Philippines in the post-war decades. According to Ileto, the publication in 1956 of Agoncillo's *Revolt of the Masses* "transgressed the proper meaning of the revolution at that time" and by doing so proved instrumental in altering the consciousness required for the student movement to take off (Ileto 1998, 185, 188–189). Agoncillo studied at public schools and dominated for decades, both by dint of strong personality and by the strength of his scholarship, the country's most important department of History: that of the University of the Philippines (UP) at Diliman. De la Costa, on the other hand, was a Jesuit who received a PhD from Harvard University. He reigned over the rival History department at the neighboring elite private university, the Ateneo de Manila University, for a long time. He was well known for his book *Jesuits in the Philippines, 1571–1768* (1961) as well as for the textbook popularly used in Catholic schools, *Readings in Philippine History* (1965). If Agoncillo was thoroughly secular, de la Costa was obviously religious. If Agoncillo promoted a 'radical' nationalist history, de la Costa was identified with a kind of history that some would derisively call a 'clerical' or pro-Church history. However, as Ileto (2017) has argued, this view needs to be refined or revised as by the 1970s, the two historians' nationalist views appear to be converging.

According to Agoncillo, then First Lady Imelda Marcos approached him twice about joining the project. The first was in 1968 and the second was in 1971 (Agoncillo and Jose 1976 in Ocampo 1995, 149–151). He was reportedly offered generous financial support as well as the freedom to decide the administration, structure, and content of the project. On both occasions, he declined, mustering all the polite gestures and alibis he could think of.[1] While he maintained a civil, if not really friendly, stance towards the Marcoses, he seemed too conscious of possible adverse consequences once he became an 'official historian,' and this weighed heavy on his decision to turn down the overtures. He declared that "the day I do that (write history for Marcos), finished, I am finished!" He added that he would "not just be a fiction writer but a prostitute" (Agoncillo and Jose 1976 in Ocampo 1995, 150).

In the case of Horacio de la Costa, the number of times he was invited to the project could not be determined, but the earliest verifiable attempt was made in 1968. As late as June 1973, the Marcos couple were still trying to win his nod, as an entry in Marcos's diaries indicates.[2] Just as in the case of Agoncillo, however, they met no success. The two historians' refusal to join the project may be, among other possibilities, a testimony to their sense of duty to uphold scholarly independence. It may also be indicative of the sharp political division in the Philippines, which made it risky for some scholars to work openly with and for Marcos. On the other hand, that Marcos went a long way to convince them to lead the project, offering generous support and promising unhampered movement, revealed much about his evolving and complex motivations in pursuing a history-writing project. It may not be assumed that undiluted self-interest was all there was. For if that was the case, why should he approach Agoncillo and de la Costa, whose reputations, of which Marcos was fully aware, made them difficult to influence or manipulate?

46 Genesis of Tadhana project

Not the type to give up easily, Marcos continued to seek people who could help him realize his dream. Meanwhile, a project called the *Filipino Heritage* (FH) was underway. Under the stewardship of Alfredo Roces as Editor-in-Chief, FH was an initiative of the Hamlyn Group, an Australia-based publishing company. Conceived before Martial Law was declared in September 1972, the Hamlyn Group entered into a partnership with the *Manila Times*, a leading daily newspaper. The original plan was to produce 102 articles on Philippine history and culture. Well-known experts were to be commissioned to write these articles, and these would be serialized in the *Manila Times* for two years. However, when almost all newspapers, including the *Manila Times*, were shut down in the wake of the declaration of Martial Law, the project was repackaged into a ten-volume opus, with public schools in the country the main projected markets. Given the altered political landscape, the FH team had to ask for official approval from the government in 1974. As part of their effort, they sought an audience with then President Marcos to present the initial outputs of the ongoing project.[3] Marcos was reported to have exploded in rage upon seeing someone surnamed Roces heading the list of editorial board members and advisers. Apparently, Marcos mistook Alfredo Roces for Joaquin 'Chino' Roces, who was Marcos's staunch critic and the owner-editor-in-chief of the *Manila Times*. Not long after the incident, the head of the Hamlyn operation in the Philippines, Kevin Weldon, received a letter from the Malacañang Palace, the seat of presidential power in the Philippines. Juan Tuvera, the Presidential Assistant, signed the letter which stated that Marcos would take over the position of editor-in-chief from Alfredo Roces. In addition, FH manuscripts should be submitted to Malacañang for evaluation. Despite Roces's offer to give way so as to maintain the economic viability of the project, Weldon did not budge under pressure from Malacañang. The FH manuscripts were submitted as per Malacañang's instruction, but after the negative appraisal, to be discussed further below, came out a few weeks later, Weldon instructed Roces to pack and transport the FH-related materials. In due time, Roces found himself and his family in migratory flight to Sydney, where (alongside Singapore) he worked for the completion of the project. FH eventually saw publication in 1978.[4]

For a few weeks upon submission of the FH manuscripts to Malacañang, on the instruction of Marcos, a group of scholars were busy poring over the pages and preparing reviews. To this group belonged younger scholars from the UP whose PhDs were from prestigious universities in Europe and the United States. Leading the group was Serafin Quiason, who obtained a PhD in History from the University of Pennsylvania and was the director of the National Library from 1966 to 1986. Before taking a post at the National Library, he was a lecturer at the Department of History of UP. His stint in academe before working as a bureaucrat prepared him for the role of intermediary between Marcos and the group of scholars who took part in the project. He acted as the Assistant Project Director. Upon his shoulders fell the task of recruiting participants—a task in which he was allowed a free rein.[5]

Initially, he gathered around him four other scholars, all young assistant or associate professors at UP. They were Samuel Tan, Zeus Salazar, Alex Hufana, and Cesar Hidalgo.[6] Together, they constituted the group whose initial task was to review the FH manuscripts. As events would have it, they would later form the core group of Tadhana project. Like Quiason, Samuel Tan and Zeus Salazar were historians by training. Hufana, on the other hand, was in literature and Hidalgo was a linguist. When Tan was initiated into the group, sometime in 1973–1974, he had just returned from Syracuse University armed with the latest multi-disciplinary approach to historical analysis. Salazar, on the other hand, had completed a few years earlier a PhD at the University of Paris Sorbonne. He trained in ethnology and history and he gained fluency in a number of European and Austronesian languages, a feat rare for Filipino scholars, then as now. Hufana for his part was an accomplished, multi-awarded writer in English. He undertook his Master's degree at Columbia University, while Hidalgo obtained a PhD in linguistics from Georgetown University. Hidalgo's early departure in 1976 from the group set the stage for the entry into the core group of another scholar, Rodolfo Paras-Perez. He was an established painter and a premier art historian who trained at Harvard University for a PhD in Art History. Like the rest, he was a lecturer at UP. The choice of people whose academic expertise and background varied was no accident. The intention was to produce a history that was multi-dimensional, one that transcends the traditional, big men-centered and politics-focused narrative. Bonds of friendship and other personal ties also informed the choice of people to be invited as it was thought to enhance the quality of working relations (Tan 1993, 85). Tan, Salazar, and Hufana, for instance, were all Quiason's close friends. Hidalgo was a friend of Hufana as Tan and Paras-Perez were of Salazar. In addition, Quiason was Salazar's *compadre,* a godfather or sponsor in the baptism of Salazar's eldest child.

The task of reviewing the FH manuscripts came as an annoying task to the members of the group. They were unclear why they were doing it. An informant recalled that he was surprised they had to review all these manuscripts.[7] Another participant vaguely remembered that Marcos had to decide whether FH should be given an official endorsement for use in the public schools, and he needed a group of scholars to help him reach a decision.[8] Apparently, none in the group knew that Marcos had the intention to wrest the editorship of the FH from Roces and that they were tasked with evaluating the FH in preparation for a possible take-over. Based on their understanding, they were recruited to write history, not just evaluate or review one.

The verdict was not long in coming and it was decidedly unfavorable. One complaint was that the perspective adopted was inappropriate—that it was not Filipino enough. It seemed bent on "pleasing the foreigners" rather than demonstrating the "internal dynamics" within the Philippines.[9] Another complaint was that the framework adopted to provide a unifying thread for all the articles written by various contributors was not coherent[10].

One may ask what would have happened had the outcome of the reviews been more favorable. I surmised the following possible scenarios: there would have been no Tadhana for there was no need for an entirely new project. With Marcos wresting the editorship of FH, its framework already set, and substantial progress already made in writing manuscripts, it was likely that only fairly limited changes, or additions, would be made to accommodate his preferences. Another possibility was that Tadhana would have pushed through just the same, as people behind FH were firm in their resolve not to allow Marcos to take over the FH.

In hindsight, however, it may have been naïve to expect that FH could ever receive sympathetic reviews from the group of scholars tasked by Marcos with undertaking the evaluation. There was a gap between the scholarly orientations of the major members of this group and that of the scholars who worked with the FH. The historians, for instance, who worked for the FH, such as de la Costa, Agoncillo, and Corpus, represented various streams in what some would call the 'old schools' in Philippine nationalist historiography. On the other hand, Salazar and Tan seemed eager to assume the role of Young Turks, brewing with new ideas and keen to offer alternative historiographic views and approaches to address what they saw as problems that had long bedeviled Philippine historiography.[11] The outlet for their pent-up intellectual energy precisely came when Marcos broached the idea of a history-writing project. Between acting as editors or evaluators for an ongoing history-writing project, on the one hand, and acting as trailblazers of the still uncharted historiographic terrain, on the other hand, the choice was obvious for these scholars.

It was also possible that at some point, the group got a hint that the review of FH was somehow related to a possible take-over of the project, in which case, there was even less of a chance for a favorable review of FH. Given Tadhana's core group's avowed rationale for taking part in the national history-writing project, it would better serve their interest and afford them maximum freedom to start a clean-slate project rather than take over one whose parameters had already been defined more or less. This is particularly clear in the wonderment of one of the members of the core group as to why they 'wasted' time reviewing FH when he, for one, already had a clear idea of how to proceed with the writing project.[12] Like Salazar, he had a well-defined historiographic agenda, as evidenced in an article he published in 1976 (see Salazar 1974; Tan 1976). It was just the opportunity to undertake research and write that he was waiting for. Giving FH a favorable review would mean a lesser opportunity for them to accomplish their objectives as Marcos might be enticed all the more to take over FH.

As Marcos lost interest in FH owing perhaps both to Weldon's obstinate stance and the group's patently negative appraisal of it, the way was paved for the birth of an entirely new project. This time, he was not content to act as a patron or a sponsor of a commission, as was the case a few years back. Neither was he interested in merely becoming the editor-in-chief, as was the case for FH. He wanted no less than authorship, in fact, sole authorship of the entire multi-volume project. What initially started as a supposedly modest desire to help advance scholarship on Philippine history by sponsoring a commission to write a history ended in a very ambitious appropriation of the role and the power of scholars. The attempt to fuse knowledge and power seemed unmistakable.

Motivations

The Tadhana project emerged from a confluence of several factors. In popular imagination, however, what easily dominated was the perception of the project as part of Marcos's grand design to perpetuate himself in power, made possible by his declaration of Martial Law in September 1972 (e.g. Veneracion 1993). The timing of the project—having taken off around 1974 when other books ghostwritten for Marcos (e.g. Marcos 1973a, 1974) appeared—tended to reinforce this view. Moreover, the trajectory of Philippine historical development, as outlined in *Tadhana*, which is to be discussed in detail in the next chapter, coincided almost perfectly with Marcos's interest in presenting Martial Law and the New Society it spawned as a natural or a necessary part of the evolutionary process in the development of the Filipino nation. The choice of the title *Tadhana*, which means 'destiny,' says it all: that the Philippines was destined to see the rise of a New Society characterized by peace, prosperity, and national pride. In addition, parts of the reform package offered to justify the declaration and maintenance of Martial Law were anchored on a "history concerned with the indigenous as a principle of assimilation and growth"—exactly the idea that underpinned Tadhana (Marcos 1982, 6).

Notwithstanding all these considerations, however, the situation was more complex. For one, Marcos was already toying with the idea of a history-writing project years before Martial Law was declared or seriously thought about, or before his regime was seriously challenged by the radicals. His extemporaneous speech in 1967, noted above, showed him rather ambivalent as to whether he would, in fact, write a history, but he was categorical about his 'wish' to do so at some point in time (Marcos 1967). There are those who claimed that as early as his first term in office (1966–1969) Marcos was already planning to extend his rule (e.g. de Quiros 1997; Muego 1988), which implies that his interests in history-writing as early as this period were already in line with his long-term plans to perpetuate himself in power for as long as possible. However, modern historical analysis precludes eschatological speculations. In his earlier offer to Agoncillo and de la Costa in 1968, Marcos did not plan to be the 'author'; he was willing to allow the two leading scholars freedom to carry out the project as they saw fit. For another, an elaborate network of excuses backed by well-oiled propaganda machinery had already been in place to address the need of justifying the Martial Law. In addition, a 21-volume history seemed too difficult, too time-consuming, too unwieldy, and perhaps not too effective a medium if the sole or primary purpose was a justification of his continued stay in power. A political agenda was certainly there, as will be further discussed below, but there must be other factors to consider as well.

One such factor was Marcos's deep personal interest in history. Practically all informants who had a chance to engage with him at close range have attested in glowing terms to the keenness of his knowledge of and interest in history. He was described by one of the core group members, for instance, as "somebody you cannot tinker with your expertise" and by another as "a voracious reader whose prodigious memory was indisputable."[13] They all remembered, some of them with fondness, their nocturnal discussions about wide-ranging historical topics with Marcos—discussions that sometimes lasted until early in the morning. They all said that Marcos had a developed sense of history and that he exuded a deep respect for historians and the historical profession. Cynics would be quick to wonder how they could have easily allowed themselves to be captivated, or conned, by Marcos. However, being professionally trained historians, with PhDs from prestigious universities at that, one could at least give them the benefit of the doubt; there may be something more than a superficial impression in such observations.

A corollary of Marcos's 'interest' in history was his awareness of the usefulness of history for administrative purpose and, of course, for personal aggrandizement. Typical in his speeches, for instance, was a declaration like "I am interested in history not only for the wisdom and the book learning it conveys, but also for its value as a basis for actual decision, policy-making and implementation" (Marcos 1973b, 3). While this might seem like no more than the empty rhetoric common among Filipino politicians, informants who worked with or for Marcos confirmed his voracious appetite for historical research as part of the routine decision- or policy-making process. An informant recalled, for instance, that she was asked to undertake research on the technological contributions of China to world history as well as Chinese influences on the Philippines before Marcos undertook a state visit to China in 1975.[14] Another participant in the project claimed that she worked on the historical basis of claims of Sabah and of the US bases agreement.[15] Still another was the case of Jose Almonte who was instructed to study how martial law was implemented in Pakistan (de Quiros 1997, 338).

Marcos has rationalized his penchant for this type of research by saying that the best advisers inhabit the pages of history who, because they were long dead, had no interest to protect or advance (Marcos 1982, 13–14). While one expects that he would be less than forthright about history's self-aggrandizing function, he was candid enough to admit on one occasion that "it is sometimes convenient to be able to write down your own side of history" (Marcos 1982, 5). This was after paraphrasing Winston Churchill: "If they won't write history the way it should be written after making history, I will write history" (Marcos 1982, 5). At the very least, Marcos was well aware of what history can do. As he said, referring to history, "no matter what others say, the written word is still a powerful instrument and the pen is still mightier than the sword. Words will always be able to achieve what the bullet cannot" (Marcos 1982, 26).

Still another contributory factor was the perceived prestige that goes with the authorship of a scholarly work. Marcos was very much interested in promoting himself as an intellectual or as a scholarly president (Reyes 2018). A key participant recalled that, of the few thousand copies of the first published volume of Tadhana, only about 500 circulated in the Philippines. The rest had been earmarked for distribution abroad, to be given as personal gifts from Marcos to ambassadors, heads of state and other high-ranking officials, friends and acquaintances whom he met in his fairly extensive travels abroad. Marcos also seemed desirous of immortalizing himself through the project. A participant quoted Marcos as saying in one of their meetings, "You know, after the end of my term, the people will forget everything that I have done, my infrastructures, etc…but the only thing that will last is this (showing a copy of the first printed volume of *Tadhana*)."[16]

Perhaps another side to Marcos's apparent genuine interest in history was his fear of, or anxiety about, it. His diaries contain passages that indicate his nagging sense of unease as to how he and his regime would be judged in history. An entry dated Oct. 8, 1970, for example, states:

> I often wonder what I will be remembered in history for. Scholar? Military hero? Builder? The new constitution? Reorganization of (the) government? Uniter (sic) of the variant and antagonistic elements of our people? He brought light to a dark country? Strong rallying point or a weak tyrant?

The diary also indicates that Marcos was fearful and distrustful of historians. After reading Bailey's book *Presidential Greatness*, which, Marcos notes in his diary entry for 19 December 1971, "explains the bias of historians and how they get it," he concluded that "history should not be left to the historians." This was corroborated by what Marcos declared in the 1967 speech in which he rationalized his desire to write history by citing the need to correct what he thought to be an erroneous and overly negative picture of him in the media. Perhaps Marcos was thinking that through Tadhana, he would be able to 'straighten' what he believed to be a distorted history perpetrated by his detractors, including historians, some of whom he described as 'contentious' (Marcos 1982, 1).

In my interview with one of Marcos's closest aides, the one whom he asked to write a memo that served as the germ of Tadhana project, he revealed that the project was undertaken primarily as Marcos's vehicle to explain himself and the declaration of Martial Law to the Filipino people, not of the contemporary period but in the future a century hence. Given the highly fractious political sphere in the 1970s, Marcos knew full well, he averred, that the public would not take the project seriously. In a hundred years, so

52 Genesis of Tadhana project

Marcos believed, people would already be far removed from the political contentiousness of the 1970s and they would be in a better position to judge without bias whether what he did was right or wrong.[17]

Still another possible factor was Marcos's sense of nationalism. He routinely utilized nationalist tropes to serve his personal agenda, and so cynics would be justified in doubting the sincerity of his nationalism. However, many in his generation grew up "in a period which took special delight in the culture and history of other countries" and consequently developed a "sense of alienation from (their) country's past," and at least some of them probably longed for redemption from such a "crisis of identity" (Marcos 1976, ii). Marcos could very well be one of them. The truth is, even if we grant that he was not one of them, many others in his own and succeeding generations were well aware of such a crisis of identity which called for a kind of history that would address it. In other words, there was a fairly broad constituency to whom the writing of the so-called 'truly' nationalist history would appeal, and Marcos was quick to respond.

The motivations of the scholars who took part in the project varied depending on their academic standing and personal circumstances at that time. The main 'designers' of the project, Salazar and Tan, claimed that what attracted them to it was the opportunity to do what they loved doing—scholarship—in an atmosphere unhampered by day-to-day concerns. Both of them had a rather well-defined historiographic agenda, and they saw an opportunity for realizing these by taking part in the project. Tan (1976), for instance, wanted to address the long-standing neglect of the Muslims and other cultural communities in traditional historical narratives, which, almost without exception, were badly skewed towards the numerically dominant Christian populace. He had a particular interest in demonstrating the interaction between the 'great' traditions of Christianity and Islam, on the one hand, and the 'small' traditions of the tribal groups, on the other. Furthermore, as a reaction to the predominance of descriptive political history, he wanted to inject into the historical narrative a multi-disciplinary analytical approach whereby, as appropriate, the analytical tools of the social sciences were woven into the historical narrative. He believed this would enable him to emphasize the dynamism of history as a counterpoint to the rather static images that gathered around traditional historical approaches.

Zeus Salazar, on the other hand, wanted to develop a more holistic and complete picture of Philippine history. In the context of seriously inadequate historical scholarship that 'silenced' various periods, notably the centuries spanning the pre-Hispanic era and the first 200–250 years of Spain in the Philippines, this was understandable. Asked if it bothered him to work for Marcos, who was despised by many, he put it strongly:

> If I'd be offered by anyone—even by a criminal—a whole institute to allow me to write my history [referring to complete Philippine history], I'd accept. I wouldn't mind even if he's a criminal. The important thing

is that I be able to do it. After all, this is more important than one single individual. So for me, there are no moral issues here because one of the attainments of historiography is that you no longer judge in moral terms.[18]

The same informant also wished to employ and experiment with new perspectives aimed at correcting the long-standing approaches heavily tinged with a colonial hangover. That Salazar and Tan had in fact succeeded in pushing their agenda can be seen in the framework adopted for the whole project. Through their combined effort, the original outline of the project was drawn (Tan 1993, 86), discussed by the group, and presented to Marcos for discussion. Marcos accepted it without asking for a revision. In the words of Samuel Tan, "Marcos swallowed it hook, line and sinker,"[19] Not long afterwards, the detailed outline was circulated in public as a 62-page pamphlet simply entitled *The Tadhana Outline* (Marcos 1976).

The nationalist packaging of the project also made it attractive. The upsurge in Filipino nationalism in the 1960s and 1970s, the meanings and defining parameters of which were contested, provided a pliable template upon which Marcos's partnership with the scholars materialized. Marcos was bound to strike very sympathetic chords not only among many scholars but among common people as well when, in justifying Tadhana project, he declared: "The need to refresh one's perspectives on the past is particularly acute for a people whose written history is mainly the legacy of nation, or nations that once subjugated them" (Marcos 1982, 3). Salazar recalled that when Quiason approached him and invited him to the project, the latter described it as a "very important, nationalist undertaking" (Salazar 1989, 194). Romeo Cruz, who joined the project much later in 1980, echoed the same words as Quiason's time-tested bait to entice prospective participants. Cruz recalled in particular that one thing that lured him to the project was the impressive manner by which topics which were seemingly difficult to situate within a nationalistic framework (such as geological origins and the pre-Hispanic period) have in fact been successfully interpreted along this line. He cited as an example the chapter on *Adam in the Philippines*, which posited the local process of humanization, rather than merely relying on the postulate of the diffusion of the human race from, say, Africa (Cruz 1989). For Rod Paras-Perez, a Harvard-trained art historian, while he was similarly attracted to the nationalist intent of the project, he also felt disturbed by the overly politico-economic conceptualization of nationalism that informed much of the Philippine nationalist history. He bewailed the common practice of treating culture like an appendix to the politics-centered narrative, if included at all. In joining the project, he felt he was being given an opportunity to help correct the imbalance. Specifically, he was interested in showing the centrality of culture and in weaving into the historical narrative the cultural, values-centered aspects of the development of the Filipino nation.[20]

Another factor was compensation. Whether this carried a heavy weight in their decision to participate, however, depended much on scholars' personal circumstances during that time. For the Harvard-trained art historian mentioned above, who already had a name as an established artist (painter) and thus had a reliable source of income, it was easy to be cavalier about matters of compensation. He recalled that when Salazar asked him how much salary he wanted just for him to accept the invitation, he casually asked his assistant how much. He said in jest that his assistant sold him cheaply.[21] Others, however, were not as fortunate. Those who served auxiliary functions, such as research assistants and part-timers, readily admitted that the compensation package was an attraction. Luis Dery, one of the researchers, for instance, claimed to have received from the project a salary which was more than double his salary as an Instructor at the UP Baguio. He claimed to have received 2,500 pesos per month from the project as a research assistant, compared with 900–1000 pesos as an Instructor at UP. Without his work on the project, he claimed, it would have been much more difficult to accumulate savings that enabled him to pursue doctoral studies while at the same time providing for the needs of his family. He admitted he owed much to his participation in Tadhana.[22]

Another participant, Reynaldo Ileto, attested that he received an honorarium (around 600 pesos) for editing a 'badly written chapter.' It was a substantial addition to his salary of about 1,500 pesos per month as Assistant Professor at UP. He said he was very happy to have been paid well for that piece of work, and he believed that "for most of those who took part in the project, the pay was the big attraction."[23]

In talking about salaries, core members, such as Tan, Quiason, and Salazar, invariably took a different view from the group of minor players. If the latter happily emphasized the substantial difference in salary between what they receive from UP and what they received from this project, the former tended to downplay the financial factor in the project, underscoring that the difference between UP pay and that of Tadhana hovered 'only' at around 20–30 per cent. In the absence of exact figures, which they hesitated to give, this is not easy to verify. It is very likely, however, that they were being modest about it. If that claim by the UP Baguio Instructor noted above was true that he was getting more than twice his UP salary, then those who occupied more senior positions, such as Salazar and Tan, were probably getting proportionately more. Given that a UP Assistant Professor was getting P1,500/month, and an Associate Professor about P2,000/month, it seems unlikely that the senior researchers were getting only P2,000 to P2,600 (following the 20–30 per cent differential claimed by Tan et al.), while the UP Baguio Instructor who was only a research assistant received P2,500. On the other hand, even if what the core members claimed was accurate, the difference could still be substantial considering they received fringe benefits such as travels abroad to gather materials to which they were the only ones entitled as members of the core group.

The attitude of the members of the other core group can best be understood in the context of widespread rumor that they received handsome amounts of money just to join the project, a claim they all summarily rejected. In jest, laughing heartily, Samuel Tan said, "How I wished I got that much!"... "If that was true, how come I was driving a car handed down to me by my brother?"[24] Zeus Salazar's retort was more stinging. He said that those who were spreading the rumor, as well as those who believed it, were perhaps thinking of themselves: "they are too inferior... they would accept it because of the money. (For) they would not be asked otherwise..."[25]

Still another attraction was the opportunity provided by the project for professional or academic advancement, specifically access to valuable historical documents. For a fresh graduate in history and for another who was a PhD student, being able to gather data while having a gainful employment was an opportunity one could hardly refuse.[26]

Finally, a variety of pragmatic reasons also played a part. Salazar, for example, candidly admitted that Quiason convinced him to join the project by saying, among other things, that participating might pave the way for rescinding the travel ban imposed upon him by the Martial Law regime (Salazar 1989). This ban, alongside detention, Salazar claimed, was a penalty for 'mocking' or criticizing Marcos's book *Today's Revolution: Democracy (TRD)*. In a separate interview, Salazar offered a different story, in which he was arrested not for mocking Marcos's book but as a consequence of the widespread arrests by the military upon the implementation of Martial Law in September 1972 (as noted in Gaerlan 1998, 255–256). In this version, he recalled that he was incarcerated for three months and was released with the help of a friend, Leticia Ramos Shahani, who was Gen. Fidel Ramos's sister. It was Ramos, one of the main implementers of Martial Law as the Philippine Constabulary Chief, who worked for Salazar's release.[27] His release, however, carried a condition that he was not to leave the country or even the vicinity of Metro Manila. This prevented him from accepting invitations for conferences or fellowships abroad, which irritated him considerably as he had a standing offer of fellowship from the French government. His desire to regain his freedom of movement proved strong enough that any opportunity to restore it was enticing.

Yet another case is that of a woman historian-activist who had a child to feed and a husband whose painful experience in jail during Martial Law made him unable to work and who had to be taken care of. She too was detained for involvement in activism, and her release carried the condition that she should work for a government agency.[28] For someone whose chance of getting a better-paying teaching job anywhere was slim, a job with a history-writing project with a good salary proved irresistible.

In sum, the partnership between Marcos and the scholars was made possible and was sustained by mutual needs—financial, political, intellectual, and even psychological. Both sides needed each other. The convergence of their needs was nurtured by the rising wave of anti-colonial nationalism

Genesis of Tadhana project

that pervaded the atmosphere in the 1960s and 1970s. To understand this partnership, its products, and its implications more deeply, we shall look into various aspects of the project as it unfolded.

Dynamics

After the outline has been completed and approved, the members of the core group divided the tasks. For practical reasons, the group initially focused their effort on Vol. II, which consists of five books covering the periods from 1565 to 1896. They figured out that they had as yet insufficient resources to tackle Vol. 1 (Geologic times up to the early 1500s), also with five books, whereas they felt they had enough for Vol. II. So, Salazar was assigned to Part I (Encounter), encompassing the period 1565–1663. Part II (Reaction), covering the period 1663–1765, was given to Hidalgo, whose early departure from the group in 1976 paved the way for the entry of Paras-Perez. Part III (Transition), which spans the period 1766–1815, was assigned to Hufana. Part IV (Transformation) was allotted to Quiason, while Part V (1872–1896) was the responsibility of Tan.

Each of the core members was assisted by two or three research assistants—usually graduate students—whose tasks included scouring for books and documents in the archives as well as, in certain instances, writing manuscripts. There were also those who worked on a part-time, per project basis. They were hired on the basis of their specific expertise. It was on this account that the likes of Ben Austria, who did a PhD in Geology at Harvard, and Reynaldo Ileto, who obtained a PhD in History at Cornell, were invited. The composition of the group was fluid at most times, wherein some people were hired, stayed for only a few months, and then disappeared to be replaced by new hirees.

From a formal administrative viewpoint, the project was under the jurisdiction of the National Library, then under the directorship of Serafin Quiason. It was classified as a 'Special Research Project.' The group was assigned the top floor, the 5th floor, for their workplace. There, almost every working day for several years starting in 1974 they worked and gave shape to the project. Every morning, there was a shuttle service that ferried the participants from their abodes at UP-Diliman and elsewhere to the heart of Manila, where the National Library was (and still is) located. At the end of the day, and sometimes, even the early hours of the morning, when they were having discussions with Marcos, the same shuttle service brought them back to their residences.[29]

The importance Marcos attached to the project may be clearly seen in the quality and quantity of resources he made available to the researchers. Informants described with nostalgia the working environment as 'ideal.' The group was provided with efficient clerical and technical staff, allowing them to concentrate on their scholarly pursuits. All the materials in the National Library were made available to them, and staff were specifically tasked with bringing in whatever the group needed from the collection. They also did not have to do typing, one thing very much appreciated by the participants. Once a handwritten manuscript was completed, they just gave it to the typists, and by the following morning or even the afternoon of the same day, it was on the desk, ready for editing. Even when required materials were found only in other libraries or institutions, and thus access to them was not normally easy, participants said it took only one call from the Malacañang to facilitate the release and delivery of such materials to the workplace.[30] One participant recalled that there had been nothing else like that in his experience as a scholar in the Philippines. He added that he had had a taste of such an ideal working environment only when he was invited as Visiting Researcher at the Australian National University way back in the 1980s.[31]

Reinforcing the 'ideal' working environment was the almost unlimited financial support for expeditions to gather primary sources in relevant archives overseas. Such conditions allowed the project to amass an impressive collection of documents, pictures, and other historical materials hitherto unavailable in the Philippines. Luis Dery, one of the researchers, describes the collection in the following terms:

> How impressive the Tadhana collections were!! Rare microfilms of William Howard Taft Papers, Alexander Robertson Papers! ... It was really well-funded! 3–4 times they (members of the core group) went abroad...to gather materials. We had complete photocopies of dissertations about the Philippines that were not available in local libraries... everything was latest... The documentation was massive...however, because they did not install an air-conditioning system in the National Library, those microfilms 'melted' and were rendered useless! What a waste! It cost millions! Just imagine one set of William Howard Taft Papers, how many hundreds of reels were that? There were probably 600 reels...[32]

Samuel Tan attested that Marcos did not seem to entertain second thoughts in approving their proposal to visit archives and libraries in Europe and the United States to collect relevant materials. The decision quickly came down only after a few days.[33] Marcos's full and generous support was apparent not only in quick approval of the proposal but also in that no limit was set on the amount of money that the group could spend in buying these materials. As the same core member happily recounted, so long as the materials were deemed useful, there was no question about the cost.[34] Considering Marcos's well-known tendency to be stingy, the generous provisions he allowed the scholars were a testament to the importance he attached to the project. Perhaps, such amenities for historical research remain unequalled in the history of Philippine historical scholarship up to the present. It is no wonder that Tan described the resources as the "(t)he most rewarding part of the project."[35]

It is not easy to determine how much of the contents of Tadhana could be attributed to Marcos. That Juan Tuvera, the Executive Secretary and later Presidential Assistant, did the editing (some say 'just' style editing) for Marcos further complicates the issue of attribution. Tuvera was the overall Project Director. He was the only one trusted to edit, as he had a very intimate knowledge of Marcos's writing style, among other things. Through his consummate hand passed all the manuscripts, before they were given to Marcos for final scrutiny before publication. If asked, the core members—Tan, Salazar and Quiason—unanimously asserted that Marcos did not have anything to do with the substantive content of the project. It was only on two occasions, Salazar claimed, that Marcos intervened, and such intervention involved alteration or inclusion of very minor details. He accommodated Marcos's request, Salazar recalled, just to humor Marcos and his own self (1989, 199). Another core member concurred with Salazar's view. In his words: "Marcos did not influence Tadhana, ideologically or theoretically. The only participation he had was when he read the manuscripts and ... had marginal notes... and questions asked. But more on factual parts of history." Boldly, he claimed that "(i)n fact it was the other way around... the Tadhana (was) the one that shaped Marcos views of history... and later on his perception of future itself."[36] Such a confident declaration seems not totally unwarranted. The influence of Tadhana framework is manifest, for example, in later books attributed to Marcos, such as the *Introduction to the Politics of Transition* (1978b). Compared with the framework of history laid out by Marcos in his diary entry for 17 February 1973, before Tadhana project took shape, the difference was stark. The *Introduction to the Politics of Transition* (1978b) adopted Tadhana's deep emphasis on the pre-colonial periods and used them as the anchor and repository of the country's authentic roots and identities. On the other hand, the diary entry noted above still follows the traditional periodization, where colonial periods define the key features of the Philippine history.

Notwithstanding the strong protestations of the core members of the group that Marcos did not substantively intervene in the project, there are indications to the contrary. Fe Mangahas was assigned to write the chapter called "Radical Alternatives," which covers Marcos's years from 1966–1972. She recalled that she was told to revise the manuscript, the contents of which apparently did not sit well with Marcos's interest. Somebody from Macalanang came one day, and Quiason asked her to join them in a closed-door meeting. During the meeting, she was told by the emissary from Malacañang that the approach she had employed was problematic. Being the author, Marcos's voice should be the one heard, not reduced to just one among several voices, as she had written the chapter. Quiason, she recalled, asked her if she was willing to revise it. She responded, "Sir, if you can get somebody to re-write it, please just have it re-written." The impasse was broken when Quiason said to the man from Malacañang not to worry, that he would fix the problem.[37]

Genesis of Tadhana project 59

There are a number of things worth noting in this episode. First, that despite the maximum level of freedom Marcos allowed the scholars to do as they pleased, when it came to certain historical questions or a period that was utmost in his political design, he would really insist on having his way. Second, a manipulator like Marcos did not need to manipulate the whole stretch of history or significant parts of it. Giving carte blanches to those working on earlier centuries allowed the scholars to preserve their sense of independence. Third, that the research assistant mentioned above could say no, at the risk of losing her job, which was very dear to her considering that she was the breadwinner, bespoke an array of possibilities, but these certainly included her sense of responsibility to uphold measures of historical methodology and professional decorum. One can argue that by doing so she in a sense "spoke truth to power." Fourth, that Quiason did not pressure her, despite his avowed duty as the Deputy Director of the Project, to uphold or represent Marcos's interest could also mean a lot of things, but one possibility was that, being a scholar himself, he shared with her an understanding of the scholarly context that served as pretext for her defiance, and he did not dare cross the line of such an understanding.

One of the team's core members, who on several occasions strongly affirmed that Marcos did not have anything to do with the content of Tadhana, did, in fact, admit at one point that he explicitly showed a desire to influence its shape. Salazar claimed that they were given instruction to emphasize the negative images of the Catholic Church: this instruction was reversed when there was a thaw in the icy relationship between Marcos and the then Cardinal Sin.[38]

The overall progress of Tadhana project turned out to be slow. By 1980, only four volumes had been published. These were, Vol. 1, Part I (Archipelagic Genesis, 1980) and Vol. 2, Part I (Encounter, 1976); Vol. 2, Part II (Reaction, 1978); and Vol. 2, Part III (Transition, 1979). Cruz claimed that much progress had already been accomplished on the remaining volumes (Vol. 3 and 4, consisting of nine books), and the manuscripts had been submitted to Tuvera for editing (Cruz 1989, 201). But it was Tuvera and Marcos, as the Deputy Director of the project confirmed, who were the bottlenecks.[39]

Tuvera's core duties as Executive Secretary or Presidential Assistant were simply too much: he hardly had time to devote to editing Tadhana manuscripts. Asked why Marcos did not employ somebody to help Tuvera, Quiason said that Tuvera was the only one trusted by Marcos.[40] Marcos's illness compounded the problem. That no more than five of the originally planned volumes saw print, even though the other volumes had already been drafted, suggests that Marcos would not allow publication of the remaining without sufficient scrutiny by Tuvera and himself.

Realizing the improbability of completing the 19 volumes, Marcos asked the group to focus on a two-volume abridgement.[41] The first abridged volume covered the earliest period up to 1896. The other one spanned the period from 1897 to the Marcos years in the early 1980s. The team set aside their

60 Genesis of Tadhana project

work on the still-unfinished volumes and concentrated on the abridgement. Samuel Tan recalled that they merely summarized the contents of published parts as well as the unpublished drafts to come up with the abridged version.[42] The first volume was published in 1982, and the other one was almost ready for publication when the EDSA uprisings in 1986 swept the project away, along with the Marcos regime. The second volume never saw print, and the subsequent disappearance of the manuscript was a source of deep bewilderment and amusement among those who were involved in Tadhana project. Piecemeal and sometimes contradictory accounts of the whereabouts of the manuscript in the last days of the Marcos regime circulated. According to Samuel Tan, the page proofs were given to Tuvera for Marcos's final approval. In turn, Tuvera turned them over to the National Media Production Center (NMPC), the printing arm of the government.[43] For his part, Serafin Quiason said that the manuscript was in the office of Tuvera in Malacañang, which was ransacked by anti-Marcos elements in the dying days of the Marcos regime.[44] Fe Mangahas, on the other hand, claimed that she went to the NMPC office after the EDSA events and asked the clerical staff about the whereabouts of the page or galley proof of the manuscript, but the staff said they had no idea.[45] Recently, I heard from one of the former members of Tadhana team that a copy of the second abridged volume has been kept by the Marcoses. It will be interesting to find out when it will be made accessible to the public and what exactly its contents are.

Questions arise as to the original agreement regarding the disclosure of the role of the scholars. According to a member of the core group, there was, in fact, an intention to acknowledge and publicize the names of the scholars, but this was to be done in the last volume completing the project. Since the events at EDSA took over and swept the still-unfinished project away, there was simply no opportunity to do so.[46] It was curious, however, why they had to wait until the project was completed. This explanation leaves one wondering if there was indeed such an intention. The same informant clarified that because the composition of the group was fluid, crediting the scholars before the project was finished might cause inaccuracy in acknowledging all the individual contributions. Why that should be the case was unclear, considering that the volumes appeared one after another, and the group knew very well who and to what extent each participant had contributed to the work on each volume. If there was indeed a plan to reveal the identity of the researchers, it would surely have been better to do so as each volume appeared since the problem of inaccuracy would loom much larger if they waited for the completion of the entire project. Then they would face the difficulty of accurately keeping track of the contributions of various participants within the span of ten years or more.

Another intriguing question is why Marcos installed himself as the author while he could have opted to serve as the editor or just a patron. This was a puzzle even to scholar-participants themselves. If Marcos's primary intention was to provide a 'scholarly' justification for his hold on power, the project would have been more credible and effective had he stayed on the sidelines and let the scholars carry their by-lines. To recall, couched in the offer extended to Agoncillo and de la Costa was Marcos's apparent intent to act as a mere patron or sponsor of the project. What caused the shift in his thinking can only be surmised.

Perhaps, in the case of the offer to Agoncillo and de la Costa, Marcos might have inferred that given their stature the chance that they would write for him (Marcos) as the declared author was minimal, whereas asking them to lead a commission as editor-in-chief stood some chance. It seemed that he really wished the project to prosper, so to avoid the danger of nipping the project in the bud, he opted to take the safer route.

It is also possible that what he considered as a 'success' in his early foray into 'writing' thoroughly gratified him and consequently emboldened him to do more daring things, such as 'authoring' a 21-volume Philippine history. *Today's Revolution: Democracy* (TRD) was the first major book-length work that was supposed to have been authored by Marcos, and it appeared in September 1971.[47] Entries in his diaries shortly thereafter showed him overjoyed with the alleged 'ripples' 'his book' had made. He stated, in an entry for 11 September 1971, that there were many people, even those not given to reading books, who "insist(ed) on having my book and discussing it," and he relished that "(e)verybody (was) talking about the book." Other books followed the TRD, such as *Notes on the New Society of the Philippines* (1973a), *Introduction to Politics of Transition* (1978), and *Towards a Filipino Ideology* (1979). These books were written for Marcos by a stable of intellectuals or in-house ideologues or propagandists, as many are wont to call them (Reyes 2018). Against the backdrop of the wondrous things that Marcos had wanted the people to believe he was—the most bemedaled war hero, a bar exam top-notcher, author of various books, savior of the nation, the best president the country ever had—authoring a 21-volume Philippine history was much in the same vein. More than anything else, perhaps it was his enormous capacity for self-deception (de Quiros 1997, 331), or what Rempel (1993) calls Marcos's 'delusional' tendencies, that enticed him to install himself as the author of Tadhana and believed that people would take him seriously for it.

At any rate, Tadhana, for the most part, was a scholarly undertaking. Whatever political intent Marcos had in mind could not negate its scholarly characteristics, which was exactly what made him politically interested in the project in the first place. His opting for a partnership with professional historians, with impressive credentials at that, points to his desire to produce a scholarly history, presumably a history that carries authority.[48] One can surmise that this authority emanates from at least the appearance or public perception of objectivity or truth. Marcos could have easily resorted to military historians, like Uldarico Baclagon, who Alfred McCoy (1999) considered as Malacañang's resident military historian. But Marcos did not. He may have thought that their work would likely not appear credible or authoritative for they did not have the quality and imprimatur of scholars with PhDs. Though not without limitations, these academic credentials enjoy esteem in society. They signify the affirmation of our society's capacity to know.

Questions arise then, what need did Marcos have for a scholarly history? From what source did such a need arise? Who or what created the source, to begin with? As the most powerful person in the Philippines at that time, it is easy to suppose that he could well afford to ignore any kind of history, let alone academic or scholarly history, to justify or keep himself in power. Why did he bother at all? Following the anonymized informant noted earlier, Marcos wanted to use Tadhana as a medium to explain himself and to convince the future generations of Filipinos and other people that what he did, such as martial law, reforms, and New Society, were right or necessary. It appears that in Marcos's mind, a history that could serve the purpose was a scholarly history, one that in his view could withstand time and critical scrutiny. And this kind of history could be written only by an army of brilliant scholars. What Marcos's 'case' was and how Tadhana fit into his grand scheme will be discussed in the next chapter.

Also possible is Marcos's deeply felt need to persuade, assuage, or comfort himself, more than anyone else. I speculate that he needed reassurance that what he was doing or planning to do was the 'right' thing, in the most morally comforting way. Used as we are to view dictators like him as downright greedy, immoral, or evil, it is easy to forget that, like everyone else, they feel governed by moral conscience, as the fascinating book *The Nazi Conscience* by Claudia Koonz (2003) shows. The idea that even Nazis had consciences could strike many as repulsive, but, as Koonz's study show, it was the case. This conscience requires constant appeasement. When we simply take dictators' moral justifications as a ruse to convince or brainwash other people, we readily ignore the possibility that more than others, it may be their own selves that they are trying to convince. For a sense of well-being, dictators, like other people, need to think and feel good about themselves. They need to feel that they are right, not just in a social, cultural, or political sense but, more importantly, in morally transcendental terms. Entries in his diary suggest that Marcos was overly anxious about the ultimate judgment of 'History.' History functioned for him like a secular god, dispensing reward or punishment for a life lived well or ill. Fastidious as he had shown himself to be in so many areas, it is not surprising that he would seek no one but the best available scholars to help him develop the strongest arguments not just to win his case before the judgment of History but also for his own sense of moral redemption.

If that was indeed the case, so be it. But what does it mean that Marcos felt compelled to argue and win his case? Why was there a 'case,' in the first place? And why did he invoke history, of all knowledge? The next chapter will clarify the historiographic and political contexts that render intelligible the framework and contents of Tadhana and its place in Marcos's political design. It will also help us address these questions.

Notes

1 Agoncillo recalled the first attempt, which was in 1968: "She (Imelda) told me that perhaps it was a good idea for me to write the history of the Philippines, from the Republic, July 4th 1946 when we became independent, to Marcos." Then Agoncillo replied, "...mahirap ito, Mam... (it's risky, Ma'm) if I were to write, people will not believe me...because people will suspect that you paid me, and it will boomerang on you...And the President realized it was correct" (Agoncillo (1976) in Ocampo (1995, 150–151)). Regarding the second attempt, in 1971, Agoncillo quoted Imelda as saying that the Marcos Foundation has invested ten million, and "we don't know how to spend the interests. And so, perhaps a multi-volume history of the Philippines could be financed out of the profits and we thought of you as the Editor-in-Chief. You can get the men you want and maybe there is money in this." In his attempt to get away, Agoncillo said that he was teaching at UP and was handling courses that no other professor could teach. Then, he said, Imelda realized that he didn't like the job, and so, she immediately changed the topic (Agoncillo 1976 in Ocampo (1995, 149–150)).
2 The Marcos diaries, at least the version I was allowed to see, covered the period from 1968 to 1984. They were deposited in the Presidential Commission on Good Government (PCGG) library in Quezon City. Typewritten (or using an early version of word processing), it has no systematic pagination and no date of publication. According to Rempel (1993), the extant copies of Marcos's diaries are heavily sanitized. That the entries in the last three years (1981–1984) were very sparing gives the impression that many entries or several pages were taken off.
3 Communication via email with Alfredo Roces, 19 November 2001.
4 Communication via email with Alfredo Roces 19 November 2001.
5 Interview with Serafin Quiason, 19 April 2004, Manila.
6 According to Romeo Cruz, he was asked by Quiason to join the project in 1973–1974, but he had to beg off because he became the dean of a branch of the UP at Clark airbase in Pampanga. He could have been a member of the core group had he opted to join then. He eventually joined the project in 1980 (Cruz 1989).
7 Interview with Samuel Tan, 12 March 2004, Quezon City.
8 Interview with Zeus Salazar, 19 January 2004, Quezon City.
9 Interview with Zeus Salazar, 19 January 2004, Quezon City.
10 Interview with Samuel Tan, 12 March 2004, Quezon City.
11 It is noteworthy that some of those who worked for FH also worked for Tadhana (e.g. Paras-Perez, Tan and Dery). There is therefore an overlap in the composition of the teams that worked on the two projects (one of the examiners of the thesis upon which this book is based should be acknowledged for pointing this out). I should clarify that those who made considerable difference in the designs of the two projects belonged to two significantly different groups, in generational and in historiographic terms. Tan and Salazar defined the shape of Tadhana, and they had a very different vision of Philippine history, as will be spelled out in Chapter 3. Tan may have been a contributor to FH, thus, constituting one of the overlaps, but his historiographic agenda—what matters to the analysis here—hardly figures in the overall scheme of FH. Paras-Perez was an Associate Editor in FH and thus contributed significantly to the design of FH, but having joined Tadhana at a later stage, he did not have as much impact on the original, overall design of Tadhana. Dery served as contributor to FH and research assistant in Tadhana, rather minor roles that afforded him a fairly limited role in the overall design of the projects. In short, notwithstanding the overlap in the composition of the

64 Genesis of Tadhana project

members, such overlap hardly mattered in defining the distinguishing characteristics of the two projects or in smoothing out the differences between them.
12 Interview with Samuel Tan, 12 March 2004, Quezon City.
13 Interview with Samuel Tan, 12 March 2004 and 19 April 2004, Quezon City.
14 Interview with Rowena Boquiren, 10 March 2004, Manila.
15 Interview with Fe Mangahas, 23 April 2004, Manila.
16 Interview with Samuel Tan, 12 March 2004, Quezon City.
17 Interview with an anonymized informant, 23 February 2005, Makati City.
18 Interview with Zues Salazar, 30 January 2004, Quezon City.
19 Interview with Samuel Tan, 19 April 2004, Quezon City.
20 Interview with Rod Paras-Perez, 4 November 2004, Mandaluyong City.
21 Interview with Rod Paras-Perez, 4 November 2004, Mandaluyong City.
22 Interview with Luis Dery, 21 January 2004, Manila.
23 Communication via email with Reynaldo Ileto, 9 March 2004.
24 Interview with Samuel Tan, 12 March 2004, Quezon City.
25 Interview with Zeus Salazar, 30 January 2004, Quezon City.
26 Interviews with Rowena Boquiren and Luis Dery on 10 March 2004 and 21 January 2004, respectively, both in Manila.
27 Tatad's version, as cited in de Quiros's Dead Aim (1997, 332), is quite different. According to this version, friends of Salazar approached Tatad, and he briefly discussed with Marcos the circumstances surrounding Salazar's arrest and detention. Upon being informed of the rather amusing grounds for Salazar's arrest, Marcos 'magnanimously' ordered his release.
28 Interview with Fe Mangahas, 23 April 2004, Manila.
29 Interviews with various participants of the project.
30 Interviews with various participants of the project.
31 Interview with Zeus Salazar, 30 January 2004, Quezon City.
32 Interview with Luis Dery, 21 January 2004, Manila.
33 Interview with Samuel Tan, 12 March 2004, Quezon City.
34 Interview with Samuel Tan, 12 March 2004, Quezon City.
35 Interview with Samuel Tan, 12 March 2004, Quezon City.
36 Interview with Samuel Tan, 20 September 2004, Quezon City.
37 Interview with Fe Mangahas, 23 April 2004, Manila.
38 Interview with Zeus Salazar, 7 March 2004, Quezon City.
39 Interview with Serafin Quiason, 19 April 2004, Quezon City.
40 Interview with Serafin Quiason, 19 April 2004, Quezon City.
41 Interview with Serafin Quiason, 19 April 2004, Quezon City.
42 Interview with Samuel Tan, 12 March 2004, Quezon City.
43 Interview with Samuel Tan, 12 March 2004, Quezon City.
44 Interview with Serafin Quiason, 19 April 2004, Quezon City.
45 Interview with Fe Mangahas, 23 April 2004, Manila.
46 Interview with Samuel Tan, 12 March 2004, Quezon City.
47 This book was written for Marcos by Adrian Cristobal, one of the brilliant intellectuals who worked intimately with/for Marcos. Interview with an anonymized informant, 23 February 2005, Makati City.
48 Interview with an anonymized informant, 23 February 2005, Makati City.

References

Agoncillo, Teodoro. 1956. *The Revolt of the Masses: The Story of Bonifacio and the Katipunan*. Quezon City: University of the Philippines.
———. 1960. *Malolos: The Crisis of the Republic*. Quezon City: University of the Philippines.

Agoncillo, Teodoro, and Oscar Alfonso. 1960. *A Short History of the Filipino People*. Quezon City: University of the Philippines.
Agoncillo, Teodoro, and Fracisco Sionil Jose. 1976. Solidarity Interview with Agoncillo. Reprinted in Ambeth Ocampo, *Talking History*. Manila: De La Salle University, 1995.
Churchill, Winston. 1956. *A History of the English-Speaking Peoples*. London: Cassell.
Cruz, Romeo. 1989. "Ang Paggagawa ng Tadhana Mula 1980 (The Making of Tadhana since 1980)." In *Paksa, Paraan at Pananaw sa Kasaysayan (Themes, Methods and Perspectives in History)*, edited by B. Abrera and D. Lapar, 200–203. Quezon City: UP Likas/Bakas.
de Quiros, Conrado. 1997. *Dead Aim: How Marcos Ambushed Philippine Democracy*. Pasig City: Foundation for Worldwide People's Power.
Ileto, Reynaldo. 1998. "The Unfinished Revolution in Political Discourse." In *Filipinos and Their Revolution*, edited by Reynaldo Ileto, 177–201. Quezon City: Ateneo de Manila University Press.
Ileto, Reynaldo. 2017. "Horacio de la Costa, SJ, the Filipino Historian, and the Unfinished Revolution." In *Reading Horacio de la Costa, SJ: Views from the 21st Century*, edited by Soledad S. Reyes, 117–142. Quezon City: Ateneo de Manila University Press.
Koonz, Claudia. 2003. *The Nazi Conscience*. Cambridge, MA: Belknap Press.
Marcos, Ferdinand. 1967. "History and National Progress." *Historical Bulletin* 11 (4): 345–352.
———. 1973a. *Notes on the New Society of the Philippines*, Vol. 1. 2 vols. Manila: Ferdinand E. Marcos.
———. 1973b. "Towards a New Social Order: The Rationale of Martial Law in the Philippines." *Historical Bulletin* 17 (1–4): 1–26.
———. 1974. *The Democratic Revolution in the Philippines*. Englewood Cliffs, NJ: Prentice-Hall International.
———. 1976. *Tadhana: History of the Filipino People: The Encounter. Vol. 2, Part 1*. Manila: Ferdinand E. Marcos.
———. 1982. "A Sense of National History." *Historical Bulletin* 26 (1–4): 1–15.
McCoy, Alfred. 1999. *Closer than Brothers: Manhood at Philippine Military Academy*. New Haven, CT and London: Yale University Press.
Muego, Benjamin N. 1988. *Spectator Society: The Philippines under Martial Rule*. Monographs in International Studies, no. 77. Athens, OH: Ohio University Center for International Studies.
Nakpil, Carmen. 1971. "Why a Historical Commission?" In *Lectures on Great Filipinos and Others, 1967–1970*, 3–7. Manila: National Historical Commission.
Ocampo, Ambeth R. 1995. *Talking History: Conversations with Teodoro Andal Agoncillo*. Manila: De La Salle University Press.
Rempel, William C. 1993. *Delusions of a Dictator: The Mind of Marcos as Revealed in His Secret Diaries*. Boston, MA: Little, Brown.
Reyes, Miguel. 2018. "Producing Ferdinand E. Marcos, the Scholarly Author." *Philippine Studies: Historical and Ethnographic Viewpoints* 66 (2): 173–218. doi:10.1353/phs.2018.0017.
Salazar, Zeus. 1974. "Ang Pagpapasakasaysayang Pilipino Ng Nakaraang Pre-Ispaniko (The Filipino Historiography of the Pre-Hispanic Past)." In *Kasaysayan: Diwa at Lawak (History: Ideas and Scope)*, edited by Zeus Salazar. Quezon City: University of the Philippines Press.

———. 1989. "Ang Historiograpiya ng Tadhana: Isang Malayang Paggunita-Panayam (The historiography of Tadhana: A Free-flowing Recollection-Lecture)." In *Paksa, Paraan at Pananaw sa Kasaysayan (Themes, Methods and Perspectives in History)*, edited by B. Abrera and D. Lapar, 193–199. Quezon City: UP Likas/Bakas.

Tan, Samuel. 1976. "A Historical Perspective for National Integration." *Solidarity: Current Affairs, Ideas and the Arts* 10 (2): 3–17.

———. 1993. "Tadhana: History of the Filipino People." *Philippine Encyclopedia of the Social Sciences*, Volume 1, History, edited by Philippine Historical Association (PHA), 85–87. Quezon City: Philippine Social Science Council.

Veneracion, Jaime. 1993. "Historiography, 1950–1986: Trends and Directions." In *Philippine Encyclopedia of the Social Sciences*, Vol. 1, History, edited by Philippine Historical Association (PHA), 52–68. Quezon City: Philippine Social Science Council.

3 Tadhana in political and historiographic contexts

In Philippine historiography, a number of areas have traditionally served as the focal points of contestation. They are the nodal points through which some of the most important defining characteristics of historical scholarship in the country flowed and took shape. As a project wanting to be recognized as important and with authority, Tadhana could not but locate itself at the cutting edge of historiographic development. At the same time, it had to accommodate and engage with enduring traditions in historical scholarship.

I shall discuss in this chapter only aspects that are vital both to the historiographic agenda of the scholars who were prime movers of the Tadhana project and to Marcos's political interests. First is the pre-historic and pre-colonial origins of peoples and cultures of the Philippines. This issue often relates to the supposed autonomy and strength of local culture vis-à-vis foreign elements in the process of historical change as well as national identity. The second deals with perspective and the concomitant issues related to periodization. And finally, I will discuss the disputed character of Philippine nationalisms that manifests in different, though related questions pertaining to the 1896 Revolution. The aims of the whole exercise are to demonstrate the historiographic terrain within and beyond which Tadhana as a scholarly project may best be understood, to lay bare how the scholars have tried to secure a niche for the project and for themselves, and to explain in what ways the contents and overall framework of the project served Marcos's political interests.

Pre-historic and pre-colonial origins

As planned, Tadhana was remarkable for the depth and breadth of its scope and for the conceptual coherence through which it wanted to weave the entire stretch of the Philippine history. The vision that underpinned this project remains unparalleled for aiming to cover the widest span of time and for trying to provide a more detailed treatment of each period. The project was particularly noteworthy in its attempt to deal with the pre-Hispanic periods (pre-1500s), which up to now remain underdeveloped in Philippine

68 *Political and historiographic contexts*

historiography. Hampered by the severe scarcity of extant pre-Hispanic written sources,[1] as well as by the mindset that nurtures the persistent belief that Philippine history began only with the arrival of the Spaniards, the little interest in pre-Hispanic periods can be gleaned from general surveys of Philippine history published up to the 1980s. As shown in Table 3.1, standard surveys of Philippine history allotted no more than a few pages, if any, to this period. They covered only a short stretch of a hundred years, or even less, before the coming of the Spaniards. It is noteworthy, thus, that Tadhana devotes over a quarter, or five of the projected 19 books, to these periods, covering hundreds of thousands of years before Spain came. The ten-volume *Filipino Heritage* (1978), the Australian-funded project discussed in Chapter 2, is equally noteworthy for having three of its volumes devoted to pre-Hispanic periods and thus may be said to give a proportionately comparable emphasis to this period.

The first book of Tadhana, entitled *Archipelagic Genesis*, was the only one of Vol. 1's planned five books that saw actual publication. It covers the

Table 3.1 Coverage of the Pre-Spanish Period in Some Philippine History Textbooks

Title and Author	Year of Publication	Number of Chapters/Pages/Volume. for Pre-Hispanic Period	Total Number of Chapters/Pages/Volumes
Zafra, *Readings in Philippine History*	1947 & 1949 (Mimeograph)	0	300 pages
Zafra, *Philippine History Through Selected Sources*	1967	Less than a chapter (6 pages)	336 pages
Zaide, *Philippine Political and Cultural History*, 2 vols.	1949, 1953	5 chapters (64 pages)	46 chapters (812 pages)
Alip, *Political and Cultural History of the Philippines*, 2 vols.	1949, 1952	3 chapters (65 pages)	36 chapters (713 pages)
Benitez, *History of the Philippines: Economic, Social, Cultural, Political*	1954	Less than a chapter (less than 6 pages, mainly geographical and climatic)	24 chapters (533 pages)
Roces, ed., *The Filipino Heritage*	1978	3 volumes	10 volumes

Sources: Data culled from various textbooks listed above.

period from the Big Bang to ca. 250,000 BC. It deals with cosmological and geological processes that made possible the formation of the universe and the archipelago which, in due time, would be called the Philippines. The planned second book, provocatively entitled *Adam in the Philippines,* seeks to cover the period of 250,000 BC to 9,000 BC, and it focuses on *homonization*—pertaining to the evolutionary process of becoming human or *homo sapiens*—as it played out in Philippine territory. Not long before the Tadhana project took off, artefacts were unearthed in Cagayan Valley, in the northeastern part of the country, suggesting the existence of the yet-to-be-found remains of a *homo erectus.* Archaeologists thought it may be similar to the famous Java Man. For some reason, Marcos readily shared their enthusiasm. In an entry in his diary dated 24 April 1971, he was effusive, claiming that "(t)he discoveries proved the existence of man with a civilization long before the western world could boast of any culture" (Marcos n.d.). Zeus Salazar, who was one of those responsible for conceptualizing this portion of the project, admitted that these two earliest periods were no doubt too remote to have a direct impact on the formation of a historic community which later would serve as the foundation of the Filipino nation (Salazar 1974, 189). The first volume was important nonetheless, in Salazar's view, to set the physical stage wherein the Philippine drama would unfold later on. In Marcos's formulation, the interpretation was extended to suggest that the elemental geologic, geographic, and climatologic processes had conspired to produce a unique environment that would nurture the formation of a distinctly Filipino national identity (Marcos 1980, 5). In other words, Filipino identity was thought of not just as an outcome of historical imaginings; it was anchored on the rocks and land, and this lent it a resilience that the appearance of primordiality can provide. Such a view of the very deep roots of Filipino identity was a 180° turn away from previous articulations attributed to Marcos. Reynaldo Ileto notes, for instance, that *Today's Revolution: Democracy* (TRD), one of the pre-Tadhana works that appeared under Marcos's name, indicates Marcos's belief that "Filipino identity would be found, not in the recovery of an illusory precolonial past, but in the people's struggle for liberation" (Ileto 1998a, 178). I shall return to this point later to highlight how Tadhana's re-framing and reinterpretation of Philippine history appeared to have influenced Marcos.

The second book of Vol. 1 carries a subtle message that, as participants in the universal evolutionary process, the ancestors of the present-day Filipinos share with the rest of humanity commonalities that should form the basis for racial equality (Salazar 1989). Against the backdrop of the long-drawn-out struggle against an inferiority complex that many Filipinos believed to have been created by colonialism, it is hard not to detect the subtle nationalist intent immanent in these formulations. Given, likewise, that a significant part of what had been paraded as glorious Philippine pre-history (or pre-Hispanic history) proved to be no more than romanticized myths and even hoaxes, one can appreciate the level of sophistication aspired for in this attempt to use available scholarly resources to ground the promotion of national pride and unity on a firmer foundation. The succeeding three books were supposed to pursue this effort to a fruitful end. But before we proceed to Books 3 to 5, let me clarify the historiographic context within which the first five books tried to locate themselves.

One major and long-standing problematic in Philippine pre-Hispanic scholarship revolved around the favorable portrayal of Filipinos vis-à-vis their 'others.' These include the neighboring Asian countries and their Western colonizers (the Spaniards and the Americans). Colonized by two Western powers, with a culture considered perhaps 'the most western' in Asia, and with no ancient cities to show off, not a few Filipinos felt a sense of inferiority or insecurity (Ileto 1998a). Marcos himself bewails in *Today's Revolution: Democracy* (1971, 91) the absence of ancient cities which could 'remind the intruder of his insolence.' William Henry Scott shares the view that there seemed to be a 'deep yearning' for ideas that could fill a void in their psyche, which was battered by colonial experience (1968, 130). Efforts thus focused on convincing Filipinos that they had a civilization, a glorious past prior to the coming of the Spaniards, and that they were not inferior to their 'others,' despite the notable absence of ancient urban centers like Angkor, Srivijaya and Pagan. Consequently, generations of Filipinos well into the 1990s, consumed a set of textbook information about Philippine pre-Hispanic history that was meant to massage the sense of their national self-worth. First is H. Otley Beyer's Wave Migration Theory, which explains the peopling of the Philippines, the diversity of ethnic groups therein, and the early cultural development allegedly brought by various 'migrant' groups— Negritos, Malays, Indonesians—long before the Spaniards came (Jocano 1965; Zamora 1967). Second is the purported 'membership' of the Philippines in the Srivijaya and Majapahit empires to show that the Philippines was not a political and cultural blank slate before Spain came (Hassel 1953). Third, the existence of the supposedly pre-Hispanic documents, the Codes of Kalantiao and Maragtas, ostensibly prove the existence of written laws before the Spaniards came (cf. Scott 1968). As sardonically observed by W.H. Scott, "The popular texts present a picture of law codes, membership in Asian empires, and political confederations projected against a background of 250,000 years of migrating waves of Filipino progenitors, almost complete with points of departure, sailing dates and baggage" (Scott 1968, 139). As more and more researches since the 1950s and 1960s seriously questioned the bases for these suppositions, there arose a need for a new anchor to which pride in pre-Hispanic past could be tied. While several history textbook-writers tend to ignore advances in research, in such a way that textbooks as late as the 2000s still clung to the old, discredited ideas,[2] others rose to the occasion and suggested ways to at least alleviate the problem. W.H. Scott, for one, highlighted the existence of a wealth of evidences that were ignored. These evidences remind readers that despite the scarcity of sources produced by early Filipinos, there are 'cracks in the parchment curtains,' in Scott's (1978) terms, which allow a glimpse of the lives of the natives. Left with not much other than the writings of early missionaries who tended to be biased, Scott claimed that, by reading intuitively between the lines of these Spanish documents, one can gather some bits of information that can help reconstruct at least the broad outlines or trends about the early history of the natives (Scott 1978, 174–175). Still another approach was to shift the focus away from the very distant past, towards the more recent and more 'glorious revolution of 1896' which served as a wellspring of nationalist pride (Ileto 1998a, 1998b).

While these efforts were no doubt helpful in their own specific ways, the centrality of the colonial period or Euro-centric framing of these approaches remained to pose problems. Tadhana was consciously designed to be the most comprehensive and trenchant solution to these problems. It offered a bold and creative application of advanced researches done abroad on the Austronesians by interrogating and discarding the taken-for-granted adoption of the urban-centered setting as the measuring rod in comparative analysis of cultural development. Whereas previously, historians had relied heavily on Beyer's wave migration theory and its variants to explain the cultural development and peopling of the early Philippines, the scheme adopted by Tadhana in Book 3 (*Austronesian in the Philippines*) interestingly reversed the positioning and put the Philippines in the enviable position of a possible intermediate staging point for the 'epic peopling' of the Austronesian world, covering areas as far as Hawaii, New Zealand, Madagascar, and of course the Indo-Malayan realm (Marcos 1976b, 6–7). I should note that this was not a mindless, procrustean distortion of known facts to fit into a nationalist mold, which has been quite common in nationalist writing almost everywhere. Rather, it was an application of research done mainly in Europe (where Salazar studied) which had not yet been applied during that time to the case of the Philippines (Salazar 1974, 193–96). This resulted in a refreshing effort to demonstrate the affinity and equality of the early Filipinos with the rest of the Austronesians, and, more specifically, the Malayo-Polynesians. At the same time, it underscores the primacy of internal factors—the internal dynamics—in the development of culture within the area.

The theme of 'universalization,' which assumes that peoples in different parts of the world are subject to a more or less common set of global historical forces, runs through the heart of the first two books. On the other hand, Books 3 to 5 are more concerned with the 'particularization' process as a logical outgrowth of man's interaction with the varied natural environment. Thus, Book 3 identifies the Austronesians as an entity distinctive from the other groups, such as Indo-Europeans, Hamito-Semites, and Sino-Tibetans, while Book 4 (*Southeast Asia: The World Between*) intends to narrow further the particularization process by showing the gradual formation of the 'Indonesian world' as supposedly distinct from that of Austronesian kin, the 'Oceanic world' (Micronesians, Melanesians, and Polynesians), and even more so from that of non-kin, such as Indians and the Chinese.

72 Political and historiographic contexts

Finally, in Book 5, the *Philippine Forms* gradually took shape roughly from AD 200 to AD 1565 as various differentiating factors came into play, including the intensification of inter-island (both intra-Philippines and intra-regional) trade and the centrifugal pull of the Sinic and Indic civilizations on parts of the Southeast Asian world that left the Philippines on a trajectory different from that of the rest of the region (Marcos 1976b, 6–12). It was during this period, so Tadhana suggests, that the 'proto-Filipino cultural identity' began to crystallize, and by the end of this period, "the Philippines was on the verge of transforming herself from an 'ethnographic' entity into a 'historic' polity..." (Marcos 1976b, 12). Implied in this formulation is the assertion of the primacy of internal factors and the rejection of the deeply entrenched views that cultural development in the early Philippines was brought about by foreign traders or waves of migrants. As a side note, this echoed or paralleled the efforts of scholars such as Jacob Cornelis van Leur, John Smail, and Harry Benda, who dealt primarily with the case of Indonesia.

Likewise, this period coincides with the emergence of 'ethnic states,' which, in Salazar's view, constituted one stream in the parallel development of comparable socio-cultural forces operative in different parts of Southeast Asia (Salazar 1974, 189–90). Such a masterstroke in effect puts the pre-Hispanic *barangays*—communities of roughly a hundred or more—in the same league as the famed ancient states, or *ethnic states*, as Salazar prefers to call them, such as Srivijaya and Angkor. The stark difference in the levels of their development and what such difference may signify had been de-emphasized as inconsequential. As the Tadhana framework asserts, comparative evaluation showing the superiority of Angkor and others and the backwardness of the *barangays* is based on a dubious yardstick that derives from a flawed assumption. The difference, so the Tadhana framework asserts, owes much to the variations in the outcome of the interplay among commercial, environmental, and socio-cultural factors unique to each locality as it interacted with the broader regional forces (Marcos 1976b, 10–11). As a process of state-formation, which seems to be of major importance to the designers of Tadhana, the various ethnic states were a parallel response to a more or less common set of factors. There is, by implication, no reason why Filipinos should view the abilities of their ancestors, and implicitly themselves, as inferior to those of other Southeast Asians. In other words, while the absence of Angkor- or Borobudur-like monumental structures in the early Philippines pained many Filipino nationalist intellectuals, the framework adopted by Tadhana rejected the basis of these concerns.

Another contribution of Tadhana's treatment of the pre-Hispanic period lies in its intent to find an acceptable basis for the national unity that is rooted deeply in a time long before the arrival of the Spanish. This attempt eschews the historical orthodoxy that regards the nation-formation as an offshoot of the Spanish colonial project. From the viewpoint of Tadhana, this is tantamount to settling for a superficial basis of unity that, precisely because it is superficial, cannot adequately address the persistent problems of disunity. Parenthetically, secessionism in Mindanao began to brew heatedly at about the same time the Tadhana was being conceptualized. By insisting on an affinity with the Austronesian, Malayo-Polynesian world, and by underlining the particularization process that set the Philippines apart from it, the Tadhana found in the supposedly common base culture a unifying thread among Christian, Muslim, and tribal Filipinos. Their particularities, Tadhana insists, were no more than skin-deep, primarily because these emerged only as consequences of more recent historical developments (Tan 1976). This coincides with the idea that by the time the Europeans came, the base culture was sufficiently developed such that the foreign influences that henceforth flooded in could not but be assimilated into the indigenous cultural matrix. Alternatively, they formed layers of trapping on top of a resilient indigenous culture. Specifically, the book states:

> When the Spaniards arrived... the process of state construction was already underway, and instinct of wisdom moved them to build the colonial state upon the beginnings of the native edifice... (T)he colonial state enlarged itself on the foundation of the barangay, promoting acculturation and pursuing trade and political expansion on the same principal route the native logic and tradition had established.
> (Marcos 1982a, iii)

The key, so Tadhana implies, lies in re-discovering and recuperating the indigenous foundation of Filipino identity and unity upon which the future structures of the nation would be built.

Perspectives and periodization

The search for deep roots not only of Filipino identity but also of the Philippine nation-state had a concomitant result of de-centering the colonial experience that has traditionally served in Philippine historiography as the fulcrum of historical development, as is clear in the writings of Spanish scholars and chroniclers since the sixteenth century. The colonial period was also at the center of the historical narrative among the late nineteenth-century Filipino nationalists and their immediate heirs (1880s–1920s). This trend was continued by professionally trained historians from the generations of Fernandez and Benitez (1920s–1940s), those of Zafra and Alip (1940s–1960s), and finally in the heyday of Zaide, Agoncillo, and Constantino (1960s–1980s). There were major differences, of course, in the rationale, in focus, and in tenor of evaluative assessments and interpretations, but they all agreed that the colonial period was *the* defining moment in the nation-formation in Philippine history.

That was not the case with the framework of Tadhana, as spelled out in *Tadhana Outline* (Marcos 1976b). Veneracion (1993) aptly observes that Tadhana's main difference from other Philippines histories previously written lay in its periodization, whereby the development of the Philippine nation-state is traced long before the coming of the Spaniards.

74 Political and historiographic contexts

Although Tadhana concedes that it was during the colonial period that the transformation to a 'political entity' was achieved, the colonial impetus was by no means a necessary ingredient. Such transformation, Tadhana avers, could have been attained anyway without colonization because the complex of forces operative within the broader regional context was sufficient to complete the transformative process. Besides, the colonial experience, as far as Tadhana is concerned, was little more than a thin glaze on the indigenously defined core. The singularly most important defining thread or pivotal hinge was the development of a Filipino nation-state. Actually, it was more skewed towards development of the state than of the nation. The roots of this nation-state, so Tadhana makers insist, lay in the distant pre-Hispanic past, and its future was heading towards full realization of what they envisioned to be a new society. The use of nation-formation as a pivotal point is not unique to Tadhana. Agoncillo, and a few others, also used it as the anchoring device. The main difference was that Agoncillo and others anchored the origin of the nation-state to the Spanish colonial period. As periodization of Tadhana shows (Table 3.2), while the formation of national

Table 3.2 Outline of Tadhana

	Title
Volume 1	The Roots of Filipino Heritage (Up to 1565 AD)
Part 1	Archipelagic Genesis (Pleistocene-Glacial Periods)
Part 2	Adam in the Philippines (ca. 250,000 BC– 9000 BC)
Part 3	The Austronesians in the Phil. (ca. 9000 BC–1500 BC)
Part 4	The World Between (ca. 1500 BC–200 AD)
Part 5	Philippine Forms (ca. 200 AD–1565 AD)
Volume 2	The Formation of a National Community (1565–1896)
Part 1	Encounter, 1565–1663
Part 2	Reactions, 1663–1765
Part 3	Transition, 1765–1815
Part 4	Transformation, 1816–1872
Part 5	Triumph, 1872–1896
Volume 3	The Promised State: A Nation in Travail
Part 1	Birth of a Nation, 1896–1907
Part 2	Participation and Partnership, 1907–1921
Part 3	Crisis and Consolidation, 1921–1930
Part 4	Ferment and Control
Part 5	Conflict and Direction
Volume 4	Search and Synthesis; Towards the New Society (1946–Present)
Part 1	Dilemmas of Nationhood, 1946–1951
Part 2	Nationalism and Reforms, 1951–1966
Part 3	Radical Alternatives, 1966–1972
Part 4	National Synthesis: The New Society, 1972–

Source: Adapted from Ferdinand Marcos, *The Tadhana Outline* (1976 b).

community (five books of Vol. 2) corresponded neatly to the Spanish colonial period, the 'Philippine Forms' (Vol. 1, Part 5) had already taken shape by the time Spain came. Tadhana scholars wished to show that colonial structures could not but build upon the template defined by indigenous elements. They maintained a quantitative balance in the coverage between Spanish and pre-Hispanic periods, allotting five books for each. Seen from the vantage point of other notable Filipino historians, such as Nicholas Zafra, Gregorio Zaide, and Eufronio Alip, who devoted a disproportionately large space to the Spanish period (see Table 3.1, p. 68), on one side, and Agoncillo, who deliberately allotted only three short chapters to this period,[3] on another, Tadhana represents the middle ground. Nation-state formation is the paramount concern of Vol. 3 (five books) and 4 (four books) of Tadhana. On this point, Tadhana seems unique. Its recognition of the tension between nation and state, as well as its emphasis on the state-formation as distinct from, but closely related to, nation-formation is not found in other approaches hitherto attempted in Philippine historiography.

Periodization is affected by the perspective or point of view adopted by the authors.[4] Early on, spirited discussion focused on the dichotomy between 'colonial' and 'Filipino' viewpoints. At various times, these viewpoints assumed different meanings, but they remain framed, as might be expected within the us-versus-them matrix. The Propagandists led by Jose Rizal, for instance, countered the Spaniards' pejorative bipartite view of history with a tripartite view. The bipartite view posits the pre-Spanish period as the 'age of darkness' that was superseded by the 'age of enlightenment' with the onset of the Spanish period. The tripartite view, on the other hand, reversed the prism and viewed the time before Spain came as the 'golden' age, the Spanish colonial period as the 'age of darkness', and Spain's departure as the redemption or the beginning of a new era (Salazar 1983). Just as the bipartite view informed the morally loaded evaluative framework adopted by Spanish scholars all through the centuries of the colonial period, the tripartite view casts a very long shadow over many historical works by Filipino scholars up to this day. The good and the bad were clear-cut and central to the analysis.

Subsequent assessments of American, as well as Spanish, colonial periods proved to be ambiguous. For generations of scholars appreciative of the legacy of Spanish and American colonizers—for example, Christianity, education, public health, science and technology, and democratic institutions—the colonial experience cannot be an undiluted curse. While such scholars as Leandro Fernandez (1919, 1925), Conrado Benitez (1926, 1954), and Gregorio Zaide (1949, 1959) may be branded as advocates of colonial scholarship primarily for their favorable, even admiring, views of the impact of American colonization, one can also find an avid proponent of the Filipino viewpoint in no less than Agoncillo himself, who was categorized as 'pure nationalist' (Cruz 1982) but was sanguine about American legacies. In the same vein, one can find this view in Gregorio Zaide (1959,

1979) and Nick Joaquin (1988), to mention but two, who were sympathetic to the Filipino viewpoint and at the same time appreciative of, even nostalgic about, the legacies of Spain. In other words, the terms *colonial* and *Filipino viewpoints* ceased to serve exclusively as markers for the dichotomy between those who had a favorable view and those who had an unfavorable view of the colonial legacies. The issue on viewpoint became more about the question of who was at the center-stage and who was at the margins of the historical narrative. The earlier emphasis on moral judgment gave way to methodological issues. Here, Teodoro Agoncillo's provocative pronouncement that there was no Philippine history before 1872 came to the fore.

In a lecture published in 1958, Agoncillo recalled that he had been telling students since the 1940s that Philippine history must be rewritten because much of what was claimed to be the history of the country was in fact not Philippine history but a history of Spain in the Philippines (Agoncillo 1958). He boldly asserted that the history of the Philippines *proper* began only in 1872 with the martyrdom of the three Filipino priests, Mariano Gomez, Jose Burgos, and Jacinto Zamora. Popularly known as Gomburza, they were garroted by the Spanish authorities on a trumped-up charge of complicity in a mutiny in Cavite, a province south of Manila (Agoncillo 1958). In Agoncillo's view, it marked the beginning of Philippine nationalism. Before then, it was foreigners who wrote about the Philippines, and because of the writers' skewed perspective, the Filipinos can hardly be seen in their narratives. Agoncillo was, of course, reacting to the common tendency among his contemporaries to include much material of tangential relevance to the Filipinos. In his words:

> Filipino historians...discuss with alacrity such irrelevant subjects as Spanish expeditions to the Mollucas, the Marianas, French Indo-China and other places, in which the Filipinos' only role was that of rowers... (S)ubjects not related to the development of the Filipino nation, I dismiss in a few words.
>
> (Agoncillo 1958, 6)

Standard accounts of Philippine historiography recognize Agoncillo as a pioneer of the "Filipino viewpoint" in writing Philippine history. This brand of Filipino viewpoint, while it can be subsumed under the tripartite view noted earlier, is in important ways different from it. Rather than being primarily concerned with the question of whether an event or a period was good or bad for Filipinos, it is more interested in whether it is relevant to the formation of the Filipino nation. If not, it falls under the rubric of colonial historiography, and it deserves to be relegated to the background, if not left out altogether. Efforts to demonstrate the internal dynamics among the Filipino people, and to foreground them as the prime movers in the historical process, are all offshoots of this type of Filipino viewpoint.

Gregorio Zaide's works complicate the picture, since he had a different version of the Filipino viewpoint. Despite being dismissed, either politely or bluntly, by many historians (particularly at UP) for his 'colonial' and pro-Church tendencies, his idea of what a Filipino viewpoint may arguably be resonant with the views of the silent public. His many textbooks were best sellers from the 1950s well into the years after he died in 1986, which suggests wide reception or endorsement of his approaches and ideas. In his revealing article "The Rewriting of Philippine History," he explicitly rejects the anti-foreign element in the Filipino viewpoint. He writes, "One can really love his fatherland without hating other nations. One can glorify the achievements of his nation without denigrating the achievements of other nations. And one can praise his own people without slandering other peoples." He also explicitly warned historians not to be "embittered by anti-foreign bias" (Zaide 1973, 174). This was a reaction to what he perceived as the xenophobic, anti-colonial proclivities that began to permeate historical scholarship from the 1950s onward. Having enjoyed orthodox status since the pre-war years, Zaide may have found the atmosphere in the post-war decades, which proved fertile for promoting heterodox views, disconcerting.[5] Aside from their contrasting attitude towards foreigners, the demarcating line separating Zaide's from Agoncillo's brand of Filipino viewpoint lies in Zaide's emphasis on what he thought was good for Filipino people, not on whether they were at the foreground of the historical narrative, as was the case of Agoncillo.

Meanwhile, the upsurge in the influence of the radical, left-leaning groups coincided with the rise of yet another slant on the Filipino viewpoint. Cognizant of the widening gulf separating the small, highly westernized, rich, and powerful elite from the vast majority of impoverished Filipinos, observers claimed that there was a need to redefine relevance and perspective on the basis of social equity and social justice (e.g. Constantino 1966, 1975). Citizenship alone ceased to be the primary basis of the 'Filipino' in the Filipino viewpoint. The socio-economic class to which the majority belonged became the principal determinant. Believed to be the true makers and bearers of history, the 'masses,' however defined,[6] became the proprietary claimant to the Filipino viewpoint. The "revolt of the masses thesis" of Agoncillo (1956) helped paved the way for this, but it was Constantino's (1975) articulate and forceful advocacy that pushed it towards the center of historical discourses. For Constantino, the measure of relevance rests on the extent that knowledge helps liberate the 'masses' from the shackles of poverty and oppression. As far as he is concerned, "Filipino resistance to colonial oppression is the unifying thread of Philippine history" (Constantino 1975, 9).

The sharp elite-mass dichotomy in Constantino's formulation found historiographic expression in the rejection of the great men's style of history or 'history from above.' In this formulation, the common people are hardly seen in traditional historical narratives. It is usually focused on stories about presidents, military leaders, rich families, and diplomatic policies. Since the great majority of Filipinos were (and still are) poor peasants and workers, it seemed scandalous to many politically conscious Filipinos that they hardly figured in historical accounts. To rectify the situation, what is variously called 'people's history,' 'history from below,' or 'history of the inarticulate' became the aim of a growing number of historians.[7] In this quest, Renato Constantino played an important role. By imputing to the collective mass of people the power to act as an engine of historical change, he in effect put them at the center of the historical enterprise. The Marxist provenance of his formulation, with its accompanying analytical and political rigidity, laid him open to harsh criticisms of some groups and avid support from others (May 1983; Schumacher 1975; A. Guillermo 1994). Among other things, he was castigated for glaring bias and for leaving out or distorting facts to sustain his Marxist framework (May 1983; Schumacher 1975). Reynaldo Ileto has observed that for all of Constantino's zealous promotion of a people's history, the people in his history hardly think, feel, speak, and decide for themselves. Someone, or certain groups, such as the elites, have had to do these for them (1979, 5). In spite of all the criticisms, or because of it, Constantino's writings, notably his two-volume synthesis of the history of the Philippines, have been immensely popular. Glenn May (1983, 70) hit the mark when he described Constantino's books as a 'semi-sacred text' among many Filipino intellectuals.

Unhappy with a people's history where the 'real' people are almost muted or left out, a new generation of historians devoted their efforts to allowing the masses to 'really' speak for themselves. Ileto's *Pasyon and Revolution* was a landmark product of this initiative. Among other achievements, it has demonstrated that despite the tyranny of the archives, so to speak, it was, in fact, possible to write history by using unusual *texts*—such as songs, folk tales, prayers, poems, and *pasyon*—that were produced by the inarticulate masses. By allowing the 'masses' to speak, the *Pasyon* recognizes the existence and autonomy of their worldview—a worldview that if seen from within its own logic is valid in its own right. Questions may, of course, be raised to what extent *Pasyon* was able to accomplish this feat (for example, Scalice 2018). Regardless, what is crucial is the idea that the perceptions and behavior of the inarticulate may be understood on their own terms, not as an irrational variant of, or an aberration from, the elite-defined code of thoughts and conduct. Through Ileto's rather essentialist formulation, the conceptual gap that divides the 'elites' and the 'masses' was made virtually unbridgeable, a formulation that would be elevated to a seemingly dogmatic position by the *Pantayong Pananaw* (From-us-for-us Perspective) (hereafter referred to as *Pantayo School*).

The *Pantayo School*,[8] if it may really be called a school, emerged from the sustained effort of a group of historians from UP to offer an alternative to existing approaches. It is a philosophically and methodologically sophisticated project. Within the context of nationalist historiography in the Philippines, its methodological ramifications are in many ways pathbreaking. The formulation and use of concepts and analytic categories that are believed to be indigenous—and supposedly faithful to the worldview and aspirations of 'authentic' Filipino people—raised fundamental questions about many long-standing ideas and practices in historical writing and research in the country. It takes common people, including cultural minorities, as the true repository of indigeneity, which is a key element in this version of Filipino perspective. Launched in the 1970s, the *Pantayo* school grew in influence until, by the 1990s, it was poised to dominate the country's largest and most important history department in the country, that of UP at Diliman. The upward trajectory was temporarily aborted by a 'purge' that saw its proponents being eased out of the department. This painful development had the unintended consequence of widening the reach and nurturing the approach further beyond UP, into other universities and the wider community.[9] Like other elements of nationalist discourses in the country, the Pantayo School developed in parallel with, in opposition to, or in consonance with other approaches. Against the complex map of nationalist discourses, where does Tadhana fit within the whole stretch of the historiographic development?

The historiography of Tadhana constitutes a transition in the evolving quest for the definition of the Filipino viewpoint. By pioneering the systematic and comprehensive search for the deep, pre-Hispanic roots of the Philippine nation-state, it prefigured the emphasis on the indigenous that would find eloquent expression in the '80s and '90s in the *Pantayo* school. By de-centering the colonial experience as pivotal to the nation's historical development, it foreshadowed what in due time would be recognized (at least in some quarters) as a landmark historiographic achievement: the cutting of the analytics of nation-formation from the hitherto colonial ties. Interestingly, this analytic approach paralleled, even anticipated, certain important aspects of what has been trumpeted in India as Subaltern Studies or in Western and Latin American academia as postcolonial theory and the decoloniality movement. At UP, however, this approach informed the indigenization movement epitomized best by the *Pantayo* school and *Sikolohiyang Pilipino*[10] (Filipino Psychology). By eschewing Constantino's formulations and refining Agoncillo's, and by rejecting conventional approaches espoused by Alip, Zafra, Zaide, and others, Tadhana was searching for an alternative that its makers believed was more suitable to address the problems of the time. What these problems were will be explored further in the next section.

The transitional role of Tadhana can be explained by the overlapping involvement of Zeus Salazar in Tadhana and in the development of the Pantayo school. Salazar was the prime mover of the *Pantayo* school, which, according to Portia Reyes (2002, 363–364), began in 1974. The early formative period of the Pantayo School coincided with the first five years of the Tadhana project, the same period during which Salazar figured prominently in that project. Upon leaving it towards the end of 1979, he continued his historiographic crusade, gathering like-minded historians at UP until they established themselves by the 1990s as one of the dominant factions within the UP Department of History. Their dominance would not last, as already noted above, as some very complex intra-departmental politics paved the way for the easing out in the early 2000s of Salazar and almost all of those closely associated with him.[11] But that is another story altogether. What is important at this point is that despite the physical purge of the *Pantayo* group, their historiographic influence lingers and expands.

Vis-à-vis the Marxist-inspired notion of a Filipino-viewpoint demonstrated most eloquently by Renato Constantino, Tadhana was explicitly reactive, if not outright dismissive. The reason was not just political, as will be discussed in the next section—it was historiographic as well. The long tradition of framing historical questions along a dichotomous Filipino/foreigner matrix provided an unfavorable context. It required more than subtle ideological conditioning for historians to transcend. Filipino nationalist intellectuals tended to view the act of fragmenting the Filipinos into various groups defined along social class, linguistic affiliation, and so forth as weakening the purportedly united front vis-à-vis the foreigners. Despite being more at home with Agoncillo's version, as noted above, the Tadhana group were not fully happy with this version either. Agoncillo's concept of Filipino nation remained, for the most part, focused on the Christian majority. It was, in the view of Tadhana scholars, particularly Samuel Tan, not sufficiently inclusive to address the concerns or aspirations of cultural minorities. As a corrective to Agoncillo's approach, Tadhana offered a conception of the Filipino nation that embraces multi-cultural diversity as constitutive of, rather than a problem in, the process of nation-formation. Tan's (1976) idea of tri-sectoral communities—Christians, Muslims, and lumads (indigenous communities)—walking side by side with one another comprises one of the salient contributions of Tadhana in historiographic development.

It is interesting to note the divergence between Tan's and Salazar's views on this matter. In Tan's article "A Historical Perspective for National Integration" (Tan 1976), he identifies two approaches: unitary, which is preferred by Salazar, and pluralist, which Tan favored. The unitary approach assumes that there existed in the pre-Hispanic periods a common cultural or historical unity. The bases for this unity are, in linguistic terms, Austronesian–Polynesian linguistic affinity and, in cultural terms, the base-culture, which may be described broadly as Malay. This analytic tack entails searching for a "common thread in the maze of ethnic diversities and complexities" (Tan 1976, 5). The pluralist approach, on the other hand, assumes that "there are indefinite numbers of events or circumstances in the historical process which do not necessarily form into an inter-related whole" (Tan 1976, 5). Applying to the case of the Philippines, this means that before the coming of the Spaniards, communities in the islands were independent and isolated from one another, and that the only kind of unity or cohesiveness was imposed from the outside. Unity was mainly political (Tan 1976).

On the issues of histories from above and from below, Tadhana exhibits a seemingly unresolved tension of combining two fundamentally conflicting strands. On the one hand, Tadhana puts a premium on state-formation as the crux of historical development, the process that is essentially 'from above.' On the other, it traces the origin of national identity, even the state itself, to a past as distant as possible, calling the bedrock indigenous and taking the masses 'from below' as its true bearers. Tension such as this seems inherent in any effort to combine the nation and the state into the hyphenated nation-state. This is especially true in cases where geographic heterogeneity and cultural and socio-economic diversity are paramount, of which the Philippines is an example. What Tadhana does is recognize and confront the tension by attempting to synthesize the two strands. As one might expect, the results are uneasy and riddled with tensions.

By insisting on the ethnic, pre-colonial origins of the Philippine state, Tadhana posits that in the distant past, there existed an indigenous Philippine state. This state was a product of the intimate relationship between indigenous Filipinos and their environment—a state that supposedly came from the bosom of the Filipino 'nation.'[12] It is another way of saying that before, there was no hyphen, no tension, between the nation and the state. The wide gap between the two that characterized the colonial and the post-war periods emanated from the long and divisive colonial experience. Tadhana recognized this as a problem that had long been ignored by scholars and politicians alike, until Marcos came supposedly and decided to do something about it. This notion smells of politics, as will be discussed in the next section, but from a historiographic standpoint, it has its own pragmatic value. For one, the polarity between histories 'from above' and 'from below' drains itself of the tensions as the issue ceases to revolve around the questions of whether it was deliberately written from the viewpoint of either pole or an inconsistency has been committed in its attempt to combine the two. The most pertinent questions become: (1) which aspect of the Tadhana framework adopts a top-down perspective, and which employs a bottom-up viewpoint?, (2) why is this so?, and (3) at what point, if ever, might they merge as one?

The persistence of diverging perspectives within Tadhana may be taken as a reflection of the socio-economic, political, and historical reality— fragmented, uneven, contentious. It is precisely this kind of situation that breeds the calls for a new approach, historiographically and politically. Viewing it from this angle allows us to highlight the point of convergence between the interest of the state and the scholar. The New Society was not just the culminating point of Marcos's effort to re-combine the nation (people) and the state (government) in a politically creative and harmonious synthesis. It also represents historiography's Holy Grail: the use of state-formation as an overarching framework is not simply consistent with the emphasis on the indigenous or on people's history—it is precisely a mechanism for realizing such a kind of history. As a product of a partnership between the state and the scholars, Tadhana conjures up the future when a 'true' people's history will finally have been written. At that point, there would be no more need for scholars' conscious effort and state sponsorship. Until then, however, one may say that the state and the scholars are justified in taking the initiative.

1896 Revolution and contested nationalisms

Another important area revolves around the 1896 Revolution and the accompanying questions about Philippine nationalisms. Ileto considers the events surrounding the 1896 Revolution as a cornerstone of modern Philippine history and the founding myth of the Philippine nation-state (Ileto 1998b). The centrality of the 1896 Revolution in historical discourses may be seen in the persistence since the 1950s of the discourses on the 'unfinished revolution' which various groups of opposing ideologies employ to make themselves seem relevant. As Ileto succinctly put it:

> Without great monuments or a court culture to serve as an alternate focus or center of national aspirations the ensemble of events and ideas called 'the revolution of 1896' has had to serve as some sort of charter or as the legitimizing principle for subsequent calls for unified action.
> (Ileto 1998a, 195)

Like many other events or ideas of monumental significance, its meanings are contested. The 1896 Revolution is problematic and ambiguous for, as Mojares observes, it "generates a surplus of meanings, which may be hostile, ambivalent and inassimilable" (Mojares 1996, 263).

Tadhana's treatment of the 1896 Revolution is clearly reactive to the sharply polarized debates about it and the 'true' meaning of Filipino nationalism. As these debates are multi-layered and multifaceted,[13] I shall focus for the purpose of this study only on the overall attitude towards the Revolution (especially vis-à-vis the Reform Movement) as well as on the extent of the role of the elite and the 'masses' in this landmark set of events. The primary reason for this move is that, among the Revolution-related issues, these questions are of the greatest relevance to Marcos's political blueprint, as will be discussed below.

Agoncillo's assertion that the 1896 Revolution was a 'revolt of the masses' was a watershed in this debate. Spelled out in his controversial book of the same title (Agoncillo 1956), it transgressed the orthodox meanings ascribed to the revolution. At various times until then, the Revolution was viewed as a handiwork of the *ilustrados* or the elites, a reaction against the abuse of the friars, a product of 'international Masonic conspiracy,' or against the excesses of feudalism (Schumacher 1991; Veneracion 1971). Nationalism, it should be noted, did not figure in these explanations. Alternatively, the unity between the masses and the elites in their struggle against the Spaniards was also commonly posited (for example Llanes 1998, Ambrosio 1998).

Nicholas Zafra, for instance, echoed a popular, monolithic view of the revolution when he asserted, in response to Agoncillo, that "the revolution was truly national in scope and in character. The persons who participated in it were moved and inspired by a genuine love of country. They came from all classes and elements of the population" (Zafra 1956, 502). For casting doubts on these beliefs about the Revolution, Agoncillo earned the ire of some conservative institutions and scholars.[14] As evidence of the paramount importance of this work, a number of succeeding works explicitly or implicitly reacted to Agoncillo's thesis, either by further developing it, by refining it, or by rejecting it altogether. Constantino, for instance, took off from Agoncillo and elevated the masses not just as prime movers of the revolution but also as the engine of the broader historical change. In his view, the hinge on which history turns is the struggle of the masses for greater freedom from colonial bondage and from oppression by the elite. Milagros Guerrero, for her part, has assaulted Agoncillo's revolt of the masses thesis by demonstrating that it was the provincial and municipal elites who led the revolution in northern Luzon, while the masses, abused by the Filipino elites and burdened by the policies of the Aguinaldo government, had every incentive not to support the revolutionary struggle, and even rose against the elites and the elite-led Philippine republic (Guerrero 1977, 2015). Glenn May, who conducted research on the Southern Tagalog province of Batangas, concurred with Guerrero. He claimed that patron–client relationships accounted for the involvement of the 'masses.' That is, it was the elite who led the fight against the foreigners, and the retinue of their underlings merely followed suit, either under duress or in deference to the wishes of their patron (May 1991).

Rather than pitting one against another, Tadhana opted to combine the mass and the elitist elements as necessary ingredients of the revolution. It explicitly denied that it was a revolt of the masses. Rather than a manifestation of class struggle, it was presented as an "expression of the national community" and as a "product both of ilustrado and mass ideologies" (Marcos 1976b, 38). Painstakingly, it tried to provide a smooth transition from the elitist Propaganda Movement to the founding of La Liga Filipina (hereafter *Liga*),[15] a civic organization which sought to promote self-help among members and get them involved in reform efforts, to the formation of the Katipunan. Whereas Agoncillo and Constantino drew a sharp contrast between the intent and methods preferred by the Propaganda Movement and the Katipunan, and saw the Katipunan as a necessary offshoot of the failure of the Propaganda Movement, Tadhana endeavored to blur the line separating the two. This was done by underscoring the mixed membership, both elite and 'mass,' of the *Liga* as well as its transitory role in giving birth to the Katipunan. Short-lived as the *Liga* was, Tadhana seems to overstate its importance by claiming that it was a "milestone in the effort of the reformers to link the *ilustrados* with the masses" and that it constituted the "marriage of strong social forces in a new dynamic ideology of national community" (Marcos 1982a, 432). In its effort to downplay the class element in the transition from Propaganda to Katipunan, Tadhana declares, "The (Katipunan) movement was not so much a class takeover as an effort of the Filipino masses to take the leadership away from the ilustrados, who they felt, moved too slowly and too uncertainly" (Marcos 1982a, 431). With such a formulation, whatever differences existed in their methods and objectives, which to an extent reflected class differences, have been elided or effaced. This seems to pave the way for the view that partnership and complementarity, rather than contrast and oppositionality, should characterize the relationship between the Propaganda Movement and the Katipunan.

Tadhana established a complementary relationship between the Propaganda Movement (elite) and the Katipunan (mass) by several means. First, it insisted that the ideology of the nascent national community drew both from the liberal ideas propounded by the Propagandists and from the "populist-messianic sentiments of the masses," an organized expression of which is the Katipunan, according to Tadhana (Marcos 1976b, 58). Second, it claimed that the united front that made the 1896 Revolution possible was achieved when the ilustrado and mass elements were fused together, and this was made possible through the combined efforts of the propagandists and the Katipunan. Tadhana, thus, claims

> Where Rizal and del Pilar represented the *ilustrado* reaching the masses in a common struggle against the frailocracy, which in the Philippines academic discourse means the rule of the Spanish friar, Bonifacio stood for the masses struggling from below to reach the ear of the *principalia-ilustrado*.
>
> (emphasis original) (Marcos 1982a, 437)

In other words, the "(R)evolution represented the convergence of all the classes in Philippine society" (ibid. 438).

This erasure of whatever class or regional differences or conflict existed within the revolutionary movement seems deliberate. In the extended outline of Tadhana explaining the projected contents of Vol. 3, Part 1 (1896–1906), which covers the Revolution up to the early American period, no mention is made of the internal conflicts that dogged the revolutionary effort. The *Tadhana Outline* focuses on the 'pragmatic and restrained' reaction of the Filipino nation to the American incursion, stressing the cooperative stance of the Filipino leaders towards the Americans who promised them a 'Filipino State' (Marcos 1976b, 40–42). The silencing of the internal factional strife or class or regional contradictions in the analysis appears to have been completed when Tadhana blamed the "feudal orientation of the Katipunan" for the downfall of Bonifacio and for jeopardizing revolutionary efforts (Marcos 1982a, 438). The anti-foreign, anti-colonial aspects of the revolution are highlighted to the extent that internal or class-conflict elements are eliminated. Ironically, Tadhana re-asserts some fundamental views on the Revolution propounded in earlier colonial historiographies, such as those of Kalaw (1925) and Fernandez (1926).

The contentious character of the 1896 Revolution is only a reflection of the multifarious nature of Philippine nationalisms on the whole. In earlier research I carried out, I examined the contents of 16 Philippine history textbooks used in Philippine schools from the early 1900s to 2000. The study indicates that within the span of a century, it was only among textbooks used during the American period (Barrows 1907); Fernandez 1919/1932; and Benitez 1926) that fairly clear and consistent images of nationalism were discernible. In the post-war period, in contrast, images of nationalism were ambiguous, uncertain, or confusing (Curaming 2001, 2017).

Clio in the hands of power?

That Tadhana is a political project—in a conventional as opposed to a 'postmodern' sense—cannot be denied. Notwithstanding the scholars' strong protestation to the contrary, Marcos did, in fact, intend to use the project for his own political interest. While they were allowed a wide latitude in designing the project, as shown in the previous chapter, Marcos seemed to have clear ideas as to how he would utilize its output.[16] The participant-scholars I interviewed vehemently denied this, but the fact was that Marcos had appropriated the 'scholars' history' for his own political purpose, whether or not the scholars liked it or were aware of it. How and why it was achieved is, I argue, a testament not only to knowledge's malleable character as a handmaiden of power but also to historical knowledge's ability to enable and at the same time set the parameters for the exercise of power.

In Marcos's own assessment, the need for national identity, unity, and self-determination is among the 'principal national problems' that must be addressed in any governmental efforts, including the writing of history (Marcos 1982b, 5). To most Filipinos in the 1970s, these were reasonable, even desirable goals to pursue. It is no surprise then that Tadhana, as designed independently by Salazar and Tan, precisely fitted into this mold. Marcos and the scholars appeared to share the same mental universe regarding this question, which renders explicable Marcos's full acceptance of the *Tadhana Outline* when it was presented to him.

As already noted, Tadhana is widely perceived as a purely political project that forms part of Marcos's effort to justify Martial Law. Despite reasons discussed in Chapter 2 for believing that the truth is more complex, this popular perception has a *prima facie* validity to it. In declaring Martial Law and thereafter maintaining authoritarianism for over a decade,[17] Marcos summoned a host of justifications. This included the alleged effort to 'save' the Republic from the onslaught of both the leftist and the rightist elements, and the supposed need to reform the society and establish a new one where gross inequality is mitigated, oligarchic control neutralized, and colonial legacies eased. That Marcos's version of history as depicted in Tadhana coincides considerably with these justifications lends credence to such a popular perception. We should suspect, however, that we might be underestimating Marcos in supposing that it was, in fact, his only, or primary, purpose in mind. Considering his track record of propensity for the impressive, grand, and heroic, there may have been something more grandiose in his overall plans.

I have noted in the previous chapter that Marcos did not wish to appropriate the project as a medium to convince, respond to, or argue with the people of his own time. He knew all too well that there was no way his contemporaries would interpret Tadhana as other than as a self-serving political project. He carried out the project because he had set his sights on the distant future. He wanted to address the people yet to be born, Filipinos and otherwise, who, perhaps in a century hence, presumably unencumbered by the bitter polarization of contemporary politics, would judge fairly and acquit his actions and appreciate the wisdom of his decisions.[18] In other words, he was setting an eye to arguing his case before the altar of history, and he was staking a confident claim to vindication.

Several factors are relevant in understanding the harmony between Marcos's political interest and the design of the Tadhana. First is the radical politics, brewing since the 1950s, that saw mounting efforts to bring down the establishment. Second is the growing disenchantment with the liberal representative democracy that Marcos and others saw as having degenerated into rule by the oligarchs. The third is the upsurge in Filipino nationalism and the escalating contestation for its definition. Last is Marcos's faith in the power of scholarship as a legitimating tool.

Politics of indigenism

As shown earlier in this chapter, Tadhana is emphatic in its treatment of the pre-historic and pre-Hispanic periods. It proudly promotes itself, not without justification, as the "first work on Philippine history that conceives prehistory as a *necessary* part of history" (italics mine) (Marcos 1980, blurb). It also concedes, as already noted, that the indigenous principle permeates much of the framework of the project. In Marcos's own words, Tadhana is a

> history concerned with the indigenous as a principle of assimilation and growth... It became necessary for me to find out what were the native and indigenous structures that we could adopt for renewal in our New Society. How can we utilize the past in order to fortify the present and to assure the future.
>
> (Marcos 1982b, 6, 12)

From the point of view of scholars who participated, what they did was purely an act of filling a huge historiographic void. They claimed that there was nothing political about it for, as they would rhetorically ask, "How can rock formation or human evolution or development of early settlements be political?" Salazar, for instance, echoing the views of other participants, adamantly declared that it was his personal policy to work only on topics as distant from the Marcos years as possible. He believed that by focusing, say, on the pre-historic or pre-Hispanic period, periods far removed from the Marcos years, there was no way he was supporting Marcos's politics. He believed he bore no responsibility for whatever political intent was ascribed to the Tadhana project (Salazar 1989, 2004). Self-satisfied as Salazar was, he could not have been more naïve in his supposition. It was precisely in the indigenous, buried in the very distant past, that the specter of Marcos's political project lurked.

The deeply political color of Tadhana's emphasis on the indigenous can best be understood and appreciated by looking into the conditions that gave rise to the project. Ileto convincingly demonstrates in one of his articles that the radical politics from the 1950s to the 1980s provides the 'discursive frame' through which Marcos's effort at history-writing can be understood. He argues that the challenge mounted by radical students not just against the Marcos regime but also against the entire ideological bedrock upon which it rested had prompted him to wrest the revolutionary initiatives from the young radicals (Ileto 1998a). The memory of the siege of Malacañang in January 1970 by radical student activists seemed too frightening for Marcos to ignore (Rempel 1993; Marcos n.d.). One prong in his multifaceted response was to offer a supposedly revolutionary ideology designed to counter Marxism, Maoism, and Leninism, whose foreign provenance, among other things, purportedly made these ideologies inappropriate for the Philippines. At the same time, he could not hide his contempt for liberal representative democracy, which like Marxism and its variants were of foreign origin (Marcos 1971, 64).

On this point, Larkin's observation may be instructive. According to him, disenchantment with the failure of Western-inspired representative democracy as a means to improve the lot of the people may be one possible reason for the shift towards the search for the indigenous. The problems began to appear not merely as systemic, which may be remedied by changing one Western-inspired system (capitalism and liberal democracy) for another (socialism/communism); critics grew more convinced that the roots of the problem went deeply back to Western mentality itself. Rather than systemic, the problem was civilizational, and the solution lay in recovering the indigenous elements to serve as the basis for creating a new system (Larkin 1979, 9–10).

In TRD (Marcos 1971), we can see Marcos's early effort to lay the groundwork for rejecting foreign models and finding a Filipino alternative. He offered the Filipino version of democracy, what he called the democratic revolution from the center, as this alternative. As though implementing this alternative immediately, soon after declaring Martial Law, he altered the political landscape in local areas by making the *barangay* the basic political unit. One of the purported aims of the New Society was "to strengthen the baranganic culture and retrieve its cultural elements" (Marcos 1976a, vii). The New Society thus constituted a return to or a re-recreation of the pre-Hispanic past, where the *barangay* was thought to be the primeval core of nascent Filipino communities. Marcos, in his 9 January 1973 diary entry, rationalized this move by highlighting barangay's indigenous credentials: the barangay emanated "from the traditions of our race (and) (t)herefore it draws on spiritual strength." Hard to please as Marcos was known to be, it was likely that he felt less than satisfied; he might have felt the need for a more compelling set of justifications. Enter Tadhana. What Tadhana does, with its emphasis on the indigenous, is formally encode in a historical, scholarly, and presumably authoritative template what otherwise would seem to be an obviously political move. By doing so, the act seems domesticated and naturalized, and was made to appear truthful and more acceptable, or so Marcos hoped. At the same time, as Ileto noted (1998a), it foregrounds the position of history as a battlefield in his multi-cornered struggle against leftist and rightist adversaries.

There seems to be something in history that makes it prone to contestation. Distance or remoteness is a fertile breeding ground for uncertainty, which is one factor that fuels disagreement. In the absence of a broad platform upon which to base contrary or alternative views, the few who have access to 'expert knowledge' can only monopolize debates among themselves, to the effective exclusion of the general public. From this vantage point, Tadhana's emphasis on the distant past, and the employment of highly credentialed scholars to provide 'expert knowledge' about it, are strategic. To the extent that the past is lost, it is malleable and manipulable.

The dexterity by which Tadhana knits the pre-Hispanic periods into a coherent whole, from the onset of the Big Bang to the geologic formation of the archipelago and the evolution of Adam in the Philippines, all the way to the formation of Filipino identity with its deep roots in the Austronesian past—all these lend a patina of credence only serious scholarship, so Marcos may have thought, could provide to otherwise patently self-serving political project. Besides, without such an analytic move, rejecting foreign models and talking about a truly Filipino ideology seemed hollow for what was commonly thought of as Filipino was nothing more than a concoction of "three centuries in the convent and forty years under the spell of Hollywood." By anchoring the Filipino in a very distant past, it made sense to eschew foreign models and consider a 'genuinely Filipino' alternative.

One challenge, however, was how to present a consistent image of a 'genuinely Filipino' alternative, considering that the Philippine state itself, as almost everyone takes for granted, was a child of the Philippine Revolution, which, in turn, was inalienably linked to Spanish colonization. Tenuously, Tadhana confronts the challenge by tracing the origin of the New Society government not to the Spanish colonial state but to the supposedly "autochthonous ethnic states" that emerged long before the Spaniards came. As earlier noted, Tadhana asserts that the colonial state established by the

Spaniards could not but build upon the existing framework defined by ethnic states (or the barangays), making it some kind of an *indigenous state* (Marcos 1976b, 10–11). By such a stroke, the continuity of the ethnic states with the contemporary government is forged, and the supposed genuineness of its claim to Filipino-ness is affirmed. Purportedly, it becomes easier, then, to present the New Society as an appropriate vehicle for searching the "Filipino identity to solve the centuries of ambivalence in national attitudes, values and action " (Marcos 1976a, vii). In the end, Tadhana drives home the message that Marcos wanted every Filipino to imbibe: that the New Society is the *tadhana*, the destiny of the Filipino people. With the use of such a metaphysical idiom, Marcos seemed bent on strengthening his deposition before the judging eyes of Clio. Whether that would help, we have yet to see. So far, judging from the still largely negative memories of Marcos and his regime, he has not succeeded.

The choice of the title *Tadhana* was ominous. *Tadhana* is a Tagalog word, probably derived from Sanskrit, whose close equivalent in English is destiny or fate. It carries a connotation that things are beyond one's control as God or the celestial forces predetermine their course. As a nationalist project, Tadhana is expected to be teleological. It appears, however, to be more than that. By tying history to destiny, not just to the nation's destiny but also to Marcos's, the triumvirate—history, destiny, and Marcos—became inextricably linked in the metaphysical transcendence of time and space. It was a combination that was potentially formidable, and it certainly was not lost on Marcos. In his own words, "History is destiny. For long before you and I were born, history dictated the future of our country" (Marcos 1982a, 12). By collapsing the past and the future, the present—Marcos, New Society, constitutional authoritarianism, or whatever it was—became a *fait accompli*, a fate every Filipino must embrace or endure as a necessary bridge to a glorious future.

Known rightly or wrongly for fatalism, Filipinos masses were the obvious and vulnerable targets of the rhetorical device that was *tadhana*. It was an index to Marcos's political acumen to frame his life, his political career, and the life of the nation using a metaphor that was likely to appeal to many Filipinos. Predating the Tadhana project was a host of commissioned biographical works in which the anticipation of the greatness and inevitability of Marcos's achievements was encoded. As noted perceptively by Vicente Rafael, in reading or viewing Marcos's biographies, one cannot fail to sense that "biography merely confirms destiny" (2000, 128). The bio-film *Iginuhit ng Tadhana* (*Destined by Fate* or *Written in Stars*), which Marcos utilized as compelling campaign material in the 1965 presidential elections, could hardly be more transparent. What the Tadhana project intended to do was not just cap all previous efforts but also inscribe Marcos's personal ambitions in the supposedly foreordained historical trajectory. After all, what is history but truth, or so many people are encouraged or misled to believe. But other than the potency of history as propaganda, we should not forget the possible role

90 *Political and historiographic contexts*

of history as psycho auto-therapy or a form of self-propaganda—a means for Marcos to convince himself of the truthfulness, goodness and beauty of what he was, what he was doing, and what he aspired to be.

Homogenizing politics

As shown earlier, Tadhana rejects the class-based perspective, best exemplified by Agoncillo and Constantino, as well as its concomitant analytic approach to the Revolution. Such a move fits very well within the ambit of Marcos's political interests. He may have had an interminable hatred for the oligarchs, but he refused to take the side of the 'people' by viewing things exclusively from their viewpoint. That would have been tantamount to upholding the views of his leftist adversaries. Instead, he saw the oligarchs as rent-seeking intermediaries that set the masses apart from the state, thus hampering national unity (Marcos 1971). Just as the friars who mediated between the colonial state and the people had to be eliminated, so did the oligarchs. If and when that was accomplished, much progress towards national unity would have been achieved. This is another way of saying that Tadhana favors the homogeneity of the nation—homogeneity that, the book was careful to emphasize, is deeply rooted in the pre-Hispanic past. Thus, any divisive elements—class-based conflicts, regionalism, and secessionism—are seen to be anomalous, and the state must deal with them by all means possible, including the use of force. In this, Marcos's multifaceted and at times violent struggles against the leftist radicals, the oligarchs, the liberal politicians, the Church, the press, the Muslim separatists and others found justification. He seemed to say that it was not just called for by an instinct for self-preservation—it was necessary for the survival, security, and flourishing of the nation.

The effacing of any conflict or internal difference is best showcased by Tadhana's treatment of the Katipunan and the Revolution. As already noted, the Tadhana excises or silences any conflict or differences between the 'masses' and the elite, Bonifacio and Aguinaldo, and Caviteño and the rest, to mention but a few. Considering Marcos's desire to draw parallels between the 1896 Revolution and his Democratic Revolution, this is not just understandable but also expected. Faced with the ever-sharpening division on all fronts—social, political, ideological, and cultural—Tadhana, in its articulation of Marcos's definition of the usable past, had to emphasize history's homogenizing or unifying function.

As a side note, in the context of the scholars' strong protestation of their independence, the treatment of the Katipunan and the Revolution in Tadhana invites curiosity. Considering that the scholar-participants were invariably from UP, and that a good number of them were even jailed for their radical nationalism and anti-Marcos activism, one may find it rather odd that the Tadhana was so clearly designed in stark contrast to Agoncillo–Constantino's formulation. Tadhana also re-inscribes parts of 'colonial historiography' on the Revolution in a way long rejected by the scholars who wished to be identified as 'nationalists.' It was the Agoncillo–Constantino line of nationalism, reinforced by the formulation or radical nationalism in the *Philippine Society and Revolution* by Amado Guerrero, that informed significantly the whole anti-colonial, anti-state, nationalist movement in the 1960s and 1970s, of which UP was the undisputed center. While it is true that there are different shades of Philippine nationalisms, and that different stakeholders were scrambling to assert their own definitions, Tadhana's treatment of the revolution intrigues and makes one wonder if it was purely coincidental that scholars' interpretations and Marcos's political interests harmonized.

On the other hand, it is also possible that the Tadhana-makers were in fact consciously going against the tide of the Agoncillo–Constantino tradition. Common aspirations among scholars are to offer something different or new, and one way to do so is to go against dominant thoughts or approaches. Likewise, from the vantage point of the post-Tadhana historiographic landscape, it was clear that the Agoncillo–Constantino tradition had spent much of its force, and it had given way to a more indigenous version of nationalism, which Tadhana pioneered. In a sense, therefore, Tadhana constituted a transition in the development of indigenism in Philippine historiography.

On the ambiguity of power

From the historiographic standpoint, the Tadhana project was both a reaction to and an accommodation of the contested nationalist traditions in Philippine historical-writing. It was at the same time an attempt to push back the frontiers of these traditions. As a reaction, it was mindful of the problems that had long haunted Philippine historiography; it aimed to offer alternative solutions to these problems. As an accommodating move, Tadhana framed its narrative within the long-familiar nationalist, anti-colonial template, but only occasionally did it fall into old clichés that had been quite common among nationalist writings in the Philippines, as in other post-colonies. As indications of its conscious attempt to raise the historiographic benchmark, it offered, among other things, a framework that was refreshing for its scope and theoretical coherence, and for the novelty and boldness of its approaches and interpretations. It was also remarkable for the richness of the historical databank it was able to set up. It was a databank that enabled it to fill in some important gaps that had long existed in the historical narrative.[19] Though not without its shortcomings and it was admittedly a political project, the Tadhana project was arguably a quest for a higher degree of sophistication in Philippine historical scholarship.

Its progenitors intended it to be so. Salazar and Tan, among others, were conscious of the intense competition in the marketplace of historical approaches and ideas within and beyond Philippine historiography. They may not have been forthright about what was at stake for them in the whole enterprise, but considering the 'logistics and logic' (Rafael 2000, 123) of power relations within and beyond the scholarly community, they appeared to be staking a claim to social acceptance, to academic accolade, perhaps to political patronage, but, most importantly, to the symbolic and tangible power that goes with all of them. By striking a partnership with a powerful entity such as Marcos, at least some of the Tadhana scholars had thought it was strategic for gaining the broadest 'market share' for the version of history they propounded.

However, that Tadhana was viewed by many as a manifestly political project proved disastrous to such aspirations, both for individual scholars and for the project as a whole. Precisely because of the Marcos signature, Tadhana has been off-handedly dismissed by many scholars as undiluted propaganda. Whatever rigor and scholarly value the scholar-participants may have invested in it hardly mattered in the face of the adverse and persistent public perception. Then, as now, only a handful of individuals out of the Tadhana circle realized and appreciated its scholarly value, although as of late, there has been increasing signs that the legacies of Marcos, including works attributed to him, are being resuscitated. Clio and her disciples' quest for greater power appears to have backfired. Or perhaps, that is a premature judgment as things can change, while the process unfolds. Only time can tell.

That Marcos sought the service of Clio's disciples suggests the ambiguity of power relations. Anyone to whom history—both as a form of knowledge and as a discipline—matters has no choice but to play by its 'rules.' It is easy to see the effort of individuals, such as Marcos, to sway historical knowledge to their side as a sign of their power and absolute manipulability (or powerlessness) of knowledge. Easily overlooked is the more deep-seated question of why the effort to influence history is being made in the first place. Pointing to the display of power is only half the equation for one does not seek more power if one has enough of it. Who or what causes, then, the feeling of inadequacy that necessitates the quest for more?

Our access to the real world is mediated by the knowledge we humans have about it. In the case of Marcos, whose sense of history, arguably, does not find many peers among Filipino political leaders, the significant mediatory role of history can be easily posited. Against the risk of reifying history, however, it must be underscored that Marcos's understanding of history, like anyone else's, was highly personal. But to the extent that one seeks to utilize history, as Marcos did, for the purpose of political power, one cannot but contend with the social or shared, as opposed to individual, character of historical understanding. At the heart of such understanding lies the 'autonomy' of knowledge vis-à-vis the power of certain groups or individuals. In other words, the 'sharedness' of knowledge or historical understanding lends it power independent of any particular group or individual, such as Marcos. By comparing the case of Tadhana with Sejarah Nasional Indonesia (SNI), which is the focus of the next two chapters, I hope to explicate a deeper understanding of the nature of the power-knowledge relations.

Notes

1 As of 1968, only "Philippine archaeology, two medieval Chinese accounts and a comparison of Philippine languages are…valid pre-Hispanic source materials available for the study of Philippine history" (Scott 1968, 139).
2 In the article entitled "Hegemonic Tool? Nationalism in Philippine history textbooks, 1900–2000," I examine textbooks from 1900 to 2000 and find out that long-discredited theories on the peopling of the Philippines were still mentioned in textbooks until 2000. See Curaming (2017).
3 His celebrated textbook *A Short History of the Filipino People* (Agoncillo and Alfonso 1960), subsequently revised/reprinted without the erstwhile co-author, Oscar Alfonso, created a stir when it first appeared in 1960 for allotting only three chapters to three centuries of Spanish period.
4 For a useful overview of explanations or rationalization behind the use of various periodizations of Philippine history, see (Gealogo 1993a)
5 There is an extensive literature explaining the resurgence of Filipino nationalism since the 1950s. However, I find the article by Teodoro Agoncillo, "Postwar Filipino Nationalism and Its Anti-American Posture," *Philippine Historical Review* 5 (1970): 269–292, a stand out for vividly capturing the sentiments, not just the logic of the nationalist response. Perhaps his very effective prose may have much to do with it.
6 Schumacher notes rightly that one of the problems that bedevil studies on the Philippine revolution is the imprecision and "looseness of class terminology." Terms such as elites, ilustrados, caciques, *principales*, proletarian, middle class, upper-middle class, the people and the masses are all problematic. For clear explication, see Schumacher (1991). Earlier, Milagros Guerrero expressed similar observation in her PhD thesis (Guerrero 1977, 22–25) a part of which appeared as a book chapter in 1982 (Guerrero 1982). The book was finally published in 2015 (Guerrero 2015).
7 For a brief overview of the concepts as applied in Philippine history, see Gealogo (1993b).
8 *Pantayong Pananaw*:' literally, 'from-us-for-us perspective.' In Tagalog, the pronoun 'we' has two equivalents: *tayo* and *kami*. The first, is used when the speaker includes the addressee and all other members of a group, real or imagined, to which both of them belong. The latter is used when the addressee is not included in the group the speaker refers to in a certain discourse. This differentiation has far-reaching implications when applied to historiography. It identifies with whom the speaker (or the historical narrative) is engaged in a discourse. From the *Pantayo* perspective, the discourse is between or among members of a group who may constitute a 'nation.' From the *pang-kami* perspective, on the other hand, the speaker (or the historical narrative) is addressing people other than the members of his/her own group. Corollary to the question of *with whom* one is engaged in a discourse is the question of *whom* and *what* is historical knowledge *for*. From the *Pantayo* perspective, historical knowledge is for the consumption of the members of one group or nation, and it is for their better understanding of themselves. In the *pang-kami* perspective, on the other hand, knowledge is designed to enable one group to present itself to another, probably as their equal or their superior. Knowledge, therefore, is for the consumption primarily of the one spoken to, and it is for the addressee to understand the group being presented to him/her. The presenter (of knowledge) gains a sense of fulfillment from having successfully presented oneself as either equal to or better than the addressee. See Reyes (2002); Salazar (2000); and Navarro, Rodriguez-Tatel, and Villan (1997, 2015) for an explication of ideas and approaches among proponents of the Pantayo School. For

a thoughtful interpretation and critique, (See Guillermo 2003, 2009; Mendoza 2002)
9 Interview via messenger with an anonymized informant who is a prime mover of the Pantayo approach, 16 June 2018.
10 *Sikolohiyang Pilipino* (Filipino Psychology) is a parallel effort to indigenize the study of psychology. It rejects, among other things, Western conceptualization of the self. See Pe-Pua (1982), Pe-Pua and Protacio-Marcelino (2000), Paredes-Canilao and Babaran-Diaz (2013).
11 Interview via Messenger with an anonymized informant who is a prime mover of Pantayo approach, 16 June 2018.
12 The rather peculiar conceptualization of state in Tadhana appears not so idiosyncratic if seen against the backdrop of works such as *Fluid Iron: State Formation in Southeast Asia* by Tony Day (2003).
13 The complexity of Philippine nationalism may be gleaned from the fact that just within the left-leaning groups, Abinales has identified at least four streams of interpretations of the 'national question.' See Abinales (1999). Churchill (2001) also offers a useful mapping out of the various streams.
14 See Ileto (2011) for perceptive reflections on this episode. The publication of the book was delayed by eight years, and it required a presidential intercession before it finally came out. It proved controversial, even before it was published. This controversy broke out on two contentious points. First, the perceived anti-Catholic stance of the book. For this, Agoncillo found himself in a running debate with the spokesperson of the Catholic Church and a scholar in his own right, Fr. Jose Hernandez of the University of Santo Tomas (see Agoncillo 1958). Second, concerning Agoncillo's class bias and other methodological issues. This point is exemplified by the interesting exchange he had with his colleagues at UP; see Zafra (1956). For an overview and analysis of the debates and other controversies, see Hila (2001).
15 Realizing the futility of reformist efforts in Spain, Rizal returned to the Philippines and founded the *La Liga Filipina* on 3 July 1892. Three days later, he was deported to Dapitan, and the *Liga* died a natural death shortly thereafter. On 7 July 1892, Bonifacio founded the Katipunan, in effect supplanting the *Liga*.
16 Interview with an anonymized informant who served as a close aide to Marcos and who wrote the memo that set off the Tadhana project, 23 February 2005, Makati City.
17 Officially, the Martial Law did not last beyond a decade, but Marcos's grip on power did not ease, even after it was formally lifted in 1981. So, until Marcos was removed from power in 1986, the Martial Law atmosphere reigned *de facto*.
18 Interview with an anonymized informant, 23 February 2005, Makati City.
19 Marcos has noted that the unsatisfactory state of historical studies in the country owed much to the fact that 'reconstruction of the past is still incomplete… We get by with certain romantic generalisation about the past and about its relevance to the contemporary times, but in fact whole scores and even centuries of our history have not merited enough study and analysis from our scholars in order to prove or disprove these conclusions' (Marcos 1982b, 4).

References

Abinales, Patricio. 1999. "Filipino Marxism and the National Question." *Pilipinas* (32): 83–109.
Agoncillo, Teodoro. 1956. *The Revolt of the Masses: The Story of Bonifacio and the Katipunan*. Quezon City: University of the Philippines.

———. 1958. "Our History under Spain." *Sunday Times Magazine*, August 24.
Agoncillo, Teodoro, and Oscar Alfonso. 1960. *A Short History of the Filipino People*. Quezon City: University of the Philippines.
Ambrosio, Dante. 1998. "Paglalagom: Isang Pambansang Rebolusyon (A Synthesis: A National Revolution)." In *Katipunan: Isang Pambansang Kilusan* (*Katipunan: A National Movement*), edited by Ferdinand Llanes. Quezon City: Trinitas Publishing House.
Barrows, David. 1907. *A History of the Philippines*. 2nd edition. Indianapolis, IN: Bobbs-Merrill Company.
Benitez, Conrado. 1926. *History of the Philippines: Economic, Social, Political*. Boston, MA: Ginn.
———. 1954. *History of the Philippines: Economic, Social, Cultural, Political*. Revised edition. Boston, MA: Ginn.
Bueza, Michael. 2017. "Marcos and the Number 7." *Rappler*, September 21. www.rappler.com//newsbreak/iq/182836-list-ferdinand-marcos-number-seven.
Churchill, Bernardita. 2001. "Historiography of 1898 and Critical Bibliography." In *The Philippine Revolution of 1896: Ordinary Lives in Extraordinary Times*, edited by Florentino Rodao and Felice Noelle Rodriguez, 277–300. Quezon City: Ateneo de Manila University Press.
Constantino, Renato. 1966. *The Miseducation of the Filipino*. Quezon City: Malaya Books.
———. 1975. *The Philippines: A Past Revisited*. Quezon City: Tala Pub. Services.
Cruz, Romeo. 1982. "Approaches to Historical Studies." *Historical Bulletin* 26 (1–4): 16–26.
Curaming, Rommel. 2001. "The Nationalist Discourses in 20th Century Philippine History Textbooks: A Preliminary Consideration." MA Research Project, National University of Singapore.
———. 2017. "Hegemonic Tool?: Nationalism in Philippine History Textbooks, 1900–2000." *Philippine Studies: Historical and Ethnographic Viewpoints* 65 (4): 417–450. https://doi.org/10.1353/phs.2017.0031.
Day, Tony. 2003. *Fluid Iron: State Formation in Southeast Asia*. Honolulu: University of Hawaii Press.
Fernandez, Leandro. 1919. *A Brief History of the Philippines*. Boston, MA: Ginn.
———. 1925. *Philippine History Stories*. Manila and New York: World Book Co.
———. 1926. *The Philippine Republic*. New York: Columbia University Press.
Gealogo, Francis. 1993a. "Periodization in Philippine History." In *Philippine Encyclopedia of the Social Sciences*, Vol. 2, History, Philippine National Historical Society (PNHS), 34–44. Quezon City: Philippine Social Science Council.
———. 1993b. "The Writing of 'People's History' in the Philippines." In *Philippine Encyclopedia of the Social Sciences*, Vol. 2, History, Philippine National Historical Society (PNHS), 44–49. Quezon City: Philippine Social Science Council.
Guerrero, Milagros. 1977. "Luzon at War: Contradictions in Philippine Society, 1898–1902." PhD diss., University of Michigan.
———. 1982. "The Provincial and Municipal Elites of Luzon during the Revolution, 1898–1902." In *Philippine Social History: Global Trade and Local Transformations*, edited by Alfred McCoy and Ed de Jesus,155–190. Quezon City: Ateneo de Manila University Press.
———. 2015. Luzon at War: Contradictions in Philippine Society, 1898–1902. Mandaluyong City: Anvil Publishing, Inc.

Guillermo, Alice. 1994. "Mga Interpretasyon Ng Rebolusyong 1896 (The Interpretations of the 1896 Revolutions." In *Katipunan: Isang Pambansang Kilusan (Katipunan: A National Movement)*, edited by Ferdinand Llanes 29–41. Quezon City: Trinitas Publishing House.

Guillermo, Ramon. 2003. "Exposition, Critique and New Directions for Pantayong Pananaw." *Kyoto Review of Southeast Asia.* http://kyotoreview.cseas.kyoto-u.ac.jp/issue/issue2/article_247.html.

———. 2009. *Pook at Paninindigan: Kritika ng Pantayong Pananaw (Location and Disposition: A Critique of from Us-For Us Perspective.* Quezon City: University of the Philippines Press.

Hassel, E. 1953. "The Sri-Vijayan and Majapahit Empires and the Theory of Their Political Association in the Philippines." *Philippine Social Science and Humanities Review* 18 (1): 1–86.

Hila, Antonio. 2001. *The Historicism of Teodoro Agoncillo.* Manila: UST Pub. House.

Ileto, Reynaldo. 1979. *Pasyon and Revolution: Popular Movements in the Philippines, 1840–1910.* Quezon City: Ateneo de Manila University Press.

———. 1998a. "The Unfinished Revolution in Political Discourse." In *Filipinos and Their Revolution*, 177–201. Quezon City: Ateneo de Manila University Press.

———. 1998b. "Revolution of 1896 and the Mythology of the Nation State." In *The Philippine Revolution and Beyond*, edited by Elmer Ordonez, Vol. 1, 61–71. Manila: PCC and NCCA.

———. 2011. "Reflections on Agoncillo's the Revolt of the Masses and the Politics of History." *Southeast Asian Studies* 49 (3): 496–520.

Joaquin, Nick. 1988. *Culture and History.* Quezon City: Solar Publishing Corporation.

Jocano, Felipe Landa. 1965. "Beyer's Theory on Filipino Prehistory and Culture: An Alternative Approach to the Problem." In *Studies in Philippine Anthropology: In Honor of H. Otley Beyer*, edited by Mario Zamora, 128–150. Quezon City: Alemar-Phoenix Pub. House.

Kalaw, Teodoro. 1925. *The Philippine Revolution.* Mandaluyong: J. B. Vargas Filipiniana Foundation.

Larkin, John. 1979. "Introduction." In *Perspectives on Philippine Historiography: A Symposium*, edited by John Larkin, 1–11. New Haven, CT: Yale University Press.

Llanes, Ferdinand, ed. 1998. *Katipunan: Isang Pambansang Kilusan (Katipunan: A National Movement).* Quezon City: Trinitas Publishing House.

Marcos, Ferdinand. n.d. "Marcos Diaries, 1968–1984." Typed manuscript. Quezon City: PCGG Library.

———. 1971. *Today's Revolution: Democracy.* Manila: Marcos Foundation.

———. 1976a. *Tadhana: History of the Filipino People: The Encounter. Vol. 2, Part 1.* Manila: Ferdinand Marcos.

———. 1976b. *Tadhana Outline: History of the Filipino People.* Manila: Ferdinand Marcos.

———. 1980. *Tadhana: The History of the Filipino People, Archipelagic Genesis, Vol. 1 Part 1.* Manila: Ferdinand Marcos.

———. 1982a. *Tadhana: Two-Volume Abridgement of the History of the Filipino People.* Vol. 1. Manila: Ferdinand Marcos.

———. 1982b. "A Sense of National History." *Historical Bulletin* 26 (1–4): 1–15.

May, Glenn. 1983. "A Past Revisited, A Past Distorted." *Diliman Review* 31 (2): 69–79.

———. 1991. "Agoncillo's Bonifacio: The Revolt of the Masses Reconsidered." *Pilipinas* 17: 51–67.
Mendoza, S. Lily. 2002. *Between the Homeland and the Diaspora: The Politics of Theorizing Filipino and Filipino American Identities: A Second Look at the Poststructuralism-Indigenization Debates.* New York: Routledge.
Mojares, Resil. 1996. "Reinventing the Revolution: Sergio Osmena and Post-Revolutionary Intellectuals in the Philippines." *Philippine Quarterly of Culture and Society* 24 (2): 269–283.
Navarro, Atoy, Mary Jane Rodriguez-Tatel, and Vicente Villan. 1997. *Pantayong Pananaw: Ugat at Kabuluhan: Pambungad sa Pag-Aaral ng Bagong Kasaysayan (From-Us-For-Us Perspective: Roots and Meanings, An Introduction to the Study of New History).* Mandaluyong: Palimbagang Kalawakan.
———. eds. 2015. *Pantayong Pananaw: Pagyabong ng Talastatasan, Pagbubunyi kay Zeus A. Salazar (From-Us-For-Us Perspective: The Flourishing of Discourses, In Honor of Zeus A. Salazar).* Quezon City: Bagong Kasaysayan Inc. (BAKAS).
Paredes-Canilao, Narcisa, and Maria Ana Babaran-Diaz. 2013. "Sikolohiyang Pilipino: 50 Years of Critical-Emancipatory Social Science in the Philippines." *Annual Review of Critical Psychology* 10: 765–783.
Pe-Pua, Rogelia. 1982. *Sikolohiyang Pilipino: Teorya, Metodo at Gamit (Filipino Psychology: Theory, Method and Application).* Quezon City: Surian ng Sikolohiyang Pilipino.
Pe-Pua, Rogelia, and Elizabeth Protacio-Marcelino. 2000. "Sikolohiyang Pilipino (Filipino Psychology): A Legacy of Virgilio G. Enriquez." *Asian Journal of Social Psychology* 3 (1): 49–70.
Quibuyen, Floro. 1998. "Towards a Radical Rizal." *Philippine Studies* 46 (2): 151–183.
———. 1999. *A Nation Aborted: Rizal, American Hegemony, and Philippine Nationalism.* Quezon City: Ateneo de Manila University Press.
Rafael, Vicente. 2000. "Patronage, Pornography, and Youth." In *White Love and Other Essays*, edited by Vicente Rafael, 122–161. Quezon City: Ateneo de Manila University Press.
Rempel, William. 1993. *Delusions of a Dictator: The Mind of Marcos as Revealed in His Secret Diaries.* Boston, MA: Little, Brown.
Reyes, Portia. 2002. "Pantayong Pananaw and Bagong Kasaysayan in the New Filipino Historiography: A History of Filipino Historiography as a History of Ideas." PhD Diss., University of Bremen.
Salazar, Zeus. 1974. "Ang Pagpapasakasaysayang Pilipino ng Nakaraang Pre-Ispaniko (The Filipino Historiography of the Pre-Hispanic Period)." In *Kasaysayan: Diwa at Lawak (History: Ideas and Scope)*, edited by Zeus Salazar. Quezon City: University of the Philippines Press.
———. 1983. "A Legacy of the Propaganda: The Tripartite View of Philippine History." In *Ethnic Dimension: Papers on Philippine Culture, History and Psychology*, edited by Zeus Salazar, 107–126. Cologne: Counselling Center for Filipinos, Caritas Association for the City of Cologne.
———. 1989. "Ang Historiograpiya ng Tadhana: Isang Malayang Paggunita-Panayam (The Historiography of Tadhana: A Free-flowing Recollection-Lecture)." In *Paksa, Paraan at Pananaw sa Kasaysayan (Themes, Methods and Perspectives in History)*, edited by Bernadette Abrera and D. Lapar, 193–199. Quezon City: UP Likas/Bakas.

———. 2000. "The Pantayo Perspective as a Discourse towards Kabihasnan." *Southeast Asian Journal of Social Science (Now Asian Journal of Social Science)*, 28 (1): 123–152.
Scalice, Joseph. 2018. "Reynaldo Ileto's Pasyon and Revolution Revisited, a Critique." *Sojourn: Journal of Social Issues in Southeast Asia* 33 (1): 29–58.
Schumacher, John. 1975. "Re-Reading Philippine History: Constantino's A Past Revisited." *Philippine Studies* 23 (4): 465–480.
———. 1991. "Recent Perspectives on the Revolution." In *The Making of a Nation*, edited by John Schumacher, 179–209. Quezon City: Ateneo de Manila University Press.
Scott, William Henry. 1968. *Prehispanic Source Materials for the Study of Philippine History*. Manila: University of Santo Tomas Press.
———. 1978. "Cracks in the Parchment Curtain." *Philippine Studies* 26 (1–2): 174–191.
Tan, Samuel K. 1976. "A Historical Perspective for National Integration." *Solidarity: Current Affairs, Ideas and the Arts* 10 (2): 3–17.
Veneracion, Jaime. 1971. "Pagbabalik-Aral Sa Tradisyong Historikal Ng Pilipinas, 1900–1960 (Another Look at the Philippine Historical Traditions, 1900–1960)." *Katipunan*, 24–39.
———. 1993. "Historiography, 1950–1986: Trends and Direction." *Philippine Encyclopedia of the Social Sciences*, Vol. 1, History, edited by Philippine Historical Association. Quezon City: Philippine Social Science Council.
Zafra, Nicolas. 1956. "The Revolt of the Masses: Critique of a Book." *Philippine Studies* 4 (4): 493–514.
Zaide, Gregorio. 1949. *Philippine Political and Cultural History*. 2 vols. Manila: Philippine Education Co.
———. 1959. *History of the Filipino People*. Manila: Modern Book Company.
———. 1973. "The Rewriting of Philippine History." *Historical Bulletin* 17 (1–4): 162–177.
———. 1979. *The Pageant of Philippine History: Political, Economic, and Socio-Cultural*. Manila, Philippines: Philippine Education Company.
Zamora, Mario. ed. 1967. *Studies in Philippine Anthropology: In Honor of H. Otley Beyer*. Quezon City: Alemar-Phoenix Pub.

4 The making of Sejarah Nasional Indonesia (SNI)

The idea of writing national history through a collective effort was conceived rather early in Indonesia. Barely had the ashes of the war for independence against the Dutch (1945–1949) settled than a committee was appointed in 1951 to undertake a history-writing project (Kartodirdjo 1975). The committee consisted of some of the most respected scholars of the time: Poerbatjaraka (1884–1964), Mohammad Yamin (1903–1962), Aria Hoesein Djajadiningrat (1886–1960), and Gertrudes J. Resink (1911–1997). It is unclear why the plan did not materialize. The possible reasons for this, according to Taufik Abdullah (1994), include that the scholars could not agree on the concept of national history, they lacked the time to write a textbook together, and they were riddled by academic or ideological incompatibilities. Another proposal was put forward in 1957 during Prijono's (1907–1969) stint as Minister of Education, and a committee was formed in 1963 (Panitia Seminar Sedjarah 1958; Zain 1976). Perhaps due to the strained political atmosphere during that time, however, nothing came out of this attempt either. "The emergence of the Guided Democracy," so Taufik Abdullah observes "marked the waning of the pluralities of expressed ideas. The meaning and understanding of history were no longer to be continuously searched for, but rather something to be supplied by the 'revolutionary' nationalist regime" (Abdullah 1975, 99). Only after the Second National History Seminar (Seminar Sejarah Nasional II, hereafter SSN2) held on 26–29 August 1970 did concrete results eventuate. The product would be a six-volume opus simply entitled *National History of Indonesia (Sejarah Nasional Indonesia*, hereafter SNI).

This chapter narrates a story about the inception of the SNI. It clarifies the context and the driving forces of the project. It also provides snapshots of the implementation of the project with particular emphasis on the dynamics of the relationship among the important figures. The final section focuses on responses to the project. It will lay the groundwork for an in-depth investigation of the context and the contents of SNI in the next chapter. The same caveat that I specified in Chapter 2 applies here: what appears to be 'merely' gossip is an essential element in the discursive analysis of power relations that underpinned the development and responses to SNI.

Inception and driving forces

The resolutions adopted at the conclusion of the Second National History Seminar (Seminar Sejarah Nasional, hereafter SSN2) in August 1970 specifically called for a history-writing project. This situation created the impression that SNI was a product of a consensual decision among historians. Evidence indicates, however, that several months before the SSN2, the Minister of Education and Culture, Mashuri, had issued a memorandum (No. 0173/70) forming the Committee for the Writing of the Standard Book on the National History of Indonesia. The letter stipulated that the book would be based on Pancasila, that it could be used in the universities, and that it could be utilized as the basis for writing textbooks for elementary and high schools (Zain 1976).

Government operatives like Nugroho Notosusanto, who was regarded by many as the New Order's 'official historian,' had started laying the ground for this project sometime in 1968 or 1969, over a year before SSN2. Nugroho delivered a lecture sometime in late 1968 or early 1969 entitled "Indonesian Historians and Indonesia's History" at the Gadjah Mada University (Universitas Gadjah Mada, UGM). He convinced the audience that it was finally time for Indonesian historians to write their own 'standard' national history (Notosusanto 1969).

Historians in the audience were dubious about writing a national history at that time. One of the key historians recalled that he shared with fellow historians the feeling that they were not ready for it. In his assessment, the experience and the abilities of the prospective members of the team were by that time still 'so uneven.'[1] An observer who opted not to carry a by-line published in a newspaper an article entitled "Welcoming the Second National History Seminar" (Menjonsong Seminar Sedjarah Nasional Ke-II) on 25 August 1970 in the newspaper *Kompas* concurred with this assessment, claiming that the quality and quantity of output of Indonesian historians were still inadequate to produce a national history.

These assessments were not unwarranted. By 1970, the historical profession in Indonesia was still small and fledgling. There were, for instance, only two Indonesians who had PhDs in History with Indonesia as their expertise, and both were still fresh from overseas: Sartono Kartodirdjo (1921–2007), who completed his PhD in 1966 in Amsterdam, and Taufik Abdullah, who obtained his degree in 1970 from Cornell. A local university would not produce the first homegrown PhD in History until 1977, when Nugroho Notosusanto was conferred the degree by the University of Indonesia (UI).

Despite skepticism by fellow historians, Nugroho was persistent and optimistic. In the text of the lecture he delivered in UGM, he forcefully argued that without actually trying to write the national history, one could not say that they were not yet ready. For too long, he lamented, Indonesian historians had been discussing philosophy and how should history be written.

It was the right time to do something concrete, he declared. Nugroho also believed that the best way to learn and develop concepts and methods lays in the process of actually writing history (Notosusanto 1969, 8–9). Over the course of the exchanges between Nugroho and the skeptical scholars, the key historian, Sartono Kartodirdjo, received a small note indicating that the Ministry of Education had already agreed with the plan and that the Ministry would fund the project. It was at that point that he acceded to the proposal.[2] Steadfast in his conviction, Nugroho won the day, as he often did over the course of the project.

It is instructive to look at the contrasting backgrounds of the two important figures in this story, Sartono Kartodirdjo and Nugroho Notosusanto. Sartono is a towering figure in Indonesian history. He holds the distinction of being known as Indonesia's first professionally trained historian, having obtained a BA degree and *Doktorandus*[3] in History from UI in 1956. His academic achievements were impressive, even by international standards. He has a Master's degree from Yale, which he completed under the mentorship of Harry Benda in 1963, and a PhD from the University of Amsterdam, which he gained in 1966 under the supervision of W.F. Wertheim. He has a well-deserved international reputation for a number of his publications, including the well-acclaimed *The Peasants' Revolt of Banten in 1888* (Kartodirdjo 1966). He was the first recipient of the prestigious Harry J. Benda Prize in Southeast Asian Studies, given in 1977. He dominated the 'academic' history landscape in Indonesia for decades. By the time he died in 2007, almost blind but still sharp and lucid, his achievements, if not also *de facto* influences, remained unsurpassed (Nursam 2008, 102–237; Vickers 2007). To many among his peers in and outside of the country, he embodies 'scientific history' as opposed to 'politicized history' (the origin and local meaning of this dichotomy to be discussed in the next chapter), for which much of Indonesian contemporary history-writing has been known (Curaming 2003).

Nugroho stood in notable contrast. He used to be a literary figure in the 1950s, an author of short stories, before he decided to become a historian. Academically, his credentials were less stellar than those of other Indonesian historians of his generation. Some observers, friends and critics alike, would tend to harp back to his literary background, his not being a 'pure or true historian' (*sejarawan murni*), for his putative 'sins against history.'[4] These 'sins' allude to his well-known reputation as supposedly an apologist for or an official historian of the New Order regime. He went to the School of Oriental and African Studies (SOAS) in 1960 on a Rockefeller fellowship, purportedly to do a Master's degree in Philosophy of History, but he left and returned to Indonesia in 1962 without completing the degree.[5] While he went on to become the first Indonesian to obtain a PhD in History from a local university, from the UI in 1977, the circumstances surrounding the conferment of the degree raised some questions on its merit, as the following stories would indicate.

A cautionary note is in order before I proceed. The stories put together here were gathered from my interviews with participants of SNI who belonged to both camps. Admittedly, they include gossip and hearsay. Notwithstanding the limitations of this kind of sources, they help in establishing the discursive frame and in illustrating the dynamics of power relations between Nugroho and his critics. The use of these oral data lies less in their truth value or accuracy (without implying that they cannot be accurate) than in how they constitute Nugroho's and his critics' reputations, both positive and negative. After all, these 'perceived truths' influenced the opinions and the behavior that Nugroho's defenders and critics developed towards him.

Sometime in 1977, after completing a draft of his PhD thesis, Nugroho approached Sartono as the main supervisor and asked that he (Nugroho) be promoted to PhD. After examining the draft, Sartono realized that it was not even ready for submission. Further work was necessary. So, he declined the request for defense. He insisted that revisions had to be made before he could approve the thesis for submission and oral defense. Subsequent events, however, indicated that Nugroho did not want to revise. After quite some time, the Department of History at UI notified Sartono that there would be a change in the composition of Nugroho's thesis committee. Harsja Bachtiar, a sociology professor at UI who was also affiliated with history, was appointed as the new main supervisor. This meant that Sartono was being demoted as the co-promoter or co-supervisor. The promotion day was set, but mysteriously, Sartono was not properly informed. He asked the UI personnel for the venue, date, and time of the promotion, but he did not receive a response. Meanwhile, Sartono had to go to Istanbul for a conference. While he was away, Nugroho's promotion was carried out and he was conferred the PhD degree not long after.[6]

That a plot may have been hatched may be inferred by putting together this story and some relevant information from an informant who was close to Nugroho. This informant said that some people at UI and the History Department had interpreted Sartono's refusal to promote Nugroho as an indication of brewing professional jealousy on the part of Sartono and between the UGM and UI Departments of History. During that time, Sartono was the only Professor of History in the whole of Indonesia, and he was with UGM, a rival university of UI. Some scholars at UI thought Sartono was being unreasonable in preventing Nugroho from getting a PhD, to the continued disadvantage of the UI Department of History vis-à-vis UGM's.[7]

The same informant also attested that Harsja Bachtiar gave Nugroho's thesis the lowest passing grade, just enough for Nugroho to be conferred the degree. Out of surprise, this informant asked Harsja Bachtiar, "Why did you give Nugroho the lowest passing grade. You're his promoter. A promoter usually gives the highest grade?" "It was what the thesis deserved," he quoted Bachtiar's response. This low mark suggests that there were indeed problems with the thesis and that Sartono was, after all, not being unreasonable in declining Nugroho's request for a promotion.

Not long after being conferred a PhD degree, Nugroho became, in 1980, the first Indonesian professor of history at UI and the second in Indonesia after Sartono (*Kompas* 1980).[8] He was a dominant figure in the Department, and his influences cast a long shadow over it, even after he died in 1985.[9] His influences extended beyond the academe and into society at large. Observers credited him for popularizing history and making it more accessible to the public, with measures he undertook as Minister of Education and as a leading historian at the Armed Forces History Center (Pusat Sejarah ABRI; thereafter History Center) (Suryanegara 1985). He was appointed to lead the History Centre in 1964 and began almost two decades of loyal service to the military (McGregor 2007, 60).[10] His military service formally ended only when he was installed as Rector of UI in 1983. While in the military, he maintained his ties with UI as a Professor of History, even at some point acting as the Head of the Department. Many are convinced that his devoted and loyal service to the military earned him military commendations and apparently political appointments in the government as well.[11] On the other hand, these government appointments made some people doubtful of his integrity as an intellectual. He is described, for example, as "one of the most important propagandists of the New Order regime" (McGregor 2007, 39). As far as orientation in writing history is concerned, he favored the conventional chronological-narrative approach with heavy emphasis on military and political aspects. This point will be discussed further in the next chapter. A lengthy treatment of Nugruho and Sartono is necessary to lay the ground for understanding the contents of, and dynamics within, the SNI project.

A confluence of factors encouraged fellow scholars, despite their initial skepticism, to undertake the project. At the broadest and most fundamental level, the nationalist atmosphere provided a template that brought all the participants together, as in the case of Tadhana. With the perceived colonial orientation of existing history books, the scholar-participants shared a desire to contribute towards decolonization of the 'colonized history.' Because it was a nationalistic undertaking, they all believed that they were doing something good which they could be proud of. They believed that the undertaking was a historic act; they were not just writing history, they were making it at the same time, which was what in fact a news item in the newspaper *Sinar Harapan* on 3 September 1970 affirmed.

Beyond the limited circle of scholars, support for the project came from various segments of the society. Press coverage of the 1970 national history seminar, for instance, focused heavily on the supposed main objective of the conference. which was to take stock of research in history with the view of producing a national history (Siswadhi 1970). This level of interest was

104 *The making of SNI*

not surprising considering that decolonization efforts in social, economic, and political spheres were mounting in Indonesia as elsewhere in Asia and Africa, and history was seen as among the most important areas that badly needed it. Even Sartono, who doubted the timing and the chance of success of the project, concurred, and he was persuaded to lead the project because of its nationalist importance. In his opening remarks in the conference, he had noted that there had not yet been a coordinated effort to write a national (for example, non-colonial) history and that the existing history textbooks were 'chaotic' and afflicted by too much commercialism (*Sinar Harapan* 1970). He also noted that Indonesia was being left behind by neighboring countries in its efforts to write national history. Apparently, this realization came from his participation in the International Association of Historians of Asia (IAHA) conference, held in Kuala Lumpur in 1968.

From the political standpoint, the 1970s was auspicious for the Indonesian state to undertake a history-writing project. At this time, it was going through a period of political consolidation after the tumultuous 1960s. One way to consolidate power and legitimize itself was by sponsoring a history-writing project.

It was not clear whether it was Nugroho's personal initiative to undertake the project, or it was an order that came from the higher authorities. According to Katharine McGregor, the project was undertaken at the behest of the military (2007, 153). The establishment of the History Center in 1964 and the history-writing project it undertook after this to counter the efforts of the PKI (or affiliated groups) to write a history that elides the shameful role of the PKI in the Madiun Uprising in 1948 lends some credence to this view (Ibid., 55–59). Beyond this piece of information, however, there is no available proof of the direct role of the military. In the 1970s, the SSN2 and its supposed brainchild, SNI, was widely understood to be a product of the collective decision among historians. As already noted, Nugroho was already toying with the idea, and he began in late 1968 or early 1969 to convince groups of scholars who would eventually form the backbone of the project.

In an interview with journalists in 1976, Nugroho recalled that prior to the idea of forming a team to write national history, an idea was floated to have a nation-wide history-writing contest whereby worthy entries would form various chapters in the projected book. After due consideration, however, the members of the core group realized that entries to the contest would not guarantee the quality of the prospective book. It was then that the option to form a team of writers was taken up instead (Zain 1976). The shape of the team readily followed the six panels in the conference: pre-history, ancient period (Hindu-Buddhist period), Islamic kingdoms (1500–1800 AD), colonial period, national awakening, and the Japanese period up to the New Order. The heads of the various panels became the respective editors of the six volumes.[12] For details, see Table 4.1.

Table 4.1 Outline of SNI 1975 and Members of the Team

Volumes	Coverage	Members of the Team
I	Prehistory (Prasejarah)	Soejono (editor), T, Asmar. D.D. Bintarti, Hadimulmuno, T. Yacob, I.M. Sutaba
II	Hindu-Buddhist Period (I M-1500 M) (Zaman Hindu–Buda)	Buchori (Editor) Bambang Sumadio, Ayat Rochaedi, Edi Sedyawati, Hadimulyo, Wuryantoro, Hasan Djafar, Oei Soan Nio, M.M. Soekarto, K. Admodjo, Soejatmi Satari
III	Islamic Kingdoms (Kerajaan Islam) (1500–1700)	Uka Tjandrasasmita (Editor), Hassan Ambarry, A.B. Lapian, M.P.B. Manus, Sagimun M.D., Tujimah
IV	18th–19th century (Abad 18th–19th)	Sutjipto (Editor), Djoko Suryo, Sartono Kartodirdjo, Thee Kian Wie
V	National Awakening (Kebangkitan Nasional) (1900–1942)	Abdurrachman Surjomihardjo (Editor), Deliar Noer, Taufik Abdullah, Yusmar Basri
VI	Japanese-New Order Periods (Jaman Jepang-Orde Baru) (1942–1970s)	Nugroho Notosusanto (Editor), Ariwiadi, Emilia B. Wiesmar, M. Marbun, Rochmani Santoso, Saleh As'ad Djamhari

Source: Information culled from Kartodirdjo, Poesponegoro and Notosusanto (eds) (1975) 6 Volumes.

The team was headed by three general editors: Sartono Kartodirdjo, Marwati Djoened Poesponegoro, and Nugroho Notosusanto. According to Taufik Abdullah, they merely followed the hierarchy of officers at that time in the Masyarakat Sejarawan Indonesia (Association of Historians of Indonesia; henceforth MSI) to determine the main editors.[13] Since Sartono was the Chair, he became the General Editor; Marwati Djoened Poesponegoro was the First Vice Chair, and Nugroho was the Second Vice Chair—thus, they were assigned general editors as well. Marwati Djoened Poesponegoro did not have an active role in the project. In my conversation with another informant, he recalled that Merwati was supposed to act as style editor, but "she didn't do anything." She was already in her 60s during that time, and her area was European history.[14] If Sartono earned his place in the leadership for his academic reputation and Merwati for seniority, one may speculate that Nugroho was assigned to the core group as an acknowledgment of his important position both in the government and in academia.

Implementation and dynamics

The available details about the earliest stage of the project are at best fragmentary. Djoko Suryo (1939–), who was one of the young lecturers in the Department of History of UGM and a close associate of Sartono, had the opportunity to observe Sartono up close when he was conceptualizing

106 *The making of SNI*

the project. He was the first to see the designs of the project because he typed the manuscript, being Sartono's assistant.[15] He witnessed Sartono meticulously drawing up a grand plan, from identifying the general questions and specific themes to justifying the perspective, drawing up periodization, identifying the methods of processing materials, and projecting the substance of the written output. "(A)rguments, theories and perspectives, everything was there!" It was "very, very idealistic."[16]

Toward the end of 1970, the whole plan worked out by Sartono was completed.[17] A few meetings were then held among the members of the core group (volume editors and general editors) as well as within each volume-team to formalize the division of labor and to discuss the suggested outline and overall framework (Sagimun 1972). The first task was to survey and gather available published materials for the respective periods. Meanwhile, Soedjatmoko, then Indonesian ambassador to the United States and an enthusiastic supporter of the project, recommended to Sartono that an intensive six-month preparation overseas be undertaken.[18] Through the intercession of Soedjatmoko, funding was secured from the Ford Foundation to allow Sartono, Nugroho, and the six volume editors to go to the United States and the Netherlands. The objectives were to undertake a 'crash course' on various aspects of social science theories and historical methodologies as well as to gather materials. The trip materialized in November 1971. Sartono planned for the group to revise or refine the framework after the intensive training overseas (Kartodirdjo 1972). Prior to the group's departure, Sartono went to the United States alone to look for an appropriate university with which they could affiliate. He visited Cornell, Wisconsin, Yale, and Berkeley, among others. He finally chose University of California, Berkeley because the weather in Berkeley was more suitable to the members of the group, most of whom have not been overseas yet. In addition, in Sartono's assessment, Berkeley's Department of History was very strong in social history, the approach very much preferred by him (Ford Foundation 2003).

Almost every working day, from November 1971 to March or April of the following year, they devoted their mornings and afternoons to reading. They usually spent evenings on discussions among themselves and with historians from Berkeley. With generous support from the Ford Foundation, each person was able to buy around 20 to 30 books. The topics they covered included the social science approach to history-writing, social science theories and methods, recent research abroad about Indonesia, and the experience of other nations in writing national history (Tjandrasasmita 1972). They had 99 sessions in all.[19] He was quoted by one the informants as saying that he had "never read so many books in so short a time."[20] Others, however, were overwhelmed by the training. Trying to learn so much in such a short time could result in an overload.[21] In April 1972, the team moved to the Netherlands primarily to gather materials. In early May of 1972, after staying in the Netherlands for a month, the team went back to Indonesia (Ford Foundation 2003, 123).

Perhaps as a portent of what was to come, the team encountered difficulties in this early stage of the project. The preparations in Berkeley did not go as smoothly as Sartono had hoped. Nugroho, for instance, stayed only for two months because, as Head of the History Center, he had other heavy responsibilities (Ford Foundation 2003, 123). Buchori, the editor of Vol. 2, for unspecified reasons, stayed for two to three months in Cornell instead of joining the group in Berkeley. Another member of the team joined only in the Netherlands, according to Surjomihardjo (1987b). Abdurrachman Surjomihardjo, who was the editor of Vol. 5, offered a version of the story slightly different from Sartono's. He said that of the six volume editors, only three managed to join Sartono for the whole stretch in the United States. One only stayed for a month (apparently Nugroho), another (possibly Buchori) joined only at the fourth month in the United States, and the last one joined only in the Netherlands. In Abdurrachman Surjomihardjo's view, writing over a dozen years later, these instances foreshadowed the formidable challenges the team would face (1987b).

From 6 to 10 June 1972, about a month after returning from overseas, members of various groups attended a seminar-workshop in Tugu, Bogor. At this workshop, each group reported their progress as well as the problems they had so far encountered.[22] Sartono also discussed the multi-dimensional approach to history and how this might be applied in the writing of the six-volume national history book (Kartodirdjo 1972). The succeeding plenary meetings were held in Bogor, Puncak, and Jakarta, and were held at least once every six months, coinciding with the semestral break from teaching in the university.[23] For each group, meetings were held more frequently as needed (Sagimun 1972).

Taufik Abdullah recalled that the plenary sessions involved intense scrutiny of each team's plans for their respective volumes. He recounted that having just returned with a PhD from Cornell (in his words, "fresh from the oven"), he was eager to display his knowledge. He earned the annoyance or fear (or both) of several in the group because of his rather confrontational questions and stinging criticisms. He particularly remembered his unforgiving critiques of Nugroho's presentation, wherein the latter proposed an eschatological or predetermined emplotment of Indonesian history. Nugroho, Taufik racalled, even proposed that the group should decide on whether to regard Sukarno as a traitor or a hero! Admitting a lack of wisdom owing to youthful impudence, Taufik remembered lambasting Nugroho and reminding him that empirical data should decide the conclusion, not the other way around. Nugroho, he surmised, was deeply hurt by this, being humiliated in front of the whole team, including several of his young associates at the History Center. Taufik speculated that Nugroho might have never forgiven him for what he did.[24] One of Nugroho's close aides at

108   *The making of SNI*

the History Center, who himself was present during the workshop, said that although Nugroho was not the type of person who divulged what he felt, it was very possible that he might have indeed been offended by what Taufik did, as narrated above.[25] Djoko Suryo's account was consistent with Taufik Abdullah's. He described plenary discussions as exhilarating intellectual experiences, especially for someone as young and as eager to learn as he was. He also could not forget how his contemporaries who were assigned to Vol. 6 under Nugroho and who were working at the History Center, had to endure 'panic attacks' whenever Taufik was around to witness their presentations. Djoko recalled Taufik as always giving biting criticisms or raising difficult questions. While the rest of the team pitied them, the reactions of Nugroho's protégés were also a constant source of amusement for the group.[26]

The membership of each group was based mainly on the area of expertise. Each volume editor, however, seemed to have enjoyed the freedom to decide who to invite to become part of his team. Nugroho, for instance, chose to employ his protégés from the History Center, who were all young and rather inexperienced. Against the backdrop of high hopes and expectations for the project, no one voiced suspicion, if there was any, that Nugroho's choice may be part of an undisclosed political motive behind the project. Members of the team were too engrossed with their own tasks to be concerned about whatever political motive there might be behind the composition of the Vol. 6 team. Suspicions would arise only later on.[27]

Most members of the team I interviewed claimed that they had freedom while writing their respective assignments. Under no circumstances, they emphasized, were any government officials to watch over the proceedings, nor were there guidelines from the government as to what they were permitted or discouraged to write about, or how specific events should be interpreted.[28] This freedom, however, seemed to apply only to volumes in which the New Order regime had a remote interest. As far as Vol. 6 was concerned, it appeared not to be the case. One of the members of Vol. 6 team confirmed that they wrote the volume in compliance with a "military mission," which specifically was "to shear (the nation of) Sukarno."[29] Believing that it was only by doing so that the nation could move on, the regime wanted to cleanse the collective national memory of anything good that Sukarno had done or stood for (more on this point in the next chapter).

The framework drawn up by Sartono was based on a 'multi-dimensional' approach to history-writing. Sartono pioneered this approach in Indonesia, and for decades, it has been considered as a methodological 'holy grail' among emerging academic historians. The framework, which I shall discuss in detail in the next chapter, was explained thoroughly during the plenary meetings. However, as actual output indicated, it was not, or could not be, faithfully followed by many members of the team.

There may be three reasons why the framework was not satisfactorily carried out. The first possible reason was that, in terms of academic preparations, Sartono was well ahead of other members of the team. Not only was

The making of SNI 109

the multi-dimensional approach demanding—it was also very unfamiliar to most other members who were either absolute neophytes or were reared in the conventional narrative approach to history. It must be noted that by 1970, it was barely 15 years since history departments in Indonesia had begun turning out graduates of history. In terms of actual experience, therefore, even in conventional narrative or antiquarian history-writing, the pool of intellectual resources was very limited. The survey of historical works up to the 1980s undertaken by Adrian Lapian and Sedijono corroborates this assessment (Lapian and Sedijono 1992).

The second possible reason was Sartono's personal leadership style. Because his demeanor was so gentle, soft-spoken, diffident, and unassertive, he did not or could not bear to push hard enough for the implementation of the framework.[30] Perhaps, upon seeing his fears and his doubts of the overall readiness and capabilities of the team being realized, he felt helpless about it and just let things be.

The third possible reason is political, and this especially applies to Vol. 6. As noted above, one of the members of the Vol. 6 team, Nugroho's very close aide, has admitted that since their primary purpose in writing Vol. 6 was to fulfill what he called a 'military mission,' the narrative approach would serve the job better than Sartono's multi-dimensional or structural approach. With a narrative approach, the messages would have a better chance of being understood by the target audience.[31] The move to expunge the succeeding edition, starting with the 1984 edition, of the use of the structural approach in favor of the narrative approach, supports this information (details to be discussed in the next chapter).

Other problems plagued the project. One was leadership accountability. While Sartono was supposed to be the main editor, Nugroho was, in fact, running the project. In setting timetables, for instance, Nugroho earned the ire of some members, even eliciting mutinous reactions from them when, for example, he proceeded to print unfinished manuscripts. He justified his decision by implying that since the deadlines have been moved back twice or thrice already, those who remained unfinished had lost the moral authority to complain. He claimed that there should be no problem as the books would undergo revisions later on.[32] (See also Zain 1976.) It seemed that for Nugroho, the priority was to complete the project as soon as possible.

Some details of this incident should be spelled out to allow us a glimpse of the dynamics between Nugroho and the other members of the team. In the article based on an interview with Nugroho in *Sinar Harapan* on 1 October 1980, he claimed that the original deadline for manuscripts was set for June 1973. Because a number of groups were still not finished, it was decided in the last plenary meeting (possibly also in June 1973) to move the deadline to September 1973. Nugroho also claimed that in this meeting, it was decided, among other things, that he would be in-charge of preparation for publication. The main duty of the person-in-charge was to finalize the drafts which were supposed to have already been examined by Sartono (for scholarly aspect) and Merwati (for writing style) (*Sinar Harapan* 1980b). Such a plan was not carried out. Sartono was not given a chance to examine the manuscripts, and Marwati Poesponegoro did not style-edit them.[33] By September certain groups were still not finished, and so the deadline was pushed back once again to April 1974. By then, however, there remained an unfinished group (the Vol. 5 group). Nugroho averred that on 8 July 1974, Sartono, being the overall editor, decided that printing should proceed after 31 July 1974. Any new manuscript or any revision in old manuscripts submitted after that date would no longer be accepted.[34]

Did Sartono in fact give his approval to publish the still unpolished, even unfinished manuscripts? He was embarrassed to admit that he could not prevent Nugroho from doing what he wanted.[35] What Sartono personally wanted was to, after finishing all the manuscripts, assign three persons or more to proofread, edit, and style-edit them before printing. He also thought that in cases of historically controversial questions, they had to offer alternative conclusions. On both counts, Nugroho did not assent and did as he pleased.[36]

This incident showed who was in control. Anyone who knows Sartono can infer that his diffident personality may have much to do with this. One might speculate that had his personality been at least as forceful or as straightforward as Nugroho's, he could have put up a stronger resistance. On the other hand, Nugroho's standing in the military-dominated scheme of things during the New Order, not to mention that the project was possibly his initiative under the behest of the military, exerted a strong influence on how others dealt with him. Sartono's subservience boded ill for the stance of the scholarly community that he represented vis-à-vis the state power that Nugroho signified, to follow the usual dichotomous positioning. The reference above to Sartono's type of personality gains credence if we look at how the stronger-willed Taufik Abdullah and Abdurrachman Surjomihardjo fared in their encounters with Nugroho.

Nugroho's decision to print unfinished manuscripts, in particular, Vol. 5, which was under the editorship of Abdurrachman Surjomihardjo, puzzled many (for example, Taufik Abdullah, Sartono Kartodirdjo, Adrian Lapian, and Djoko Suryo). On the other hand, such behavior was also well understood by others who knew Nugroho up close. He was said to have justified his decision by claiming that the time and money allotted by the sponsor of the project, the Ministry of Education, had already been well exceeded. He seemed to have felt embarrassed about the delays for which he held himself personally responsible to the Minister.[37] Nugroho was known to be faithful to his promises, and hard worker as he was, he demanded that results be delivered on time. Since he believed that the deadline had been moved a number of times already, he did not think it should not be transgressed anymore.[38]

The trouble was, Nugroho's notion of a 'deadline' seemed not shared by others in the group.[39] When Taufik Abdullah's group, for instance, failed to meet the 'absolute' deadline, Nugroho sent the manuscripts to the printer, and they were shocked upon hearing that the volume had already been printed.[40] Taufik Abdullah joined Abdurrachman Surjomiharjo in protesting at not being consulted in the publication of their volume. What further enraged them was that the chapter written for Vol. 5 by their colleague Deliar Noer was unceremoniously removed from the printed version. It turned out that this was due to his critical remarks about the New Order regime that incensed Suharto.[41] As a consequence, Deliar Noer was expelled from the teacher's college, where he was serving as a professor, in addition to being banished from the project. Combining their sympathy for their friend with their resentment for Nugroho's rash judgment, Taufik and Abdurrachman both withdrew from the project and renounced any responsibility for Vol. 5.[42] Their contributions, however, were not taken out, and the succeeding printing (the one that actually circulated widely in public) carried the name of Yusmar Basri, giving the impression that he was the real editor and writer of Vol. 5, whereas in fact he was not. Yusmar Basri was one of Nugroho's young protégés at the History Center.

That Taufik and Abdurrachman resigned in protest indicated that they would not tolerate Nugroho's transgression of their principles. They stood by their desire to protect their integrity as scholars and individuals. That Nugroho, however, was undeterred, had his way, made use of their contributions under somebody else's name, and got away with it indicated the stronger constellation of power that emboldened him to act as he did. That it would take another five years before, in 1980, Abdurrachman could retaliate against Nugroho in the open—via newspaper articles—and give voice to the hitherto muted contempt he had for the latter suggested his relatively weaker position vis-à-vis Nugroho.[43]

Nugroho's impudence had yet to peak. When a later edition of the SNI appeared sometime between 1980 and 1983,[44] only the names Nugroho Notosusanto and Marwati Djoened Poesponegoro were printed as editors on the cover of the books. Sartono's name was taken out. Rumors circulated that he, following Taufik and Abdurrachman, had also withdrawn from the project.[45] Both vocal and silent critics of Nugroho's handling of the SNI applauded Sartono's supposed 'withdrawal.' They speculated that he could no longer bear to feel responsible for the books that they felt in many ways did not uphold scholarly standards (Atmakusumah 1992; Soeroto 1980). As a fairly logical explanation, it was no wonder it persisted as a widely upheld truth. Observers such as Syamdani (2001), who was writing in 2001, referred back to that incident to emphasize the very problematic character of the SNI. Even historians who were still alive (at the time of the interview in 2005) and were closest to Sartono, such as Djoko Suryo, Adrian Lapian, and Taufik Abdullah, did not have any idea of what really happened.

It turned out that Sartono never withdrew, but he was removed.[46] He kept quiet about it for so long, he said, because nobody asked him before I did. Actually, sometime in 1987, a journalist from the newspaper *Kompas* asked him why he withdrew from the SNI project. He politely evaded the question (see *Kompas* 1987). Perhaps, he did not like to make an issue out of it, or he did not want to be pitied. The reason for his removal appeared to be related to his suggestion to Nugroho to not put the names of the three main editors in the front cover, creating the impression that they were the authors of the volume. In his view, it was more ethically appropriate to indicate the names of the volume editors and writers in front, while the names of the main editors could be placed inside. Nugroho did not agree.[47] When Sartono stood by his position, Nugroho removed his name in the subsequent editions without any explanation or warning whatsoever.[48]

These incidents, however, ought not to be interpreted as a brazen display of power on the part of Nugroho. In the world where Nugroho, Sartono, and other protagonists existed, there were subtle ways to smooth out the rough edges of the power play. In fact, despite what Nugroho did, bitter critics such as Taufik Abdullah and the mildly critical Sartono described him as a 'likeable' or 'good person.'[49] It would thus be inaccurate to depict Nugroho as a rough, power-wielding individual who would flaunt his power at every turn. Perhaps his conduct, sometimes at the expense of ethical principles, suggests that he felt lacking in power and that he was in pursuit of more of it. It is pertinent to address where he stood in the topologies of powers during that time.

Taking the lead from a statement of his adjutant, Nugroho had a military mission to accomplish.[50] Instances cited above thus may be understood as suggestive of his determination to overcome all possible obstacles to accomplish the 'mission' and complete it as quickly as possible.[51] One may speculate that his efforts to railroad the publication of the manuscripts and his refusal to subject them to a thorough editing could mean that he was concerned not only about the time (deadline) but also about the content of the books. He seemed especially careful not to subject Vol. 6 to scrutiny by other members of the team. That could also be an important reason why he rejected Sartono's plan to assign three or more proofreaders and editors, through whom all manuscripts should pass before printing. One of Nugroho's close friends recalled that he asked Nugroho why he published Vol. 5 ahead of the rest while it was still unfinished. He quoted Nugroho as replying, "It's alright! It's (already) good!" He seemed convinced that the volume was already suitable and that he wanted to show the people, the Ministry of Education, especially, that a quality output was soon forthcoming from the project. Considering that rigor or "accuracy was not one of (Nugroho's) strong points," such a judgment on his part seemed unsurprising.[52]

Another possible reason rested in the dynamics between Nugroho and the members of the Vol. 5 team. One close to him speculated that Nugroho might have suspected Taufik and Abdurrachman of deliberately delaying the project. Afraid of the impact of delays on the overall success of his brainchild, Nugroho launched what amounted to a pre-emptive strike by publishing the volume hastily.[53] When the two were enraged and withdrew,

Nugroho averted a potential crisis (of accountability for Vol. 5) by naming Yusmar Basri as the volume editor/author. A prevailing perception among members of the team was that if any volume was ready for publication at that time, it was Vol. 1, not Vol. 5.[54]

Possibly, a combination of these considerations prompted Nugroho's actions. However, once we examine in the next chapter the contents of the books, we will be in better position to decide. At this point, what is important is to underline that Nugroho, aside from being a historian, regarded himself as a soldier who sought recognition for being good and dutiful (McGregor 2007, 55–58).

Reactions

Despite the tumultuous episodes involving some members, the project was completed and officially launched on 15 December 1975. Apparently elated at the completion of the project, Nugroho Notosusanto declared that it constituted a 'national pride' and that it proved beyond doubt that Indonesians could write their own history (Zain 1976). He also proclaimed that SNI was the best Indonesian history yet written, as *Kompas* reported on 19 March 1976. As if to sharpen further the significance of the occasion, he juxtaposed the publication of the SNI with what he called the 'failure' of the two previous attempts during the Sukarno period (Zain 1976).

The importance given by the government to the project was evident in the ceremony held on 18 March 1976, wherein the books were formally presented to President Suharto. The event bannered the headlines of major dailies the following day. It was also televised nationwide via the government television, the Televisi Republik Indonesia (Republic of Indonesia Television) TVRI (*Kompas* 1976). In attendance during the formal presentation were the Minister for Education and Culture, Sjarif Thayeb, and the three main editors, along with each volume's respective editors (Siswadhi, Leirissa, and Atmakusumah 1976). On this occasion, Suharto reiterated his call for increased attention to the teaching of national history in schools. SNI was declared by Nugroho, the Minister, and the President alike as a standard reference text of Indonesian national history (*Kompas* 1976; Zain 1976).

Notably excluded in the immediate press coverage was Sartono's categorical pronouncement in his preface to the books that "none among the members of the team regards this book as a standard, far from it" (Kartodirdjo 1975, viii). Actually, the question of whether to consider the SNI a standard work was raised in the early stages of the project. Uka Tjandrasasmita noted in his paper for the Tugu workshop in 1972 the problematic character of the term 'standard.' He recalled that in their discussion with foreign experts in Berkeley and the Netherlands, it was repeatedly raised. He urged a reconsideration of the intention to consider it a standard work (Tjandrasasmita 1972).

114 *The making of SNI*

Sometime later, two journalists, Atmakusumah (1976) and B.M. Diah (1976), took note of Sartono's pronouncement. Like a call in the wilderness, however, their voices were ignored amidst the obedience of the media and the public school system to government directives regarding the SNI. The injunction lasted all throughout the New Order, even beyond. The SNI was officially (mainly symbolically) withdrawn only in 2002, when the government could no longer resist the mounting public clamor.

That the government conferred on the SNI the status of the "standard history book" and maintained it for decades notwithstanding its shortcomings may be considered an act of political power trying to define historical knowledge. The crudity of this move did not escape some observers in Indonesia, but, as with Sartono's pronouncement, their criticisms could only find limited support among small segments of the population. It would take a long time, and gradual little steps, before sufficient pressures built up to undermine the status of the SNI as official history.

Hardly had the books entered public circulation when, barely three weeks after their presentation to Suharto, the SNI began its travails in the hands of critics. B.M. Diah, a well-known journalist and owner of *Merdeka*, one of the national dailies in Indonesia during that time, launched the first major salvo. He wrote a passionate and lengthy critique of the books in his newspaper. Practically all my informants readily remembered Diah's piece, at least vaguely, which suggests the lasting impression it left on the reading public. In the article, B.M. Diah lambasted the SNI for several reasons. First, according to him, it was grossly biased against Sukarno. Second, Diah bewailed that contrary to its purported aim of writing a truly Indonesian history, significant parts of it remained largely dominated by "Western viewpoints" and filled with Western sources. Third, the historical methodology was inadequately employed. He even went as far as calling for the withdrawal of the book from circulation (Diah 1976). The reasons for these criticisms will be discussed further in the next chapter in conjunction with the overall historiographic and political contexts. At this point, it is important to note one thing. Diah keenly observed that the biased treatment of Sukarno in Vol. 6 cannot seem to be accounted for by a simple problem of innocent subjectivity on the part of the writers, Nugroho specifically. Diah suspected that it emanated from a more deeply felt desire to assert one's personal beliefs at the expense of methodological imperatives. Diah seemed to be hinting at the position of Nugroho in the scheme of things in Indonesia and implied that there was nothing innocent or accidental in the treatment of Sukarno.

In June 1976, Atmakusumah wrote a mildly critical review of the SNI for *Kompas*. This review prefigured a more expansive review article which would appear in *Prisma*, a periodic magazine, two months later. He identified various editorial weaknesses of the book. These included the notable absence of illustrations or photos in some parts and inappropriate, misplaced, or unlabelled photos in others; numerous typographical errors; inconsistent terminologies; and inappropriate layout. More important, however, was his observation that many of the SNI's controversial assertions were haphazardly formulated, without sufficient effort to provide evidence, much less critical evaluation of competing possibilities. Another was that the authors of Vol. 6 wrote as if they were journalists, in a hurry to finish a deadline and delivering information that they subconsciously 'knew' to be good only for the day. Atmakusumah wondered what could be driving the authors to be in such a hurry. That the entire project was finished in four years was an extraordinary feat, he mused. He speculated that the authors (especially referring to the Vol. 6 team) perhaps wanted to reconstruct recent history while evidence, both written and oral, was still fresh; soon, such evidence would be lost forever (Atmakusumah 1976).

Two months later, a review appeared in *Prisma* written by the trio of Siswadhi, Leirissa, and Atmakusumah (1976). It was subdued and politely appreciative although forthright about some of SNI's notable weaknesses. Corroborating many of Atmakusumah's observations cited above, they pinpointed the weaknesses as follows: (1) editorial inconsistencies and problems, such as absences or faults in documentation; (2) contradictory interpretations; (3) one-sided interpretation or interpretations based on highly selective treatment of evidence; (4) apparent absence of an overriding theoretical and unifying framework; and (5) grossly inadequate research on some periods. The reviewers were invariably quick to forgive the authors for these lapses, saying that this was the first attempt and that revisions would follow as promised by the authors. The title of the review is quite interesting: "Buku Babon Sejarah Nasional Indonesia: Objektivitas yang Ideal?" ("Standard Text of National History of Indonesia: Ideal Objectivity?") The question mark (after the word 'objectivity') makes one wonder what lay beneath the circumspect and appreciative tone of the reviewers. It does not categorically uphold Diah's biting critique, but it obviously made an impact on the reviewers, especially Atmakusumah, who did the review of the controversial Vol. 6.

In November 1976, Abdurrachman Surjomihardjo published the first in a series of critiques of SNI in *Kompas*. Such critiques would not abate until the late 1980s when he died. While this first salvo was much milder than what he wrote later in the 1980s, it gave a foretaste of what was to come. He noted, for instance, the irregular circumstances surrounding the 'birth' of the SNI and alluded to broken goodwill and ethical norms that were transgressed in the process. He also quoted an unnamed historian who was supposed to have used a metaphor of a defective baby (*bayi yang cacat*) to refer to the SNI.[55] What was more, he did not hold back, saying that it was just a draft and that the word 'standard' was a very smug way of describing it (Surjomihardjo 1976).

In the succeeding two decades, from 1977 to 1997, the SNI occasionally figured in the media, usually coinciding with the announcement of the plan to revise it or a new edition came out.[56] They also cropped up around the

116 *The making of SNI*

time a new national history conference was being planned or held, as well as when a government-initiated, history-related project was being mulled over.[57] In 1980, an initial exchange between Sartono Kartodirdjo and Taufik Abdullah, on the one hand, and Nugroho, on the other hand, ended up rousing an indignant rejoinder from Abdurrachman Surjomihardjo. This encounter was set off by mischievous responses from Sartono and Taufik Abdullah to a journalist from *Sinar Harapan*, who asked what they could say about the ongoing efforts (in 1980) to revise or improve the SNI-6. Sartono was quoted by a news item to have responded, "I can only laugh. Hahahaha." Taufik Abdullah, on the other hand, responded that if Prof. Sartono had said that, then he might as well say, "Hihihihi" (*Sinar Harapan* 1980b). Nugroho appeared to have been offended, as evidenced in an interview that appeared in the same newspaper on 1 October 1980. The title of the interview was telling: "Agree with Sartono's Ideas, Except the 'Hahaha." (*Sinar Harapan* 1980c)

In this interview, Nugroho mentioned numerous things that impelled Abdurrachman Surjomihardjo to respond. The response appeared in the same newspaper 15 days later. It was a scathing critique of an unnamed person, but it was obvious that Abdurrachman was referring to Nugroho. His pent-up anger palpable, he lambasted his unnamed target for an '*asal bapak senang*' (so long as the boss is happy) mentality and for lying (Surjomihardjo 1980). He further described the history-writing in Indonesia as 'chaotic' or in 'crisis' (*kemelut*), and he categorically stated that Vol. 6 did not satisfy the requirements of scholarship. It was, he claimed bitterly, a humiliating chapter in the history of history-writing in Indonesia (ibid). What appeared to be an overheating altercation led to an editorial from the same newspaper, with a view to dousing the fiery exchange.

Not long after the 1984 edition came out, the front-page article entitled "Some Problems Found in the Standard Text National History of Indonesia" appeared in *Sinar Harapan* on 12 April 1985. It highlighted the lingering as well as newfound problems, such as error-laden index and bibliography, and photos without captions and sources in the latest edition of the SNI. Due to the problems, observers expressed bemusement or doubt about the status of the SNI as 'buku babon' or standard text.

Surjomihardjo proved to be a continuing and hard-hitting critic. Joining the public discussion aroused by Suharto's call in May 1987 to formulate an official, 'objective' history of the period 1950–1965, Surjomihardjo rekindled the controversies when, on 20 May 1987, he published in *Kompas* a translation of selected parts of Klooster's book *Indonesiers Schrijven Hun Geschiedenis* (Indonesians Write Their History) (Klooster 1985). The book was published two years earlier (1985), and it documented and analyzed the process and the outputs of the efforts of Indonesians writing their own history, covering the period 1900 to 1980. Taufik Abdullah, in a separate article, described it as the "most comprehensive and exhaustive study" of Indonesian historiography and, despite some notable problems, a "real contribution to our knowledge" (Abdullah 1988, 334). What Surjomihardjo opted to translate were portions detailing the process and the problems encountered in making the SNI. In his introduction, he noted that being a foreigner, Klooster was an outsider in the SNI project and thus he was a detached observer. His book deserved to be paid due attention (Surjomihardjo 1987a). What Surjomihardjo seemed to have in mind was to reaffirm, even intensify, his earlier critique of SNI by proxy. In a sequel to this article (the article was published in two parts), he highlighted Klooster's observations that SNI lacked research; that the writing was uneven; and that it had failed to carry out the prescribed, multi-dimensional, social science approach (Klooster 1985 as summarized in Surjomihardjo 1987b).

In 1992, in consonance with the reported plan to revise SNI, a number of more openly critical articles appeared. In the two articles written by Masduki Baidlawi in the news magazine *Editor*, the title was telling: 'Looking at History that Smacks of Politics' (1992a) and 'Negligence that goes on and on' (1992b). An article written by Atmakusumah, whose articles in 1976 have been discussed above, was even more direct: 'SNI VI: A Political Book' (Atmakusumah 1992).

In the first article, Baidlawi cited the significant declaration of the then Minister of Education, a high-ranking government official named Fuad Hasan, that the SNI-6 would be the primary focus of revision because it had numerous weaknesses, and it received considerable attention from the critics owing to its controversial character. The second article, on the other hand, reiterated the problems—factual mistakes and skewed interpretations—that persisted in the SNI and the history books based on it, despite already having undergone several editions or revision. It called for the books' total overhaul (*perombakan total*). Significantly, it concluded with a lesson: "it is important to separate political interest from historical interpretation" (Baidlawi 1992). Against the backdrop set by all previous articles that dealt with SNI, these two articles were notable for their candor, specifically in linking political interests with the shape of history. Even Diah and Surjomihardjo, who were both strident critics of the SNI, were not as explicit in their earlier reference to the political character of the SNI. That the times may have indeed changed seemed evident in the third article, in which the previously cautious Atmakusumah shed many of the inhibitions apparent in his 1976 critiques of the SNI. Without mincing words, he declared that "the editor of Volume 6 no longer played the role of an observer of history but rather a politician" and that the SNI-6 gave the impression that it was not a historical but rather a political book (Atmakusumah 1992). Perhaps these candid critiques were motivated by the atmosphere of openness ('keterbukaan') that was seen in the early 1990s, which proved to be short-lived.

As stated earlier by Nugroho, SNI did undergo revisions to address its problems or weaknesses. However, the way revisions were undertaken left much to be desired and to be suspicious about. Out of the seven or eight

118 *The making of SNI*

editions, there were in fact only two major revisions, in 1984 and in 1993. The 1977 and 1980 editions were only very slightly different from the 1975 original edition. These little differences consisted of improvement in language use; the addition of a glossary, index, or bibliography; and correction of typographical errors. Editions that appeared between 1985 and 1991 were almost the same as the 1984 edition. The 1993 edition's primary difference lay in having an additional seventh volume that was specifically devoted to the New Order regime.[58] Likewise, the chapter about the Japanese period, which was originally part of Vol. 6, was moved to Vol. 5. Thus, the coverage of Vol. 6 had been shortened to the period from the onset of independence in 1945 up to the end of Guided Democracy.

Out of the six volumes, only Vol. 6 underwent substantive changes. A few chapters of Vol. 2, 3, and 4 were also re-written, and some materials were added, but the changes did not go anywhere near those made to Vol. 6. Even less consequential were the changes in Vol. 1 and 5, at least until the 1990 edition

Summing up

While this chapter serves as the counterpart of Chapter 3, where the making of Tadhana was discussed, the structure of the two chapters is not strictly parallel. Unlike Tadhana, which seldom figured in public discussion, SNI had for several decades been the object of recurrent public scrutiny. Discussing public critique is integral to the analysis of SNI. A number of observations need to be highlighted here. First, the critical responses to SNI were not suppressed, but the relatively small number, and the sporadic character of their criticisms, meant limited impact. Once the appellation 'standard' had been officially imputed on SNI, it stuck in the mind of many people, despite claims and verifications to the contrary made by scholars and journalists who knew better.

Second, the criticisms had been narrowly focused on the first edition (1975) of SNI. The fact that the succeeding two editions, 1977 and 1980, were little more than reprints may have misled critics into thinking that other later editions were also not much different. This can be inferred from B.M. Diah's re-issue in 1985 of his 1976 review of SNI without any substantive change. The same article was later reprinted as a chapter in the book *Straighten History (Meluruskan Sejarah)* (Diah 1987). Had he looked closely enough at the 1984 edition of SNI, he would have been startled and even more infuriated with the changes.

Finally, perhaps partly as a consequence of the singular focus on SNI, other sources of more blatant propaganda escape the critics' notice until much later. The most notable of these were the versions of SNI that Nugroho and his team prepared for high schools, which will be discussed in next chapter. These were purportedly mere summaries of the original SNI 1975 edition. The titles of the textbooks were *Sejarah Nasional Indonesia untuk SMP* (1976) (National History of Indonesia for Junior High School) and *Sejarah Nasional Indonesia untuk SMA* (1979), which included three volumes each (National History of Indonesia for Senior High School). That no critical commentaries appeared in the media about the highly propagandistic contents of these textbooks until the late 1980s may be partly attributable to the critics' skewed focus on SNI. Like the general public, critics seem to have believed in Nugroho's pronouncement that these textbooks were just summaries or simplified versions of SNI, adapted to suit the pedagogical needs of the high school students. As will be shown in the next chapter, this was not so, and the possible implications are analytically and politically significant.

Notes

1 Interview with an anonymized informant, 23 & 25 June 2005, Yogyakarta, Indonesia.
2 Interview with an anonymized informant, 15 December 2005, Yogyakarta, Indonesia.
3 Patterned after the Dutch system, Doktorandus in Indonesia roughly corresponded to a post-bachelor's degree or honors, or a Master's degree. After about three years of Bachelor's degree (Sarjana Muda), some students study for two more years and write a thesis to obtain Doktorandus.
4 In my interview with Taufik Abdullah (10 June 2005, Jakarta), he narrated a running joke between himself and Abdurrachman Surjomihardjo, another important historian. That is, Nugroho lacked rigor because he was not from the Department of History but from General Studies (also in UI). Apparently, in the 1950s and 1960s, students who were still undecided were allowed in UI to stay in the General Studies program and decide later on what specialization to pursue. Nugroho used to be much more interested in literature, and only in later years, he opted to move to history. Another respected Indonesian historian, concurred, "(Nugroho) started in literature and then majored in History. So he didn't have a full course of History. Only one year." (Interview with an anonymized informant, 8 June 2005, Jakarta).
5 The reason for prematurely returning to Indonesia remains unclear. In my interview with Irma Notosusanto, Nugroho's wife (8 August 2005, Jakarta), who joined him in London, she recalled that at the height of the crisis on Irian or Papua in 1962, Nugroho suddenly told her that he wanted to go home, saying that war was breaking, and he didn't like to be overseas when it broke out. So, off they went home. Later, however, she thought that the real reason lay in the problem of severe lack of lecturers in the Faculty of Arts at UI as well as in the increasing polarization of campus politics that left no one interested in occupying the position of Dean of Student Affairs, which was given to him.
6 Interview with an anonymized informant, 23 & 25 June 2005, Yogyakarta.
7 Interview with an anonymized informant 8 June 2005, Jakarta.
8 That Nugroho was considered the first Professor of History at UI needs clarification. Only a professor can supervise and promote a PhD student. In the 1970s, only Harsja Bachtiar held that rank in the History Department of UI, which probably explains why he was the one who acted as promoter of Nugroho to PhD, after Sartono, who was the original supervisor, appeared to have been unceremoniously sidelined, as noted earlier. Harsja Bachtiar's PhD, however, was in Sociology, not in History. He was, thus, not strictly considered a Professor

120 *The making of SNI*

of History. When Nugroho himself declared publicly that there were only two professors of history in Indonesia up to the early 1980s, he and Sartono, he must have not considered Harsja Bachtiar as a historian, even if he was teaching Sejarah Masyarakat (Social History or History of Society). See *Sinar Harapan* (1980a).

9 Interview with Tri Wahyuning Irsyam, one of the historians at UI, 8 August 2005, Depok.
10 The most comprehensive and thorough account of Nugroho's life and career is found in Chapter 2 of McGregor (2007).
11 Many of my informants, including his very close former adjutant, who asked to remain anonymous, believe that Nugroho's appointments, first as Rector of UI and later as Minister of Education, were a sort of 'reward' for his loyal service to the military.
12 Interview with an anonymized informant, 8 June 2005, Jakarta.
13 Interview with Taufik Abdullah, 10 June 2005, Jakarta.
14 Interview with an anonymized informant, 8 June 2005, Jakarta.
15 Interview with Djoko Surjo, 22 June 2005, Yogyakarta.
16 Interview with Djoko Suryo, a historian at UGM and who worked closely with Sartono Kartodirdjo in the SNI project, 22 June 2005, Yogyakarta.
17 I could not find an extant copy of the detailed framework supposedly entitled "Kerangka Konseptuil Sejarah Nasional Indonesia" (A Conceptual Framework of Indonesia's National History) which Sartono told me was published in an Indonesian journal. Perhaps, the title was different, and I may have already found it among the two articles written by Sartono himself that discuss what seem to be a framework of SNI (see Kartodirdjo 1970, 1972).
18 Interview with an anonymized informant, 15 December 2005, Yogyakarta.
19 Interview with an anonymized informant, 15 December 2005, Yogyakarta.
20 Interview with an anonymized informant, 15 December 2005, Yogyakarta.
21 Interview with Djoko Suryo, 22 June 2005, Yogyakarta.
22 For details of what was discussed during the workshop, see the three volumes of proceedings: *Lokakarya Buku Standar Sedjarah Indonesia*, Jilid I-III (The History of Indonesia Standard Text Workshop), Volumes 1–3).
23 Interview with an anonymized informant, 15 December 2005, Yogyakarta.
24 Interview with Taufik Abdullah, 10 June 2005, Jakarta.
25 Interview with Yusmar Basri, one of the historians at History Center, 18 December 2005, Jakarta.
26 Interview with Djoko Suryo, 22 June 2005, Yogyakarta.
27 Interview with Djoko Suryo, 22 June 2005, Yogyakarta.
28 Interview with several anonymized informants, June-December 2005, Yogyakarta and Jakarta.
29 Interview with an anonymized informant, who was close to Nugroho, 22 August 2005, Depok. The interview, done in Bahasa Indonesia, was sometimes interspersed with phrases in English. This was one of those phrases this informant uttered. In his words "to shear Sukarno "
30 Interview with an anonymized informant, 22 & 25 June 2005, Yogyakarta.
31 Interview with an anonymized informant, 22 August 2005, Depok.
32 Interview with Magdalena Manus, 26 July 2005, Depok.
33 Interview with anonymized informants on 23 & 25 June 2005 and on 8 June 2005, Yogyakarta and Jakarta.
34 It puzzles why Nugroho would write a letter to the Minister of Education, dated 17 May 1975, stating that by April 1974, all the manuscripts were already polished and ready for printing, whereas he himself attested that the ultimate deadline had been reset for 31 July 1974 precisely because there was still a group that was not finished by April 1974. Abdurrachman Surjomihardjo thinks that this

episode indicated Nugroho's desire to please the boss and gain commendation in the process (Surjomihardjo 1980).
35 Interview with anonymized informant, 23 & 25 June 2005, Yogyakarta.
36 Interview with anonymized informant, 23 & 25 June 2005, Yogyakarta.
37 Interview with four anonymized informants who knew Nugroho personally, June to August 2005, Jakarta/Depok.
38 Interview with anonymized informant, who was close to Nugroho, 8 August 2005, Depok.
39 Interview with anonymized informant, 23 & 25 June 2005, Yogyakarta.
40 Interview with Taufik Abdullah, 10 June 2005, Jakarta.
41 Interview with Taufik Abdullah, 10 June 2005, Jakarta.
42 Interview with Taufik Abdullah, 10 June 2005, Jakarta.
43 The newspaper article "Sejarah Kontemporer dan Kemelut Penulisan Buku Sejarah Nasional Indonesia" (Contemporary History and the Chaos in Writing SNI), which was published in *Sinar Harapan* on 15 October 1980, was not the first Abdurrachman Surjomihardjo wrote about SNI. On 17 November 1976, he wrote a short piece in *Kompas*, "Penulisan Sejarah Mutakhir (Recent Historical Writings)," whose tone was subdued and politely critical. The 1980 *Sinar Harapan* piece mentioned above was decidedly fiery and was clearly directed at Nugroho himself, without, of course, explicitly identifying him.
44 Designating the year each edition appeared is not straightforward. One reason is that, as they appeared on the title page, edition and reprinting numbers are mixed up or inconsistent. The first edition clearly appeared in 1975, the second in 1977, the third in 1980 and the fourth in 1984. However, in between 1975 and 1984, and beyond 1984, reprints appeared that were indicated also as 'edition.' Say, 1976 edition (which was just like 1975) and 1990 edition (just a reprint of the 1984 edition). I didn't see any 1981–1983 editions, but Klooster (1985) mentioned that they were very similar to the 1980 edition.
45 This is widely believed both in Indonesia and abroad. Many times, when I gave a presentation, both in Indonesia and overseas, and mentioned this incident, there were participants who asked for clarification of the matter because the common belief was that Sartono withdrew from the project.
46 Interviews with an anonymized informant, 23 & 25 June 2005 and 15 December 2005, Yogyakarta.
47 In an interview with Nugroho (see *Sinar Harapan* 1980c), Nugroho has noted that Sartono expressed a contrary view on where to put the names of the editors. However, he was silent on the 'ejection' of Sartono. Instead, he made an impression that Sartono indeed withdrew ("keluar") from the project by not negating the journalist's assumption that he did so.
48 Interviews with an anonymized informant, 23 & 25 June 2005.
49 Interviews with an anonymized informants, 23 & 25 June 2005 and 10 June 2005, Yogyakarta and Jakarta, respectively.
50 Interview with an anonymized informant who was close to Nugroho, 22 August 2005.
51 Another possible indication that Nugroho was really in a hurry may be glimpsed from a perceptive observation of an author of an article that appeared in *Kompas*. He observed the SSN2 (Seminar Sejarah Nasional 2) appeared to be hastily organized. He inferred such a claim from the fact that the seminar had been moved four months earlier; it had been originally planned for December 1970 and was moved to August 1970. He suspected that political reasons ('alasan-alasan politis') might have been behind this (Siswadhi 1970). I have found no proof that such a move was at the behest of Nugroho. The relevant point is that there were people who, as early as 1970, harbored a suspicion about the political motivations behind the national conference.

52 Interview with an anonymized informant, 8 June 2005, Jakarta.
53 Interview with an anonymized informant, 8 June 2005, Jakarta.
54 Interview with Taufik Abdullah informant, 10 June 2005, Jakarta.
55 Sartono was the one Abdurrachman was referring to. Sartono felt guilty having uttered those words to refer to SNI. As late as 2005, he was still wondering whether Nugroho, who had a 'special child,' might have misconstrued what he meant and felt insulted. As a reprisal he expelled Sartono from the project (Interview with an anonymized informant, 23 & 25 June 2005, Yogyakarta).
56 For example, in 1992, the then outgoing Minister of Education announced that there would be a revision of the SNI. See Taufik Abdullah (1994, 203–204) for an overview of different views expressed in the media, seminars and private conversation about the plan to revise the SNI in 1992.
57 For instance, in 1987, Suharto declared the need to take another look at the period 1950–1965, and to come up with an 'honest and objective' reassessment of the period (Abdullah 1987a, 1987b; see also news articles in *Kompas*, "History of Indonesia's New Era Needs to be Re-written" (Sejarah Zaman Baru Indonesia Memang Perlu Ditulis Kembali)," (5 May 1987) and "Government Needs to Prepare Reference Guide for History of 1950–1965" (Pemerintah Perlu Menyusun Buku Acuan Sejarah Indonesia 1950–1965) (27 May 1987).
58 A foreword of Vol. 7 indicates that the decision to form a separate volume specifically for the New Order period emanated from the decision of the Minister of Education in 1992, upon the recommendation of a working committee tasked to take another look at history-writing. This appears to have a link to the clamor raised sometime in 1987 for a new history book on the 1950–1965 and New Order periods.

References

Abdullah, Hamid. 1987a. "Beberapa Kendala Penulisan Sejarah (Some Obstacles in Writing History)." *Suara Merdeka*, June 11.

———. 1987b. "Dilema Sejarawan Nasional (The Dilemma of National Historians)." *Suara Pembaruan*, July 14.

Abdullah, Taufik. 1975. "The Study of History." In *The Social Sciences in Indonesia*, edited by Koentjaraningrat, 89–166. Jakarta: Indonesian Institute of Sciences (LIPI).

———. 1988. "Review of Indonesians Write Their History: The Development of Indonesian Historical Study in Theory and Practice, 1900–1980 by H. A. J. Klooster." *Journal of Asian Studies* 47 (2): 432–34.

———. 1994. "In Search of a National History: Experiences of a Multi-Ethnic and Multi-Historic Indonesia." In *Constructing a National Past: National History and Historiography in Brunei, Indonesia, Thailand, Singapore, the Philippines, and Vietnam: A Collection of Conference Papers from the International Workshop on National History and Historiography*, edited by Putu Davies, 203–218. Brunei: Department of History, Universiti Brunei Darussalam.

Atmakusumah. 1976. "Mengamati 'Sejarah Nasional Indonesia' yang Dijadikan Buku Babon (Taking a Look at the Indonesian National History (SNI) which was Made the Standard Text)." *Kompas*, June 15.

———. 1992. "SNI VI: Buku Politik (SNI VI: A Political Book)." *Editor*, April 15, 30–31.

Baidlawi, Masduki. 1992a. "Kealpaan Yang Terus Berulang." *Editor*, April 15, 1992.

———. 1992b. "Meninjau Sejarah Yang Berbau Kekuasaan (Reviewing History that Smacks of Politics)."

Curaming, Rommel. 2003. "Towards Reinventing Indonesian Nationalist Historiography." *Kyoto Review of Southeast Asia*, March 2003. http://kyotoreview.cseas. kyoto-u.ac.jp/issue/issue2/index.html.
Diah, B. M. 1976. "Sejarah Nasional Indonesia Harus Tahan Uji (SNI Must be Able to Stand Scrutiny)." *Merdeka*, April 10.
———. 1987. *Meluruskan Sejarah (Straighten History)*. Jakarta: Pustaka Merdeka.
Ford Foundation. 2003. *Celebrating Indonesia: Fifty Years with the Ford Foundation 1953–2003*. Jakarta: Ford Foundation.
Kartodirdjo, Sartono. 1966. *The Peasants' Revolt of Banten in 1888: Its Conditions, Course and Sequel. A Case Study of Social Movements in Indonesia*. The Hague: Martinus Nijhoff.
———. 1970. "Sekali Lagi Pemikiran Sekitar Sejarah Nasional: Meneruskan Langkah kearah Dekolonisasi Historiografi Indonesia (Onces Again Thoughts on National History: Towards Decolonization of Indonesian Historiography)." *Lembaran Sejarah* 6: 23–35.
———. 1972. "Merenungkan Kembali Pemikiran Tentang Persoalan Sekitar Rekonstruksi Sejarah Indonesia Sebagai Sejarah Nasional (Remembering Once Again the Ideas about Reconstructing the History of Indonesia as a National History)." In *Lokakarya Buku Standar Sejarah Indonesia* (The History of Indonesia Standard Text Workshop) Vol. 3, n.p. Bogor: Tugu.
———. 1975. "Kata Pengantar Umum (General Introduction)." In *Sejarah Nasional Indonesia (National History of Indonesia)*, edited by Sartono Kartodirdjo, Marwati Djoened Poesponegoro, and Nugroho Notosusanto, Vol. 1, vi–ix. Jakarta: Departemen Pendidikan dan Kebudayaan dan Balai Pustaka.
Klooster, H. A. J. 1985. *Indonesiers Schrijven hun Geschiedenis: De Ontwikkeling van de Indonesische Geschiedbeoefening in Theorie en Praktijk 1900–1980 (Indonesians Write Their History: The Development of Indonesian Historiography in Theory and Practice 1900–80)*. Leiden: KITLV.
Kompas. 1987. "Sejarah Zaman Baru Indonesia Memang Perlu Ditulis Kembal (The History of Indonesia's New Era Needs to be Re-written)," May 5.
Lapian, Adrian, and Sedijono. 1992. "Historical Studies in Indonesia in the 1980s." *Asian Research Trends* 2: 1–27.
Leirissa, Richard, and Z. Ghazali, eds. 1993. *Sejarah Nasional Indonesia VII: Lahir dan Berkembangnya Order Baru (The Birth and Development of the New Order)*. Vol. VII. Jakarta: Departemen Pendidikan dan Kebudayaan dan Balai Pustaka.
McGregor, Katharine. 2007. *History in Uniform: Military Ideology and the Construction of Indonesia's Past*. Singapore: NUS Press.
Notosusanto, Nugroho. 1969. *Sedjarawan Indonesia dan sedjarah Indonesia (Indonesian Historians and History of Indonesia)*. Yogyakarta: Universitas Gadjah Mada.
Nursam, Mohammad. 2008. *Membuka Pintu bagi Masa Depan: Biografi Sartono Kartodirdjo (Opening Doors for the Future: A Biography of Sartono Kartodirdjo)*. Jakarta: Penerbit Buku Kompas.
Panitia Seminar Sedjarah, ed. 1958. *Laporan Seminar Sedjarah nasional 1957 (Reports on the National History Seminar 1957)*. Jakarta and Jogyakarta: UI and UGM.
Sagimun, M. D. 1972. "Masalah Konsepsi Teoretis Kerangka Panel III Chusus Bab IV sub-bab 3, 4 dan 5 (Problems in Conceptualizing the Theoretical Framework of Panel 3 Especially Chapter 4 and Sub-chapters 3, 4 & 5)." In *Lokakarya Buku*

Standar Sejarah Indonesia (The History of Indonesia Standard Text Workshop). Vol. 2. n.p. Tugu, Bogor.

Sinar Harapan. 1970. "Buku Sedjarah Nasional Dekati Chaos (National History Book Approaching Chaos)," *Sinar Harapan*, August 4, 1970.

———. 1980a. "Sejarah Demi Masa Kini (History for the Sake of the Present),", January 9, 1980.

———. 1980b. "Masalah Sejarah Kontemporer 'Hahahaha' dan 'Hihihihi (The Problems of Contemporary History Hahaha and Hihihi)," September 20, 1980.

———. 1980c. Setuju Konsep Sartono, Kecuali yang 'Hahahaha:' Wawancara dengan Prof. Dr. Nugroho Notosusanto ttg. Sejarah Kontemporer (Agree with Sartono's Ideas Except the Hahaha: Interview with Prof. Dr. Nugroho Notosusanto about Contemporary History)," *Sinar Harapan*, October 1.

Siswadhi. 1970. "Seminar Nasional Kedua di Jogya (The Second National Seminar at Jogya)." *Kompas*, September 3.

Siswadhi, Richard Leirissa, and Atmakusumah. 1976. "Buku Babon Sejarah Nasional: Objektivitas Yang Ideal?" *Prisma* 5 (Edisi Khusus): 81–90.

Soeroto. 1980. "Sejarah Harus Ditulis Jujur (History Must be Written Honestly)." *Prisma* 9 (8): 60–63.

Surjomihardjo, Abdurrachman. 1976. "Penulisan Sejarah Mutakhir (Recent History Writing)." *Kompas*, November 17.

———. 1980. "Sejarah Kontemporer dan Kemelut Penulisan Buku Sejarah Nasional Indonesia (Contemporary History and the Crisis in Writing the National History of Indonesia)." *Sinar Harapan*, October 15.

———. 1987a. "Terwujudnya Buku Standar Sejarah Nasional Indonesia (The Completion of the Standard Book National History of Indonesia)." *Kompas*, May 20.

———. 1987b. "Terwujudnya Buku Standar Sejarah Nasional Indonesia: Sebuah komentar lanjutan (The Completion of the Standard Book the National History of Indonesia: Further Comments)." *Kompas*, July 3.

Suryanegara A. M. 1985. "Sejarawan, Sejarah dan Masa Depan (Historian, History and the Future)." *Sinar Harapan*, October 21.

Syamdani, ed. 2001. *Kontroversi Sejarah di Indonesia* (Historical Controversies in Indonesia). Jakarta: Grasindo.

Tjandrasasmita, Uka. 1972. "Konsepsi Teoritis Kerangka Panel III Penulisan Buku Standar Nasional Indonesia, Zaman Pertumbuhan Dan Perkembangan Keradjaan Islam Di Indonesia (1500–1700) (Conceptualizing the Theoretical Framework of the Panel 3 of the Standard Book of the National History of Indonesia, Emergence and Development of Islamic Kingdoms in Indonesia (15000–1700)." In *Lokakarya Buku Standar Sejarah Indonesia* (The History of Indonesia Standard Text Workshop) Vol. 2, n.p. Tugu, Bogor.

Vickers, Adrian. 2007. "Sartono Kartodirdjo, 1921–2007." *Inside Indonesia*, December 15. www.insideindonesia.org/sartono-kartodirdjo-1921-2007.

Zain, Umar. 1976. "Penulisan Kembali Karya Standar Sejarah Indonesia (Rewriting Standard Book of Indonesian History)." *Sinar Harapan*, March 22.

5 SNI
Contents and contexts

As in the case of the *Tadhana* project, a complicated configuration of the social, historiographic, and political forces influenced the shape of and the responses to the National History of Indonesia (*Sejarah Nasional Indonesia*, SNI). Unlike *Tadhana*, however, which never enjoyed the public appreciation its creators had hoped for, SNI experienced vicissitudes of fortune depending on the shifting political climate. From the status of being the 'standard text' for more than two decades since the mid-1970s, promoted by the government through education and the media, among other channels, it became an object of thoroughgoing skepticism and fierce public criticism in the post-Suharto period. It reached the point that demonstrators burned the textbooks that were supposedly based on SNI to dramatize their opposition.[1]

Following the approach used to understand Tadhana, this chapter initially describes and analyzes the historiographic development in/on Indonesia within which SNI might best be understood. The mapping out of the historiographic landscape is important not just to understand the structure and contents of SNI but also to elucidate the political contexts of the project. Among other things, it shows how a scholarly approach had managed to restrict the political interests of the prime mover of the project.

Historiographic mapping

From the historiographic standpoint, there are two main areas from which SNI drew its clearest defining characteristics: the attempt to employ an Indonesia-centric perspective (*Indonesiasentrisme*) and the effort to implement the multi-dimensional, social science approach. The Indonesia-centric perspective foregrounds the role of local or indigenous actors in historical narrative. It changes the angle of viewpoint: instead of scholars looking in from the outside, this approach seeks to view historical process from within. It seeks to neutralize the long-standing approach that presents Indonesia and its people merely as an appendage, if seen at all, to the history of the Dutch, or any other foreign groups, in the Netherlands East Indies.

The multi-dimensional or social science approach, on the other hand, is a method that requires the use of concepts and other analytic tools from various social science disciplines to illuminate historical phenomenon. This approach assumes reality as multi-dimensional in its complexity. Each discipline is limited by its nature and can grasp only parts of reality. By drawing from various disciplines, it hopes to employ a holistic approach and, thus, to neutralize the tendency common in conventional historical writing to focus largely on political aspects. The ultimate aim is to capture more complete and multiple dimensions of historical experience.

Sartono Kartodirdjo was the main promoter of these approaches in Indonesia from the 1960s onwards. He envisioned the multi-dimensional approach and an Indonesia-centric perspective going hand in hand. The effort to present local people as *dramatis personae* and to foreground internal development within Indonesia lay at the heart of the Indonesia-centric perspective. Meanwhile, the use of various tools from the social sciences was meant to create a holistic picture of internal development in Indonesia. It was also a means to account for the integration of various groups within the archipelago—the elite and the common people, Javanese as well as other ethnic groups, Muslims, and other religious groups. Such integration was not seen to be merely in the political aspect, manifested in the formation of the Indonesian state, but also in cultural, social, and economic terms (Kartodirdjo 1972).

Indonesia-centrism

Long before SNI project, the Indonesia-centric approach was pursued by scholars such as J.C. van Leur, C.C. Berg, and G. Resink (Van der Kroef 1958). Oft-cited is J.C. van Leur's observation about the tendency of colonial historiography to look at Indonesia from the "deck of the ship, the ramparts of the fortress, [and] the high gallery of the trading house" (van Leur 1955, 261). Early Indonesian writers, such as Rangkuti (1953) and Soetjipto Wirjosuparto (1958), tried to employ a variant of this approach by inverting the positions of the colonizers and colonized so that the local actors described by the Dutch as rebels or insurgents were called heroes. This approach was deemed inadequate or inappropriate (Abdullah 1975, 121–122). Showing the natives as actors and prime movers in their history became the paramount goal.

Sartono demonstrates in his key scholarly works that integration is a fundamental element in Indonesia-centrism. By integration, he meant how various cultural, political, social, and economic elements came together to form a unity that served as the bedrock of national identity and the nation-state. The overwhelming diversity of Indonesia—in ethnic, geographic, religious, economic, cultural, and linguistic terms—poses a considerable challenge to scholars who aimed to present such a huge and diverse area as a unified entity. Integration as the unifying framework was a logical response to such a challenge (Kartodirdjo 1972, 1975, 2001).

In Sartono's framework, all the forces, processes, acts, objects, or tools that stimulated or facilitated interaction of people, as well as the cultural diffusion and economic exchange that facilitated the process of integration, deserve sufficient attention in historical analysis, from the pre-historic period to the present (Kartodirdjo 1972, 1975). As noted in the previous chapter, carrying out Sartono's framework was a tall order, and we shall see the limited extent to which SNI-1975 actually fulfilled the aspiration for the Indonesia-centric perspective and the structural approach. The idea here is to show that despite limitations or weaknesses in the implementation, the combined approaches helped in restricting the political goals of the regime, as represented by Nugroho Notosusanto.

In Vol. 1 of SNI-1975, the decision to do away with the technology-based traditional periodization of Indonesian pre-history (Palaeolithic, Mesolithic, Neolithic) was partly attributable to the imperative of setting a framework more sensitive to the peculiarities of the local conditions. As Soejono, the lead author of Vol. 1, clarified, one problem with the lithic-based periodization was its disproportionate concern about the advances in technological development. It was also primarily based on European cases, which emanated from conditions presumably different from those in Indonesia (Soejono 1972). The writers of the volume endeavored to plot Indonesia's pre-history using what they called a social-economic model. They broadened the basis of periodization in this model to include economic and social problems alongside technological development. The periodization was, thus, divided as follows: the hunting and gathering stage, the stage for farming and domestication of animals, and the tool-using or technology-based specialization stage. The importance of technological development, as reflected in the lithic-based periodization, was by no means set aside. It was incorporated into a model that reflects the socio-economic needs of the people at various stages of development (Soejono 1972; Moelyadi 1992).

The socio-economic model that the authors of Vol. 1 (SNI 1975-1) had adopted enabled them to include elements of Indonesian pre-history that did not fit well with the more conventional and Europe-based periodization. Indonesia, rather than Europe, offered the yardstick. More importantly, the socio-economic model gave space for demonstrating the peculiarities of the Indonesian case as it underwent the successive stages of hunting and gathering, farming and animal domestication, and technological specialization. In the process of doing this, the Indonesia-centric perspective was affirmed, if not explicitly, at least indirectly or incidentally.

In Vol. 2, the attempt to adopt Indonesia-centrism was more unequivocal, which drew praise from reviewers, such as Siswadhi (see Siswadhi, Leirissa, and Atmakusumah 1976, 82). Covering the period when Hindu-Buddhist influences arrived and were assimilated in the archipelago, the volume summarily rejected the supposed passivity of Indonesia as the recipient of Indian influences. Emphasized instead was the purported active role of

'Indonesians' in this assimilation process. Citing scholars such as J.C. van Leur and Bosch, the authors argued that it was Indonesia that set the initiative and the manner by which the process went along. They further asserted, unfortunately without due substantiation or elaboration, that the push-factor did not come just from the Indian traders but also from indigenous actors who visited India and saw the condition there (Kartodirdjo, Poesponegoro, and Notosusanto 1975, 23). It was notable that the word invited (*diundang*) was repeatedly emphasized. Likewise, the absence in the same form of key cultural features of India, such as the caste system, in Indonesia is highlighted as proof of the active role or dominance of Indonesian culture in the interaction between the two cultures (Kartodirdjo, Poesponegoro, and Notosusanto 1975, 26–27).

Unfortunately, the forceful manner in which the authors asserted the Indonesia-centric perspective was not accompanied by efforts to demonstrate such a perspective. The thinness of evidence was arresting. In a few pages where they discussed Indian influences, the authors merely noted selected views of different authors (Krom, van Leur, Bosch, Coedes) and concluded from there that the Indonesian-side was in fact active, not a passive recipient of Indian influences. Illustrative examples, save from mentioning the caste system, were notably absent, and the process of differentiation or divergence from Indian cultural patterns was not even hinted at. As the whole treatment was strikingly mechanical, and at best contrived, one could hardly see the native Indonesian as the *dramatis personae* (except as, supposedly, the one who 'invited' the Brahmans) in their interaction with the Indian cultures. Moreover, there was no explicit effort to illustrate how this period related to the process of gradual integration of the Indonesian nation. It must be noted that the authors ignored the fact that the Indonesian nation had yet to be formed by then. They used the term Indonesia or Indonesians, regardless of time periods. In the succeeding chapters, the authors were content in describing the contents of Chinese dynastic records and many inscriptions that pertain to various cities, such as Kutai, Tarumanagara, Srivijaya, Majapahit and small kingdoms in Sunda and Bali. These read less like a history than a historiographic account.

The Indonesia-centric perspective appeared to be easily lost amid the preponderance of information borrowed from the accounts of Chinese travelers or chroniclers as well as in the attributions to the Indian influences. Here and there are statements that assert Indonesia-centrism, but they were isolated, unsubstantiated and contrived to demonstrate the perspective. For instance, in the sub-section on Hindu ritual, the text states that a certain Kundunga, described as possibly the first person to be 'touched' by Indian influence, was able to maintain his 'Indonesian' (not just 'Javanese') character, but there are no reinforcing or supporting details. Moreover, the rest of the subsection is devoted to the images of how powerful and influential Indian cultural influences were, but, again, without explanation or substantiation (Kartodirdjo, Poesponegoro, and Notosusanto 1975, 34–35).

Multi-dimensional or structural approach

As already noted, the main driving force in the multi-dimensional or structural approach is the need to formulate a multifaceted explanation for historical phenomenon, such as national integration. Here, I draw from the works of Sartono Kartodirdjo (1982, 2001) to clarify the nature of this approach. The multi-dimensional approach posits that history covers much more than what is happening in the king's palace, in the courtrooms, in rich men's houses, and in trading houses. It is much more than about inter- or intra-elite rivalries, wars, laws, or diplomatic maneuverings. History is the totality of human experience.

The fundamental assumption that underpins the multi-dimensional, often also called the structural, approach is that everything that happened occurred as it did because of multiple factors and in multi-layered contexts. Given a different context, or different combinations of factors, things would have unfolded differently. Full understanding of the whole context is thus the key to understanding an event or a set of events. In academic discourse among Indonesian historians, the structural or multi-dimensional approach is often sharply differentiated from what they usually called a processual (*prosesuil*), narrative, or chronological approach, the latter being a straightforward exposition of what was supposed to have transpired. As far as this approach was concerned, an event was important because it was a part of a story that needed to be told. Explaining why an event or an action occurred as it did was less important than formulating a clear story of what happened. If the structural approach aims to explain, the processual approach seeks to narrate or describe. If the earlier requires use of various theoretical or analytic tools in the social sciences, the latter does not need these tools.

In institutional terms, the difference between the two approaches found expression in the oft-cited observations that the History Department at the University of Gadjah Mada (UGM), which was under the leadership of Sartono Kartodirdjo, had been well known for the structural approach, whereas the University of Indonesia (UI), which for some time had been under the leadership and influence of Nugroho Notosusanto, adhered to the processual-narrative approach. To an extent, this perception of difference remains to this day, though it appears not as sharp in practice as it used to be.

Under ideal circumstances, the structural and processual-narrative approaches complement each other to form a neat, lucid, and integrated account. Sartono showed how this might be done in his two-volume *Introduction to New History of Indonesia (Pengantar Sejarah Indonesia Baru)* (Kartodirdjo 1987) and *Peasants' Revolt of Banten in 1888* (Kartodirdjo 1966). In the case of SNI, however, the lack of experience of the authors was clearly manifest in the often underdeveloped, disjointed, and strained relationship between the two approaches.

The original, 1975 edition of SNI was organized in conformity to the structural approach. To varying degrees, the framing of every volume allows different aspects—social, cultural, economic, and political—to be discussed in parallel or entwined with one another. For instance, Vol. 4 discusses the geographic features, bureaucratic and political framework, trade and other economic activities, cultural development, and social organizations. This has been done either by allotting a specific sub-section for each aspect or by weaving several aspects together in discussing each kingdom (Mataram, Banjar, Aceh, and others), period (that is, liberal period, 1870–1900), or set of socio-economic practices (cultivation system, social movements, and revolts).

Another example is Vol. 1, which deals with pre-history. In each stage (hunting and gathering, agriculture, and others), aspects such as geography, technology, social organization, and culture are given ample space. Even Vol. 5 and 6, which cover the more recent periods, apportion space for discussing various aspects, notwithstanding the preponderance of 'exciting' political developments. The treatment of politics in these volumes does not by any means disproportionately dominate or crowd out the rest. There is one exception here though. Vol. 6, which covers the period from 1942 to 1965, allots about a third (the first of the three chapters) explicitly to a narrative-chronological approach. The two other chapters conform to the same structural approach as other volumes.

To what extent these approaches have been carried out in the project is a question that, as I will show later, has a bearing on the analysis of politics-scholarship interplay in the next chapter. Short of identifying all the deficiencies evident in the outputs, something that is tangential to the arguments this book seeks to develop, I shall note here a number of observations, culled from my own reading of SNI 1975 as well as that of other commentators.

Observers agree that SNI-1975 fell well short of what was expected or hoped for. The harshest publicly made comment came from Abdurrachman Surjomihardjo (1980), a respected Indonesian scholar who was also one of the key members of the team, being the editor of Vol. 5. He declared that SNI constituted a 'shameful chapter' in the history of Indonesian historiography, a claim that seemed to be largely borne out of his frustration with Nugroho's handling of the project. In his view, only Vol. 1 (Pre-History) approached the benchmark of scholarly standard (Surjomihardjo 1976). In my interview with Sartono in 2005, he frankly admitted that he was unhappy about the output, far as it was from the Indonesia-centric and multi-dimensional approaches he envisioned. The reason, he said, for writing the two-volume *Introduction to New History of Indonesia* (*Pengantar Sejarah Bahru Indonesia*, 1987 and 1992) precisely lay in his disappointment with SNI-1975. He wanted to produce an alternative to SNI and he aimed at showing what SNI could have been, had other members of the team successfully followed his vision.

That the problem had persisted in subsequent editions of SNI was evident in a seminar held in UGM in 1984 to commemorate the 27th anniversary of the First National History Seminar in 1957. *Kompas* reported on

17 December 1984 the sobering findings of the seminar: that the community of Indonesian historians was still a long way off from carrying out the multi-dimensional approach. Notwithstanding a fair share of critics, this approach remained at least until the mid-2000s a 'methodological Holy Grail' for certain groups of historians in Indonesia. In a talk he delivered in 2005, during the celebration of the UGM History Department's 55th Year Anniversary and Sartono's 85th birthday, Bambang Purwanto, one of the most important Indonesian historians, claimed that the state of Indonesian historiography, in general, and Sartono's contributions, in particular, stagnated after a certain point. In his assessment, the multi-dimensional approach remains not sufficiently understood, even misused by those who purported to apply it (Setyadi and Saptono 2006).

The first observation points to the paucity of basic research informing the project. A cursory glance at the lists of materials reveals that the authors relied on a huge number of secondary and foreign-authored sources, about which the editors for Vol. 3 (Tjandrasasmita) and Vol. 4 (Sutjipto) were forthright and apologetic, in the introductions to their respective volumes. For his part, journalist B.M. Diah (1987, 9) observed that one can count on one's fingers local sources. This is understandable, considering that no money was allotted for 'real' research and that social sciences in Indonesia were still in their formative years. The thinness of evidence, for instance, of the supposed dominance of indigenous elements (in Vol. 2) was largely attributable to lack of research. The same applies to the examination of the Agriculture Stage (Vol. 1) from the lens of what happened in neighboring countries, deviating from the Indonesia-centric perspective. These examples coincide with historian Richard Leirissa's observation that, due to a serious lack of research, the treatment of the seventeenth and eighteenth centuries in Vol. 3 and 4 unduly placed a very lopsided focus on the activities of the Dutch East Company or VOC at the expense of the more interesting and relevant things happening within Indonesia during that time. Consequently, the aspiration to showcase the primacy of internal dynamics, the essence of Indonesia-centrism, gave way to the very same Neerlando-centrism that, ironically, the whole project was supposed to counter (Siswadhi, Leirissa, and Atmakusumah 1976, 86).

Another observation focuses on the unevenness of writing, both within and across different volumes. The reason why Sartono insisted that a thorough edit—both stylistic and grammatical—must be undertaken before the manuscripts were printed was precisely to address this problem. Other than a reflection of a lack of writing experience on the part of members of the team, as pointed out by Sartono, this may also have been be due to a lack of understanding of Indonesia-centrism and the multi-dimensional approach and how these approaches might be properly applied. As exemplified by the *Introduction to New History of Indonesia,* the approach entails a well-crafted demonstration of how various aspects—social, economic, cultural, political, institutional—interact and interweave and how such interaction helps clarify or explain a phenomenon: uprisings or social movements. In the case of SNI, this approach is best exemplified in parts of Vol. 4. The chapters on uprisings against colonialism and social movements stand out as good examples of this approach (SNI-4 1975, 123–227). Richard Leirissa, an Indonesian historian, shares this assessment. He has noted that, in comparison with Vol. 3, which he also reviewed, Vol. 4 was much more integrated in the sense that parts fit well into a discernible framework of analysis. He was not explicit about how well the multi-dimensional approach has been employed, but he was categorical in praising the analysis of social movements, which he claimed was new, very refreshing, and interesting (Siswadhi, Leirissa, and Atmakusumah 1976, 84–86).

The same thing cannot be said of Vol. 2, which features a catalogue of inscriptions or Chinese records, or what scholars say or argue about them. There was a glaring lack of effort to arrange or frame these accounts to demonstrate how social, economic, political, religious, and cultural factors interacted to form a unified description of life in early Indianized states in Java, Bali, Kalimantan and Sumatra (SNI-2 1975, 29–129). Even the chapter on Singhasari and Majapahit, two kingdoms in Java in the thirteenth to fifteenth centuries, which is evidently much better written, does not faithfully conform to the structural approach (SNI-2 1975, 252–282). It is mostly a narrative of political developments—the rise and fall of Majapahit. Only in the chapters about the kingdom of Mataram and the kingdoms in Bali and in Sunda is an effort to follow the prescribed approach discernible. Even in these cases, however, the writing style of the assigned authors, exacerbated by a lack of data, hamstrung their efforts (SNI-2 1975, 75–252). Non-political aspects, such as culture, religion, and socio-economic dynamics, are discussed, along with the political, but the inter-connection among them never approached the clarity evident in several parts of Vol. 4.

Here lie the weaknesses and limitations, in scholarly terms, of SNI. In consonance with widely held perceptions, at least among liberal intellectuals in Indonesia and elsewhere, concerning the oppositional relationship between politics and 'good' scholarship, the weaknesses of SNI tend to be viewed as a major reason for its vulnerability to political misuse or abuse (Purwanto 2001a, 2001b; Curaming 2003). As will be shown in the later part of this chapter, things were more complex. Despite the weaknesses, how SNI was designed by Sartono Kartodirdjo, with the pursuit of the multi-dimensional or structural approach as the key feature, enables SNI-1975 to limit its vulnerability to politically motivated interests and thus suggests the autonomous power of scholarship. This is a point that has often been missed by scholars familiar with SNI, including Sartono Kartodirdjo himself. In these scholars' minds, Nugroho Notosusanto had fully succeeded in using the project to serve his own and the New Order regime's interests. In what ways these widely held perceptions were inaccurate will be clarified in the rest of the chapter.

Political terrain

The SNI project took off with the scholars harboring good faith and high hopes in it (Surjomihardjo 1980; Abdullah 1994). Most members of the team who I have interviewed claimed that in the beginning there was not an iota of suspicion about whatever political motive there might be behind the project. As far as they were concerned, the project was purely a scholarly undertaking, and despite the enormous challenges it entailed, they took it on simply as part of scholarly and their patriotic duties. Only to the extent that nationalism was considered political could they acknowledge the project's political intent. In the context of post-war Indonesia, to be nationalistic was hardly considered a political act. It was a natural predisposition and a moral obligation.

Nugroho's foreword in Vol. 6 (SNI-6 1975) strongly suggested that he expected readers to find a good deal of controversy in the volume. He emphasized what he had consistently declared in many of his previous writings (e.g. Notosusanto 1964, 1978, n.d.) and public declarations (Sumantri 1982; *Sinar Harapan* 1980a, 1980b; Zain 1976): that contemporary history was by nature contentious supposedly because many people who were still alive may have different experiences or interpretations that diverge from historians' accounts. In writing that foreword, he seemed to be preparing the minds of readers to regard 'selectivity' and 'subjectivity' in historical work as natural. As if saying one has to take and live with them.

The efforts to justify the New Order regime constitute the main factor that accounts for both the form of SNI and the public responses to it. This approach rested on a number of pillars: demonizing the communists, eulogizing the military, discrediting Sukarno, and discrediting the Old Order. The following discussion will focus on Vol. 6 because these pillars were covered in this volume.

As already noted in Chapter 1, the New Order regime emerged from a set of mysterious, irregular, and bloody events in 1965–1966. These were preceded by a sharply contested and protracted struggle for political supremacy among forces that included the PKI or the Communist Party of Indonesia, the pro-Sukarno groups, and the military. Central to the story of the birth of the New Order was the 'coup' or 'counter-coup' that involved the killing, on 1 October 1965, of the six generals by a group of soldiers who called themselves the *September 30 Movement (Gerakan 30 September* or G30S). The importance of this event may be gleaned not only from what happened immediately afterwards, such as the collapse of the communist party, massacre, and incarceration of hundreds of thousands of people, the fall of Sukarno, and the rise of Suharto—it may be observed in the lingering state of terror that followed in its wake, haunting Indonesian society for decades, even up to this day (Budiawan 2004; Goodfellow 1995; Heryanto 2006, 1999; Melvin 2017, 2018; Miller 2018; Robinson 2018; Wahid 2018). As there is a big corpus of published works discussing the controversial character of this event,[2] there is no need to repeat details here. Suffice to note that the main points of contention in the debates about this episode include the following questions: why were the generals killed, and who was the real mastermind, if there was any? What was the nature of this event? Was it a coup against the government or a pre-emptive counter-coup to save the Sukarno regime from the rumored impending coup by the 'Council of Generals,' whose purported members were those abducted and killed? Were the tragic killings of the generals an offshoot of intra-army or armed forces conflict, as the Cornell Paper alleged, or were they a part of the grand plans of the communists to wrest control of the government, as the New Order regime claimed? The main task here is to clarify how SNI-6 (1975) treats the G30S as a movement, how it explains the killings, and who it blames for them. Certain relevant persons or events are highlighted in order to examine how far the account provided in the book served the interests of the New Order regime. These include the supposed centrality of the role of the communists in the G30S episode and the corresponding minimal or non-involvement of the military. Because of the significant variations in the treatment offered in different editions, which were produced by practically the same group of scholars, a comparison will follow.

The SNI-6 (1975) starts discussing the G30S with emphasis on the alliance between Sukarno and the PKI. The two were blamed for the sharp polarization of the political field between friends and enemies; the friends were nurtured, and the others were set aside or 'neutralized' (119). The sins of the PKI since 1964 are enumerated: aggressive and vitriolic propaganda, willful provocation, unlawful acts, infiltrating the military, threatening national unity, fomenting social unrest, deception, and attempts at a power grab (119–121). The book denounces the acts of seizing lands (*aksi sepihak* or unilateral action) carried out by the PKI-affiliated farmers' organization in the name of land redistribution, claiming that there was no more land in Java that should be subjected to a land reform program (108). Transmigration, it adds, is the only way to give poor peasants land (119). The PKI is also blamed for allegedly influencing Sukarno toward a wayward foreign policy (for example, over Konfrontasi, the 1963–1966 confrontation with Malaysia), and it is castigated for belligerently imposing politicized standards on arts and literature.[3]

The volume also describes the allegedly double-faced strategy of the PKI, portraying its participation in parliamentary democracy as a deceptive front to gain legitimacy and respectability while preparing for an opportune moment to seize power by forceful means, such as a coup d'état (120). Infiltration of the military ranks through the efforts of the *Biro Khusus* (Special Bureau), a supposedly secret group of operatives, is part of the grand strategy. The SNI-6 (1975) claims that the PKI had learned from the debacle in Madiun in 1948 that it was not enough to have their own troops, but they also needed to neutralize the military leadership and, if needed, liquidate it. It also claims that a PKI document was found in 1964, allegedly stating that the year 1966 would be the time when the condition was 'ripe' for a forceful take-over (120). There was no explanation of why 1966, and the source of this document was not disclosed. It also notes that by August 1965, Sukarno had fallen ill and that this condition could have resulted in paralysis, if not death. This was supposed to be a pretext for D.N. Aidit (1923–1965), the chairperson of the PKI, to have decided on hastening the shift from a peaceful parliamentary approach to the use of violence (121). The discussion presents the abduction and killings by G30S of the generals as the long-planned handiwork of the communists.

The names of the military personnel who were supposed to be agents of the *Biro Khusus* are identified—Untung, Sunardi, Atmodjo, and Anwas—and they are also pinpointed as responsible for setting the targets for liquidation. They were among the members of the group, the G30S, that kidnapped, supposedly tortured, and killed the generals, whose bodies were eventually thrown into a well in Lubang Buaya. The narrative then notes briefly that Suharto decisively acted to crush the coup. The whole coverage of the event, of the history of Indonesia in fact, ends abruptly a few days after 1 October 1965, when Suharto sent troops to quell the rebels in Central Java (122–123). There was no mention whatsoever of the reaction of the people and the subsequent events leading to the demise of PKI. Nor was there any reference to the rise and notable achievements of the New Order up to the early 1970s. As the supposed official history of the New Order regime, it was a truly bizarre way of ending the book.

The paper presented by Ariwiadi, one the members of the Vol. 6 team, at the planning workshop in Tugu, Bogor in 1972 indicates that the team planned to cover up to the 1970s, to highlight the achievements of the New Order, and to present a clearly negative view of the Old Order and Sukarno. Ariwiadi calls for the need to differentiate clearly between the Old and the New Order. The team's ideas were obviously in the incipient stages, but a rhetorical pattern is discernible. The Old Order represents 'dark' times— economic crisis, paralyzing politics, whimsical rules, chaos, poverty, and underdevelopment—and the New Order was the opposite—economic development, orderly politics, and systematic laws (Ariwiadi 1972).[4] It is notable that Ariwiadi's colleague, Moela Marbun, who was assigned to write the concept paper for Guided Democracy, had a different mindset. The way she wrote the paper suggests a reluctance to paint an overly negative picture of the period. She describes the era in a level-headed manner, mentioning problems but not exaggerating them (Marbun 1972). As members of the same team under Nugroho, the contrast between Ariwiadi's and Marbun's tone and approach was striking. When actual output came out with the publication of SNI (1975), however, it was the plan as spelled out by Ariwiadi that prevailed.

One clear manifestation of the effort to paint a negative picture of Sukarno and the Old Order is the highly skewed treatment of Sukarno and his government. There is, for instance, only one sentence in the whole chapter in SNI-6 (1975) on Guided Democracy that presents Sukarno in a positive light and one other favorable sentence about the government.

136   SNI: contents and contexts

In this sentence, Sukarno was credited, alongside the military, for his decisive efforts to break the supposedly paralyzing political impasse that emanated from endless party-bickering during the period of parliamentary democracy (103). The SNI-6 (1975, 109) also made a positive reference to government efforts to increase exports, but it was quick in pointing out that these efforts did not succeed.

Efforts to demonize the PKI and to discredit Sukarno were often woven together. His purportedly wayward behavior is often attributed to the influence of the PKI. For instance, the *Konfrontasi* with Malaysia that arose from Sukarno's opposition to the formation of Malaysia in 1963, Indonesia's subsequent withdrawal from the UN, the dissolution of the leftist Murba Party which was PKI's rival, and Sukarno's distrustful attitude towards the military were all blamed on the influence of the PKI on Sukarno (110–111, 115). At the same time, its supposed notoriety, its aggressive actions, and its posturing were all attributed to the protection of Sukarno. On the one hand, efforts to demonize PKI were reinforced by emphasizing his faults, whereas efforts to tarnish him can easily be enhanced by associating whatever he did with the influence of the PKI. To his fanatical supporters, passing the blame to the PKI cannot but be a welcome move. On the other hand, the subliminal message that he was weak because he allowed himself to be influenced by the PKI can hardly escape the non-'Sukarnois.' Either way, it is beneficial to the interest of the regime.

A number of points about the treatment, as summarized above, are noteworthy. First, there is a deliberate effort to emphasize the partnership of Sukarno with the PKI and to blame the partnership for numerous problems. Second, the coverage was very scanty: just a little over four pages for the crucial period leading up to the pivotal G30S event, and nothing afterward. Third, the involvement of the military in the G30S, as well as in the kidnapping and killing of the generals, is explicitly stated, rather than downplayed, as one might expect, given the official claim that the G30S was a handmaiden of the PKI. Fourth, there was no mention of the role of the Gerwani, Pemuda Rakyat, or other PKI-affiliated groups in the killing. Finally, the coverage ended abruptly a few days after 1 October 1965, when the killing of the generals happened. The last four points would have not been striking had the other versions of SNI, as will be discussed below, not offered sharply different renditions.

A comparison with the version of SNI for high schools offers valuable insights. While these textbooks were supposedly only a simplified offshoot of the project, the differences were stark and the circumstances surrounding the birth of these textbooks reveals important information about the dynamics within SNI project itself.

Soon after the publication of SNI in late 1975, the version for junior high schools came out in early 1976. The foreword of this textbook states that as early as 28 October 1975, the textbooks had already been completed (Notosusanto and Basri 1976, 2). The first set (three volumes) was entitled *Sejarah*

Nasional Indonesia untuk SMP (National History of Indonesia for Junior High School, SMP means Sekolah Menengah Pertama or junior high school; hereafter SNI-SMP) and the second set, published in 1979, was simply called *Sejarah Nasional Indonesia untuk SMA* (National History of Indonesia for Senior High School, SMA refers to Sekolah Menengah Atas or Senior High School). It was prepared by a team led by Nugroho Notosusanto and Yusmar Basri. The foreword further claims that it was based on the newly published SNI, reworked supposedly to suit the pedagogical needs of high school students (Notosusanto and Basri 1976, 5). That these textbooks were just summaries of SNI has been widely believed: respected Indonesia expert John Roosa, for instance, claims that treatment of the September 30th Movement in school textbooks was merely a "shortened and repackaged version of SNI account of the Movement" (Roosa 2012, 31). This supposition gave him reason not to include these school textbooks in his study that sought to demonstrate the varieties or contradictions in the official history of this key event. If Roosa had included these textbooks in his examination, he would have discovered greater variations, even contradictions.

That SNI-SMP textbooks were published just few months after SNI and they began to be used in the public schools starting in 1976 or 1977 was a remarkable case of urgency. It means that the textbooks being prepared while the work on SNI was not yet fully completed. That these textbooks were written exclusively by Nugroho's team was irregular. The understanding among other team members was that the textbooks for high school would be prepared by a team of historians and history teachers appointed on the basis of merit and chosen following a set of more or less transparent criteria and procedures. At the very least, the composition of the team would be determined by a collegial body, not by a single individual.[5]

Contrary to Nugroho's declaration, SNI-SMP was not a mere summary of SNI, simplified or adjusted to suit the needs of high school students. It was substantially different, both in framework and in content. For one, SNI-SMP followed an entirely chronological, narrative approach, while SNI (1975), as noted above, tried to employ a structural, multi-dimensional approach. A chronological approach may be justified by pedagogical imperatives, as Nugroho suggested in the foreword of SNI-SMP. A structural approach is no doubt much more difficult for high school students to understand. An informant, however, indicated that Nugroho preferred a narrative approach because of, among other things, the greater ease by which it could convey the intended messages, and this, I suppose, includes political messages.[6]

A more important difference was that SNI-6 (1975) paled in comparison with SNI-SMP in the intensity and clarity of its propaganda messages. The portrayal of the Madiun Affair is a good example. The Madiun uprising refers to the revolt in 1948 in the regency called Madiun. The factors that led to, as well as the details of violence that ensued from, the uprising were complex. These include the factionalism among left-leaning groups, of which

PKI was just one part. In short, it may not be a PKI-planned revolt. However, such an important detail was easily lost amid the strong anti-communist sentiments of the government, military, and Muslim groups (see McGregor 2009 for various interpretations of the Madiun Affair). In their view, it was a treacherous move by the communists, who were allegedly more concerned about their political interests than national unity and welfare. In SNI-SMP, this episode is categorically described as a betrayal (*pengkhianatan*) by the PKI. Such description is even emblazoned as the title of a sub-heading (105). Given the details it provides (SNI-SMP, 106), the intent to link Madiun to G30S is clear and thus cements the idea that PKI was perfidious:

> The rebels... killed with impunity government officials, military (TNI) officers and party leaders or groups whom they considered enemies and the bodies of some them were put in wells...Such gruesome or barbaric acts were remembered by the people especially those in East and Central Java 17 years later with the outbreak of the G30S. The ways of killings, including the act of putting the dead bodies inside the well, were the same.

In SNI-6 (1975), there is nothing like this. It is plainly called an uprising in Madiun, and the only mention of it in relation to the G30S is made in two plain sentences, stating that the PKI had already tried in 1948 to seize control of the government, but this attempt failed, and from that point on, it struggled underground (SNI-6 1975, 119–120). The only other mention is made in two paragraphs describing the event in an unadorned way, summarized as follows: the rebels seized the city of Madiun, and Djokosuyono, who installed himself as the military governor, made a speech on the radio whereby he called for the purge of colonial and reactionary elements from the TNI. It is followed by the enumeration of charges raised by Musso, a key leader of the Communist Party, against the nationalist leaders, such as Sukarno and Hatta. After plainly stating that the government immediately crushed the rebellion, it closes with an expression of regret that those involved were not brought to trial because the Dutch were once again on the offensive. What stands out in this exposition is not the alleged betrayal by the PKI, as highlighted in SNI-SMP, but the justifications of the communists for launching the ill-prepared uprising (58–59).

The case of what happened well at the Lubang Buaya, and where the bodies of the kidnapped and killed generals were hidden, which became an iconic symbol of the treachery of PKI, is also worth exploring. SNI-SMP sharply differs from SNI-6 (1975) in mentioning the doctors' supposed postmortem, according to which the victims experienced heavy torture (*siksaan berat*) before they were killed. SNI-6 (1975) carries no such a claim. SNI-SMP (161) also states that the bodies were already decomposing by the time they were taken out from the well, which is another claim not mentioned in SNI-6 (1975). Regarding the reaction of the people to what happened in

Lubang Buaya, SNI-SMP is straightforward, noting the killings of many people that happened in the wake of the 'coup.' In contrast, SNI-6 1975 is totally silent about it, while the later editions, such as SNI-1984 and SNI-1993, are hesitant to discuss it. SNI-SMP, furthermore, states that the killings of the PKI leaders (no mention of members, sympathizers, and suspected affiliates) that ensued after the G30S in 1965 was the people's initiative, allegedly as a reprisal against what the PKI did in Madiun in 1948. SNI-SMP also notes that President Sukarno's indecisive attitude gave rise to the impatience of the people (161–162).

Another aspect in which SNI-SMP clearly exceeds SNI-6 (1975) in apparent propaganda intent concerns the image of the military. One easily expects SNI-6 (1975) as an official history to emphasize the good image of the military. It highlights, for instance, the role of the military as a partner of the government in restoring order, or in saving the republic from all sorts of threats, as well as in breaking the political impasse caused by the supposedly 'unwieldy' party politics (103, 106). However, it does not go to the extent of obliterating the role of the military in the G30S event, which SNI-SMP does. After enumerating groups—such as political parties and trade unions—that PKI allegedly infiltrated and eventually neutralized or won over, SNI-SMP authors highlighted that it was the military that remained the only institution capable of withstanding the 'PKI conquest' (151). Perhaps it was in the spirit of this claim that the authors tried to conceal that the armed forces itself was infiltrated by the PKI and that segments of the armed forces were actually sympathetic to the PKI. The height of this effort can be seen in the depiction of G30S as a purely PKI affair. Even Col. Untung bin Syamsuri (1926–1967), who was a military officer and the leader of the G30S, was not mentioned. The very faint trace of military involvement is hinted at in a sentence whose function is merely to clarify Biro Khusus's role. It states, "Biro Khusus was a secret agency that was directly under the leader of the party (PKI) whose task is to infiltrate the military and to influence and create a group sympathetic to the PKI" (SNI-SMP, 160). Any student who had no prior knowledge and read nothing other than SNI-SMP would have no notion of military involvement in the G30S episode.

SNI-SMP also demonizes the PKI in a more forceful manner. For instance, notwithstanding Sukarno's many non-communist supporters in the parliament, SNI-SMP exclusively blames the PKI for the failure of the parliament to respond to the public clamor for the dissolution of the communist party, for massive restructuring of the cabinet, and for improper handling of economic crisis (SNI-SMP, 196). In contrast, SNI-6 (1975) is silent about this point. SNI-SMP also chides the PKI for forcefully taking land from legitimate owners (152).

Given that these two texts were written almost at the same time by a small group of military historians under the supervision of Nugroho, it is easy to be perplexed why the significant differences? Regarding the difference in the intensity of pro-regime interpretations, one possibility is that the two versions might have been written by different persons who simply had diverging views about these historical events, and Nugroho did not exercise due diligence to ensure consistency of views. Yusmar Basri wrote Vol. 3 of SNI-SMP (the one under consideration here) under the close supervision of Nugroho.[7] Yusmar Basri belonged to the team that wrote SNI-5 (1975), whereas those who were responsible for SNI-6 were Yusmar's colleagues at the Armed Forces History Center, such as Saleh As'ad Djamhari, Rochmani Santoso, and Ariwiadi.

Individual writing style, or writing ability, may also have something to do with the outcome. SNI-6 (1975) and SNI-SMP, for instance, both emphasize the sins of Sukarno and the Guided Democracy regime. SNI-SMP, however, appears to be clearer or more straightforward in its message. In its attempt to discuss the sources and the gravity of economic problems during the Guided Democracy period, SNI-6 (1975) merely cites the problems—hyper-inflation, white elephant projects, corruption. No attempt has been made to explain and exemplify what they meant or to establish their causes and interconnections. There is also no explicit mention of the supposed culpability of Sukarno in all these problems (SNI-6 1975, 195, 109–10). If the idea is to demonize Sukarno, one would easily get the impression that this version was haphazardly written. SNI-SMP, on the other hand, is able to define and explain more clearly, within fewer pages, the connections between the monetary crisis, corruption, inflation and the suffering of the people (Notosusanto and Basri 1976, 152–54). There are possibly more fundamental reasons for these differences, which I shall return to below. An important thing to highlight at this point is the individuality and agency of the members of the team. Despite being supervised by Nugroho, who seemed bent on promoting the interests of the regime, each member of the team exercised their own power to produce narratives and interpretations in ways they liked and/or knew how.

It cannot be denied that political interests, particularly regime justification, are a key factor that influenced the overall shape and tenor of SNI-SMP. That it was indeed intended to be a political tool right from the start became clear in 1982, when, in an interview with a journalist, Nugroho declared, "Yes, I know that (referring to SNI-SMP) was not perfect...but its contents were already okay (sudah baik) and it *satisfies the requirements set forth by Pak Harto*"[8] (emphasis mine) (Sumantri 1982). Many scholars in Indonesia, and virtually all foreign scholars, had long suspected this was the case, but Nugroho had always been adamant in rejecting any suggestion that he was a lackey of the regime. Indeed, what he said in that interview was a very rare explicit admission that he wrote history in conformity to the order or wish of the higher authorities.

If political interest is indeed the primary reason, why would SNI-6 (1975) be any less effective as a vehicle, particularly in comparison with SNI-SMP? A possible answer lies in the contrasting set of constraints within which the two projects developed. Whereas SNI-SMP was written with Nugroho and his team enjoying full freedom, free from restriction imposed by Sartono and other members of the team, the same team of historians were hamstrung by at least three strictures in writing SNI-6 (1975). The first emanates from the pressure to conform to the structural, multi-dimensional approach agreed to, or imposed, by the team. The second was the attitude held at least by some influential members of SNI (1975) team towards contemporary history. Such an attitude springs from what I call, for lack of better term, the "contemporary-history-as-not-yet-history" mentality. And finally, the presence and the towering stature of Sartono himself, who, despite Nugroho's audacity to overrule him several instances before, remained a 'force' to be reckoned with.

Reading various papers presented in the workshop in Tugu, Bogor in June 1972, which were compiled in three volumes entitled *Workshop on Indonesian History Standard Text (Lokakarya Buku Standar Sejarah Indonesia)*, one is readily struck by the strong pressure for everyone to conform to the structural, multi-dimensional approach. Nugroho, who was known not to be a fan of this approach, could only concur. Interviews with several people close to Nugroho confirmed his preference for the narrative-chronological approach. His literary background may had to do with this preference. For him, history was a story.[9] For another, if the objective was to convey a message (moral, exhortatory, propagandistic), it could be accomplished more effectively using a story-telling approach than with a structural and analytical approach.[10] In Nugroho's paper for the workshop entitled "Period Since 1942: An Introduction" (Periode Sedjak 1942: Pengantar), he expresses agreement with the structural approach but insists on the need for a chapter that adopts a chronological or narrative approach as an introductory but integral part of the whole effort (Notosusanto 1972). That was precisely what came out in SNI-6 (1975), as described above: a chapter that spells out a chronological narrative of what happened from 1942 to 1965 precedes the two chapters devoted to the structural, multi-dimensional history of the period. It seemed a sort of a compromise. In Nugroho's foreword in SNI-6 1975 edition, he justified such a move by implying that unlike other volumes that dealt with the periods long time past—periods when lack of data made it difficult to present a clear and detailed narrative—there were simply so many sources for events that are so immediately important in the period covered by the volume (1942–1960s) that it would be a pity not to plot them in a clear narrative.

The compromise had important consequences. Confining the narrative approach to the introductory chapter left with only a limited space that precluded a detailed and passion-inciting narrative that effective propaganda entails. This is a possible reason for the less intense or less effective propaganda messages in SNI-6 (1975). Also, the narrative arc that fits the time coverage of the main chapters, from the Japanese to Guided Democracy periods (1942–1965) rendered incongruous the discussion in the first chapter of the period 1966–1970s, when many things happened that were crucial to the legitimacy of the New Order regime. Perhaps, if the New Order period (1966 to 1970s) had been included in the coverage of the two main chapters, discussing in the first chapter the achievements of the New Order would be necessary. Even in such a case, however, the primacy of the structural approach would likely preclude the need for details that could crowd out non-political aspects—elements that the structural approach aims to equally highlight. So, here, we have a case whereby the structural framework of the project seemed to have restricted the ability of Nugroho and his team to convey more effectively their propaganda messages.

That the birth and early years of the New Order were not covered in the original SNI (1975) is puzzling. Their absence cannot be deliberate as the papers for the planning workshop in 1972 explicitly stated the intent to include the period up to the 1970s. The members of the Vol. 6 team whom I interviewed claimed that they cannot remember what happened that led to the exclusion of the 1966–1970s period. I can only speculate based on available pieces of evidence.

In Nugroho's preface to SNI-6 (1975), he launched a broadside against undisclosed targets, chiding them for not being brave enough to face the responsibility of making people understand their most recent history. Such declaration would easily appear odd to anyone unfamiliar with the context. Those who knew the backstory would understand that Nugroho was referring to Sartono and other scholars who harbored skeptical attitudes towards contemporary history. Sartono was wary of the "lack of distance that is needed for an objective historical investigation." In his view, "(f)oreign scholars are in a better position to deal with contemporary history since they need not take sides" (2001, 44). It appears there was a pressure for Nugroho and his team to back-track from their original plan to include the New Order period. That this may have been the case might be glimpsed from the team members' recollections of the heated episodes during planning workshops, when Nugroho and his team had to endure Taufik Abdullah's and other members' comments and difficult questions on various issues, including the supposed need to decide on the supposedly 'bad' defining features of the Old Order and 'good' ones for the 'New' Orders.[11]

The timing and the condition under which SNI-SMP was produced, as well as its contents, suggest what SNI-6 (1975) might have looked like had Nugroho and his team worked unfettered by the restrictions imposed by Sartono and other members of the team. I speculate that one possible reason for Nugroho's hasty move to form his own team to write the high school textbooks, without conferring with Sartono and other historians, was his fear that the type of history he envisioned would not be realized with Sartono under the helm. The significant difference thus between SNI-SMP and SNI (1975) may be reflective of the extent of Nugroho's frustration with SNI-6 (1975). This disappointment appeared to have driven him to produce SNI-SMP the way they did and, in a sleight of hand, declare that it was just a simplified version or a summary of SNI (1975). The public, including the critics, seemed to have believed this claims. Their attention was focused on SNI (1976) without realizing that the truly blatant propaganda was found in SNI-SMP. The problematic character of SNI-SMP was first brought up in the media in an editorial simply entitled "Writing Indonesian History" (Penulisan Sejarah Indonesia) published in *Kompas* on 17 September 1985. Unlike SNI, which was almost instantly debated when it came out, SNI-SMP was peculiarly ignored by critics for a decade. In 1987, it became an issue that attracted a more sustained public attention, as reported by *Kompas* on 5 and 27 May 1987 (Kompas 1987a; 1987b). The Ministry of Education declared the need to take another look at the teaching of history in schools.

A number of possible reasons could explain this oversight. It is likely that not many people had actually read SNI (any edition) and SNI-SMP together. So, hardly anyone knew the difference. Also, teachers and textbook writers whom I have asked confirmed the tendency to find the easy way out. Teachers would use what was readily available, which was SNI-SMP (and its sister-textbooks SNI-SMA). Similarly, textbook writers would merely copy from sources that were popular and easily accessible. Rather than doing their own research or drawing from and simplifying the admittedly more difficult to read SNI, it was much more convenient to just consult and paraphrase SNI-SMP (and its sister-textbook SNI-SMA). The high level of similarity among a wide range of available textbooks in the 1980s and 1990s confirms this observation. Still another possible reason for the critics' neglect of SNI-SMP was that they might have believed what Nugroho and government official had declared: that it was just a simplified version, or a summary, of SNI (1975). Thus, it could not possibly be 'worse' than SNI (1975).

The 1984 edition

An examination of the 1984 edition of SNI (Poesponegoro and Notosusanto 1984) confirms the suspicion that Nugroho would have written SNI-6 (1975) very differently under unrestricted conditions. By this time, Sartono had already been removed by Nugroho, as discussed in the previous chapter. The 1984 edition is strikingly closer to SNI-SMP than it is to SNI-6 (1975) in structure, tone, and content.

The first obvious difference between 1975 and 1984 editions of Vol. 6 (SNI-6) lay in the structure that reflected the framework adopted. Just like SNI-SMP, SNI-6 (1984) had abandoned the multi-dimensional in favor of the narrative-chronological approach. The 1984 edition constituted a massive overhaul of Vol. 6. In stark contrast, other volumes barely changed through the years. The little that remained of the multi-dimensional approach had been confined to a sub-section in each chapter, often just as appendices to a lengthy account of political development. See Table 5.1 below.

144 SNI: contents and contexts

Table 5.1 Comparison of Outlines and Political Contents of Vol. 6, SNI (1975) and SNI (1984)

1975 Edition SNI-6*	1984 Edition SNI-6**
Chapter 1: Overview (124 pages) Narrative of what happened from Japanese Period to October 1965	I. Japanese Period (89 pages) Among seven sections, two are non-political: Section D (War Economy) and E (Education, Social Communication and Culture). 19 out of 89 pages are non-political
Chapter 2: Japanese Period (50 pages) Among four sections, only one for politics: A Social Change and Mobility B War Economy C Government Structure and Political Life (18 out 50 pages) D Education and Social Communication	II. War for Independence (115 pages) Among nine sections, there are two non-politics sections. Section H (Economic Blockade) and I (Education, Culture and Social Communication. 33 out of 115 pages are for non-political matters
Chapter 3: Republic of Indonesia (158 pages) Among six sections, three for non-politics and three for political themes A Social Mobility and Social Stratification B Economic Development C Government Structure and Political Life (24 out of 158 pages) D Education and Social Communication E Foreign Relations (18 out 158 pages) F National Security and ABRI's Dual-Function (8 out of 158 pages)	III. Liberal Democracy (70 pages) Among eight sections, only one is non-political: Section H (Education, Culture and Social Communication. 26 out of 70 pages deal with non-political matters IV. Guided Democracy (80 pages) One section among 6 is allotted for non-political matters, 11 pages out of 80. V. New Order (133 pages) Three sections for non-political: D (Economic stabilization), E (5-Year Development Plans) and H (Socio-cultural Development). [Note that discussion on economic stabilization and 5-Yr Plans (22 pages) is heavily underlain by political tone and motive; it was meant to draw sharp dichotomy between the New and the Old Order.] 41 pages out of 133 pages for non-politics

Notes:
* 50 out of 158 (32%) for politics
   68 pages out of 208 pages (multi-dimensional part) or 33% devoted for political matters
** 357 out of 487 (73%) consists of political matters

Having been freed from the strictures of the multi-dimensional approach and Sartono's 'contemporary-history-as-not-yet-history' stance, the 1984 edition devotes significant attention to political themes and pushes the logic of contemporaneity to its utmost, covering the years up to 1983. Out of 487 pages, 357 (73%) are devoted to political matters compared with 68 out of 208 pages (33%) in the 1975 edition.

The free-flowing narrative-approach enables the 1984 edition to provide more clear-cut images of events and personalities, including a more sharply negative depiction of Sukarno, the PKI, and the Old Order as well as a more clearly positive appraisal of Suharto, the military and the New Order. For instance, whereas the 1975 edition mentions without elaboration the sources or manifestations of economic problems during the Guided Democracy, the 1984 edition provides copious details about the economic crisis, devoting about a dozen pages to compact and relatively well-organized details about the economic problem; its alleged cause and impact (321–331), specifically hyper-inflation; and its alleged relationship with Sukarno's erratic and profligate economic policies. More importantly, the effort to connect all these facts to the suffering of the people succeeds in conjuring up an extremely negative image of Sukarno and the Old Order among readers.

As already noted, the 1975 edition's failure to go beyond early October 1965 effectively excluded events that were important to the birth and legitimation of the New Order regime. The 1984 edition addresses this 'deficiency' by, initially, providing a decisively negative picture of the period 1950–1965—gloomy, chaotic, hopeless, unstable—and then changes tone gradually, becoming more expectant and upbeat after Suharto took over power from Sukarno from March 1966 onwards. The positive tempo continues until unbridled optimism is unleashed in the coverage of the post-1967 period when Suharto was formally installed as the president. Panegyric descriptions of the gains in stabilizing the economy, putting order in the society in general, and strengthening the foundations of political stability were extensively detailed in over 100 pages of text (Poesponegoro and Notosusanto 1984, 404–519). The 1993 edition went even further, with a separate volume of almost 500 pages highlighting the accomplishments of the New Order (Leirissa and Ghazali 1993). For the purpose of this study, there is no need for a detailed examination of the contents of the 1993 edition. The additional details from this edition merely affirm, rather than complicate or alter, the trajectory of analysis based on the 1984 edition.

To be more specific, the sub-section on the period of consolidation (since 1968) in the 1984 edition starts with how conscientious the government then was in partnership with the parliament in their effort to address law-related problems. Law, it states, is "an objective guarantee to normalize the situation necessary for development" (SNI-6 1984, 426), justifying such effort. A few lines later, however, it becomes clear that this is aimed as a critique of the supposed 'lawlessness' of the Old Order. It reports on the repeal of the laws promulgated by the previous regime that were incompatible with the constitution. It also claims that, unlike the situation under the Old Order, government officials and the people in general became more law-abiding (426–427). This illustrates one of the ways by which the 'othering' of the Old Order is accomplished in the 1984 edition.

The succeeding pages parade the specific efforts of the new regime to 're-pair the damage' or 'save' the country from the ravages wrought by the former government. Highlighted are campaigns to wipe out corruption and to curb inflation, the rehabilitation of export-oriented industries and tax collection infrastructure, the recovery of 'ill-gotten' wealth, debt-restructuring, the rationalized economic planning, and the overhaul of foreign policy. Gains, big and small, in each of these areas contributed to creating a picture of progress, order, and optimism that stood in stark contrast to the depressing situations under the previous regime (426–430). Without his name being mentioned, Suharto is often cast as the hope for the future. In contrast, Sukarno represents the nightmare of the past.

It is also noteworthy that the 1984 edition is categorical about the role of the women's organization, *Gerwani* or *Gerakan Wanita* Indonesia (Indonesian Women's Movement), and youth organization, Pemuda Rakyat (People's Youth), in the purported act of torturing and killing the generals. Both were affiliated closely with PKI. In contrast, SNI-6 (1975) and SNI-SMP are silent about their involvement. Moreover, whereas the 1975 edition is quiet about the reaction of the people to the G30S episode, the 1984 version is explicit about it, describing the reactions as 'angry.' The burning of the PKI headquarters by the mob supposedly indicates such anger (395–396). Similar is a fairly detailed description of the alleged effort of the PKI to 'come back' in early 1968 (402–403)—a move that seems to highlight the 'latent danger' (*bahaya laten*) that communism supposedly posed to Indonesian society.[12] This is something that both SNI 1975 edition and SNI-SMP are silent about.

While the 1984 edition is overall more systematic, detailed, and forceful in rendering accounts favorable to the Suharto regime, it would be a mistake to assume that that there is always a linear progression from SNI 1975 to SNI-SMP to SNI 1984 edition in terms of clarity or efficacy of conveying propaganda messages. In efforts to conceal or minimize the involvement of the military in the tragic G30S event, for example, the 1975 edition serves the purpose better simply by saying so much less about it than the 1984 edition. Whereas the 1975 edition allots no more than a total of two pages (SNI-6 1975, 120–122), in the 1984 edition there is a detailed description of military involvement spread out in a dozen pages (SNI-6 1984, 390–402). For another, while later editions pinpoint Col. Untung as the leader of the movement, the 1975 edition names Syam Kamaruzaman, designated by the text as a PKI high-ranking officer, as the leader (SNI-6 1975, 121). Untung is relegated to the minor position of being just one among military men involved. The military involvement in the 'shameful' G30S event is emphasized far more in the 1984 edition than it is in either of the two other versions.

To the extent that SNI-6 openly recognizes that some military personnel were involved in the G30S, all editions are invariably careful to emphasize that these military men were misled or brainwashed by the PKI through the persistent infiltration efforts of its Special Bureau *(Biro Khusus)* (SNI-6 1975, 120; SNI-6 1984, 399). Not an iota of space is allowed for the possibility that the military officers subscribed to leftist ideas on their own volition. In comparative terms, the 1975 edition is more straightforward and emphatic about the alleged vulnerability of the military to PKI brainwashing than SNI-SMP and the 1984 edition (SNI-6 1975, 120–121). It provides, for instance, some details as to how the Special Bureau broke into the military, even mentioning specific middle-ranking officers who were supposed to be channels for the spread of communist ideas. The 1984 edition, on the other hand, merely mentions the Special Bureau's function and cites a number of brigades or battalions in Central Java as targets of attempted intrusion (SNI-6 1984, 387, 397).

Even so, despite the vehemence of SNI-SMP, in general terms and particularly against the leftists, there are instances when it proves softer than SNI-6, both the 1975 and 1984 editions. The PKI, for example, is not blamed for Indonesia's withdrawal from the United Nation or UN and the confrontation with Malaysia, as is the case in the 1975 edition. Nor is there any mention of the pressures on the artists or literary figures to toe the "Politics is in Command" line favored by the Institute of People's Culture (*Lembaga Kebudayaan Rakyat*, or LEKRA) and other leftist organizations.

Despite efforts to provide accounts favorable to the regime, these versions of official history vary and they lack a consistent progression from the earlier to the later editions, which suggests a less than controlled effort to promote the interest of the New Order regime. In places, the volumes contain contradictory messages that go against the core of the official narrative that justifies the regime.

Before the 1975 edition closes, nestled in the middle of the last paragraph, the authors declare:

> With the coup attempt of the G30S/PKI that failed, the whole of ABRI (military) opened their eyes about the consequence of inter- and intra-service (military) conflict due to the infiltration of ABRI by people who are agents of an outside political power.
>
> (SNI-6 1975, 345)

That such a statement can be found in SNI, supposedly *the* regime's official history, is very significant. This statement reiterates the blame on an 'outside political power' (presumably communists) for the cause of the G30S tragedy, which is in line with the official narrative. However, it also implies the involvement of the military and includes intra- and inter-service rivalries among the causes of the G30S. Doing so undercuts not only the whole effort to deny or minimize military involvement in the incident, as is made clear in the earlier parts of the book—more significantly, it subverts the major ideas behind the official explanation of the event, as painstakingly laid out in the book published in 1968 *The September 30 Movement Coup Attempt*. Authored by Nugroho Notosusanto and Ismael Saleh (1926–2008), a military prosecutor, this book was prepared with the assistance of the Rand Corporation, one of the key players in the US government's anti-Communist efforts during the Cold War (McGregor 2007, 65–66. The main aim was to counter the damaging implications of the analysis made by scholars from Cornell University, Benedict Anderson and Ruth McVey, which denies the major role of the PKI in the G30S and lays the blame squarely on internal dissension within the army. For its part *The September 30 Movement Coup Attempt* insists that

> the 'September 30 Movement' was not an internal Army (a)ffair. The cases did not have the characteristics of internal Army squabbles. They were neither caused by difference between the Army and the Air Force, nor between any of the other within the Armed Forces.
> (Notosusanto and Saleh 1968: 145)

This book also forcefully argues that the episode was a coup attempt masterminded by the communists to wrest control of the government.

There is something really strange here. SNI-6 (1975) was written by Nugroho Notosusanto and his team. At the same time, Nugroho was the co-author of *The September 30 Movement Coup Attempt*. Both are widely known as the New Order regime's official history (Roosa 2012). Yet one contains a passage that fundamentally goes against the main argument of the other. How could that happen? One may interpret it as nothing but an indication of how negligent, sloppy, rash or incompetent Nugroho was. He seemed to have not closely monitored the output of his close aides and rushed into publishing the volume without careful edits and oversight.

This interpretation cannot be ruled out, but I would also flag the need to pay attention to other possible important factors, such as the role and volition of military historians who tended to be ignored as no more than Nugroho's alter egos. Contradictions like this may be easily brushed aside as accidental, natural, or common, as a product of differences in perspective, hasty interpretations, or carelessness. However, that it was not accidental is indicated by the presence of similar passage in the 1984 edition. While no necessarily causal connection between the intra-military rivalry and the G30S is established, this passage sets the reader to interpret the internal rivalries within the Army (or military as a whole) as leading to the G30S episode.

> Since 1962…the 'divide and rule' politics towards the ABRI reached climax such that the process of *disintegration, rivalries and controversies* between or within different branches or services of the ABRI accelerated until such point that the G-30-S/PKI broke out.
> (SNI-6 1984, 456; italics original)

One may argue that the passages in SNI that are incoherent or even contradict official narratives do not on the whole mean anything substantive insofar as the political interests of the regime. They do not, for instance, negate the fact that SNI, particularly Vol. 6, was an official history that served the interests of the New Order regime. They also do not overturn the power relations that characterized the project, putting the scholars rather than the state operatives in the dominant position. Be that as it may, the absence of the coverage of certain key events, the existence of contrarian statements, and the less than coherent or forceful portrayal of politically important events indicate slippages that call for a more nuanced analytic approach and for teasing out their full implications.

The significant variations across the officially sanctioned texts highlight a disconnect between, on the one hand, the coherence and singularity of power that underpins the idea of official history. On the other hand is the fluidity and multiplicity of powers that shape knowledge on the ground. What needs underscoring is the agency of Nugroho's young assistant historians who wrote the relevant parts. This agency is easily overlooked when, juxtaposed with big powers like the New Order regime or its operatives, like Nugroho, scholars are readily viewed as the 'manipulated' or 'co-opted,' as if they are powerless, or they do not have their own interests to pursue.

The fact that Nugroho and his team were on the payroll of the Armed Forces heightens the impression of 'officiality,' thus overshadowing the complex power relation that accompanies knowledge production. What gets created is a simulacrum (or perception) that imputes the regime and its official history greater power than what it actually had. With the public acting as if indeed, SNI 1975 was *the* official history, the "fakery of the news" was in effect obscured by the publicly perceived truthfulness of the fake. In due time, the fake becomes the truth. What this points to is the complicity of the public in truth-making, which reinforces the need for a more nuanced analytic approach to knowledge production.

In the service of two masters?

Historians employed in a military institution are in a challenging situation. As professionals trained in historical methodologies that champion impartiality or objectivity, they are in an ambiguous position between their membership to the community of scholars and their obligations as military personnel. They are often viewed with suspicion by fellow historians and segments of the public. Trained to pursue 'objectivity' as much as possible, members of the team seemed to feel conflicted when faced with the demand of their work at the History Center. Nugroho Notosusanto and his close aide were illustrative examples.

Apparently aware of the negative public perception of him, Nugroho took pains to convince the public that he deserved to be treated as scholar-historian. In various instances, he tried to display a mastery of historical methods and utilized them as weapons in his contentious debates with critics. While he was not always convincing, he carried himself quite well in a number of those instances.[13] Meanwhile, his close aide felt guilty for what he claimed they did. Believing that Sukarno was a great leader, he felt bad that he had joined the endeavor to discredit Sukarno and besmirch the leader's memory. Perhaps as an attempt at self-redemption, after retiring from the History Center in 1995, this aide pursued a PhD in history and vowed to do a 'scientific history.'[14]

The ambiguities of military-historians' positions tend to pose certain limitations to what they can do or achieve. As historians, they have to contend with rules or conventions, and they engage in the prevailing discourses of the professional community, where they also like to be accepted, respected, or recognized. Nugroho's team had to engage with the community of historians and deal with the overall historiographic landscape as it was developing then in Indonesia. Despite being backed by the supremacy of the New Order regime, they did not have pre-eminent power or influence within this domain. They had to wrestle with, among other forces, scholarly conventions, where politics lies in scholars' being avowedly non-political or at least discreet about their political proclivities. The clash of the two domains of power was perhaps inevitable.

Aside from the limitations emanating from the military-historian's ambiguous position, the nature of history-used-as-a-propaganda also posed a considerable challenge to scholars. Even if they consciously aimed at promoting propaganda, they had to maintain at least a semblance of impartiality or objectivity and a grasp of historical methodology. Since the power of history-as-propaganda depends to an extent on the appearance of credibility, they had to strike a delicate balance between forcefulness and subtlety, immediacy and restraint. While there were instances when what Nugroho and his team published betrayed their crudity or lack of skills along this line, there were also instances when restraints upon them, self-imposed or otherwise, were apparent. Some notable examples from SNI-6 shall be discussed below to illustrate the point.

As noted earlier, the place called Lubang Buaya occupies a central position in the official narrative of the New Order.[15] It became a museum that even today serves as a memorial to the alleged treachery, wickedness, and hunger for power of the PKI.[16] Considering the pivotal position it occupies in the official narrative of the regime, one may be surprised that all versions of SNI covered in this study, including the usually virulent SNI-SMP, treats it rather mildly, particularly in comparison with what has been popularly known. For instance, none among various editions of SNI-6 contain the grotesque details meant to incite the anger of the public towards the PKI circulated through news reports from military-controlled newspapers like *Berita Yudha* and *Angkatan Bersendjata*. These reports claimed that the members of Gerwani and Pemuda Rakyat gouged out the eyes of the generals and mutilated their genitals or had women dance naked around them and even 'raped' them.[17] SNI-6 1975 edition merely states that the generals were tortured; it does not describe the torture as 'berat' (severe) or 'kejam' (cruel or gruesome), as is the case in the 1984 edition (SNI-6 1975, 122; SNI-6

1984, 390). More surprisingly, the alleged culpability, even the mere presence, of the Gerwani and other PKI-affiliated groups in Halim or Lubang Buaya is not even hinted at in the first edition.[18]

Once more, the reason for this discrepancy may have been a simple oversight or carelessness on the part of Nugroho's team. This supposition is plausible in the case of SNI 1975 edition, which, as discussed in the previous chapter, was printed rather hastily. That the level of culpability of Gerwani and other PKI groups is amplified in the 1984 edition indicates the intent to rectify the oversight. The silence, however, in both editions about the ghastly acts allegedly committed by the women—castration, poking out of eyes, dancing of naked around generals—is different. It cannot be an accidental oversight. It indicated the unwillingness of the team members to mention them. One of the members of Nugroho's team claimed that they could find no credible evidence for such alleged wrongdoings. In addition, for educational purposes, inclusion of such details was deemed inappropriate.[19]

Another case is the treatment of the episode called General Offensive (*Serangan Umum*) of 1 March 1949. This refers to the coordinated attack by Republican forces under the operational leadership of Suharto against the Dutch-controlled Yogyakarta, holding it for about six hours. The controversy surrounding this event lies in Suharto's claim that it was his brainchild, sidelining Sultan Hamengku Buwono IX as the initiator. All three editions refrain from eulogizing the role of Suharto in this event. They uniformly state that Suharto led the attack but neither exaggerate his role as the leader nor present him as the initiator. In his autobiography (Soeharto 1989), Suharto claimed credit for initiating and leading it. Instead, it is the event's significance that is highlighted in all versions of SNI. Consistently, the attack is described as 'extraordinarily intense' and a crucial factor in demoralizing the Dutch forces (SNI-SMP, 108), thus turning of the tide of war to the advantage of the Indonesian military (SNI-6 1975, 63; SNI-6 1984, 162).

The period from securing Supersemar or the Letter of Instruction that allowed the transfer of power from Sukarno to Suharto is yet another example of restraint on the part of the scholars. The first edition is totally silent about it. The narrative ends soon after the G30S incident for reasons earlier discussed. The 1984 edition is notable for not embellishing the importance of the event. Unlike the case of SNI-SMP, which states that "Supersemar constitutes a turning point in the victory of the New Order and because it was newly acquired must be defended and protected" (169), the 1984 edition simply states that "11 March 1966 was the start of the New Order" (413).

There are several other instances when restraint on the part of the historians is apparent. However, I single out these three cases as examples because they are central to the interests of the regime, or of Suharto specifically. That the supposed official history would not go as far as other propagandistic tools could mean various things. One possibility is the conscious or unconscious 'attempt' of the historians who wrote it to uphold the rules of evidence in historical methodology. Despite being dubbed as a mouthpiece or an icon of New Order propaganda, and for that bitterly criticized, SNI (especially the 1975 edition) was at best of limited forcefulness or efficacy. Perhaps, Suharto's call in early May 1987 to take another look at the history of 1950–1965 and to formulate anew an official, specifically "objective and honest" history of the New Order was in recognition of the limitations of SNI.[20]

Notwithstanding the preponderance of the regime's political motives in SNI-6, there were spaces in this project in which these motives did not dominate. This situation provides us a glimpse of the complex interplay between politics, scholarship and chance. It allows us to see scholars as agents who have their own power. Chance and the unintended exercise of power sometimes play an important role too. The wellspring of the powers of scholarship in the context of Indonesia needs to be clarified.

Deep roots of scholarship-politics tensions

The tensions between the scholarly and the political run long in the field of history in Indonesia. Early recorded episodes involved spirited exchanges about the question of objectivity and subjectivity within the 'club' of colonial historians, as Resink put it (1968a, 63). The Indonesian scholars did not participate; they were, as Resink noted with hyperbole, "totally ignorant of it" (1968b, 66). If the notion of 'subjective history' had to be fought for in Europe, in the context of a long-standing tradition of positivism, rationalism, and empiricism, the same may not be true in the case of Indonesian scholars. The subjective notion of history seemed to have easily found a fertile niche in the emerging community of Indonesian historians. Among the reasons for this, Resink spelled out, were the "pluralistic and polyinterpretable" character of Indonesian culture and the 'syncretistic traditions' that altogether nurtured the spirit of tolerance among the people. The other reason, Resink said, lay in the backwardness of historical theory as it developed among colonial scholars in/of Indonesia. That is, the colonial historiography of the earlier days did not pay particular attention to the question of historical objectivity, so it was relatively easy to embrace the notion of historical subjectivity (Resink 1968a, 66).

In the earlier stage, the question of subjectivity was not primarily linked to the influence of the 'obviously' political, such as the interest of the state or political leaders. It was rather tied to the impact of the *Zeitgeist* or the dominant spirit of the time, including the supposedly ahistorical attitude emanating from traditional culture, as bewailed, for example, by Soedjatmoko (1965) and Bambang Oetomo (1961). The same culture had, supposedly, also nurtured and sanctioned the close ties between the rulers and the court poets/clerics (*pujanggas*). It is a practice that, some would say, would be carried all throughout Indonesian history, perhaps in different forms, even up to the New Order period. Coasting along the rise of nationalism, the notion of subjectivity would in due time become decidedly political, both in tone and in intent. The proliferation starting in the late colonial period of the purportedly historical works that seemed mythical, extolling the glories of the Indonesian past, illustrated the extent to which intellectuals, such as Mohammad Yamin (1951), would choose to be carried away by a strongly nationalist atmosphere.

Against such a backdrop, one may appreciate the importance of what happened on the fateful day of 14 December 1957. In the opening day of the historic first National History Seminar, Soedjatmoko[21] and Yamin were the two presenters tasked with articulating their proposed philosophy of national history.[22] The two scholars offered what proved to be classic articulations of the two contrasting views on the philosophy of the national history of Indonesia. The primary bones of contention were the questions "History for what?" and "What should history be?" If Resink, only five years earlier, had bewailed the absence of Indonesians' participation in the debate, things would never have been the same after the Soedjatmoko-Yamin encounter in December 1957. The friction between 'scientific' and nationalist history was given eloquent expression perhaps for the first time in Indonesia's public sphere. It continued, although in a sporadic manner, in succeeding decades.

Mohammad Yamin argued passionately for the use of history to promote national unity and national pride (1968). Soedjatmoko, for his part, argued exactly the opposite. He warned against the use of history as a political tool, and he called for a 'scientific' and 'open approach' to the study of history, devoid of any preconceived political purposes. As far as he was concerned, talking about philosophy of history at a time when there was a virtual absence of empirical research was premature and inappropriate. He urged that research be done in an open space following scientific approach, and the output would frame the shape philosophy would take afterwards (Soedjatmoko 1958). The whole idea of his paper revolved around the urgent need to protect history from the impatient demands of nationalism.[23]

Soedjatmoko's eloquent articulation aside, the mantra of nationalism seemed overwhelming. Among the seven respondents invited to comment on the Yamin–Soedjatmoko exchange, hardly anyone expressed agreement with the points raised by Soedjatmoko. Two of the respondents (see Ave 1958 and Kartawirana 1958) flatly rejected Soedjatmoko's proposal and one of them, J.B. Ave, appeared to be deeply angered by it. Others either implicitly denied Soedjatmoko's views by agreeing with Yamin and being mum about any of Soedjatmoko's proposals. In his response, Soedjatmoko tried to mollify Ave by anchoring the roots of their oppositional views on the unclear nature of the theme of the panel. He said that it should not be about philosophy of national history but about issues on the writing of history. These reactions were a portent of how, in the succeeding decades, Soedjatmoko's ideas would be received by the history establishment in Indonesia, in particular, and the public, in general. While there has been a tendency in foreign (particularly American) scholarship on Indonesia to exaggerate the impact or influence of Soedjatmoko's 1957 piece, as exemplified, for instance, by Kahin and Barnett, who gushed about its supposedly being widely read and influential (1990), Indonesian historians whom I have interviewed and who studied in the 1960–1980s attest that it was hardly a 'hot' topic of discussion in their classes. That the Soedjatmoko-edited book *Introduction to Indonesian Historiography* was translated into Bahasa Indonesia and published in Indonesia only in 1995 underlined its limited readership and influence before the mid-1990s.[24]

Apparently, like many of Soedjatmoko's other compelling ideas, his message cannot but be confined, during much of Guided Democracy and New Order periods, to the undercurrents. It was considered by many, to put it in the most polite terms, as well ahead of its time.[25] It would have to wait for the rise of Sartono and the multi-dimensional school (sometimes called the UGM School) before a sustained effort materialized to bring at least parts of Soedjatmoko's message to the surface, allowing it a chance of joining the mainstream of historiographic development.[26]

The scientific and the nationalist history were not necessarily antithetical, as Soedjatmoko suggested. Klooster pointed out, rightly in my view, that a nationalist historiography can also be scientific, although he conceded that it may seldom happen. The difference between the two, he claimed, lay in the purpose. That is, while nationalist historiography aims at "cultivation of love and esteem for the fatherland," scientific historiography seeks to understand "the past in its own right" (1982, 48–49).

Parenthetically, while many foreign observers[27] were disapproving, dismissive, or bitterly critical of the nationalist historiography that developed in the Old and New Order periods, there were also others who were sympathetic or at least tolerant. In a characteristic historicist fashion, Nichterlein demonstrated the various ways by which different Indonesian authors had given substance to the idea of history consistent with the demands of the time or their understanding of those demands. 'Scientific' history, she claimed, was but one of several possibilities by which history could be written. It was not necessarily the most applicable or acceptable (Nichterlein 1974). Resink declared, "Our national attitude has to an important extent been determined historically, and it will continue to develop as a response to the challenge of the extra-national, a-national, and in some case, antinational historical attitudes of many" (G.J. Resink 1968). Frederick and Soeroto (1982) also espoused history as a product of its time, and it was not necessarily antithetical or inferior to 'scientific history.' While many Indonesians appeared comfortable with such a historicist view of the discipline, it did (does) not sit well with the views of the eloquent and the vocal few. The likes of Bambang Oetomo, Soedjatmoko, and, in the past decade, Bambang Purwanto proved to be as harsh, if not harsher, than their foreign counterparts in castigating nationalist historiography. Mohammad Ali,[28] Sartono Kartodirdjo,[29] Abdurrachman Surjomihardjo,[30] Taufik Abdullah,[31] and Kuntowijoyo[32] were also critical, but their stance seemed tempered by their sympathies for or understanding of the inevitability of national (if not nationalist)[33] aspirations. Altogether, however, they gave a clear, albeit muffled, voice in an atmosphere pervaded by the logic of nationalism. Their occasional articles, in the press and/or in more scholarly venues, kept the tension between the 'scientific' and the nationalist scholarship alive all throughout the extended period when the pressure was enormous for the former ('scientific') to bow down to the latter ('nationalist').

Where does Nugroho fit in all this? It is tempting to regard him as a carrier of the long tradition of the-ruler-and-the-poet/chronicler relationship that dates back to the *pujanggas* in the courts of Mataram, Majapahit, and other old kingdoms. Responding to insinuations that he was New Order's *pujangga baru* (new pujangga), Nugroho had time and again insisted that he was a scholar, not an 'intellectual prostitute' (Notosusanto 1978, 1981b). Whether he succeeded in convincing his critics is doubtful, but since many in Indonesia also respected and admired Nugroho, more careful and nuanced judgments may be needed. Consider, for instance, that if we liken Nugroho to Prapanca, an exemplar of a pujangga, this view is complicated by scholars' conflicting interpretations of Prapanca. While C.C. Berg dismissed Prapanca as a manipulator of history who served the political interest of his ruler, and he also questioned the historical value of Prapanca's purported work *Nagarakrtagama* (Bosch 1956), scholars like Sutjipto Wirjosuparto[34] (Wirjosuparto 1982) defended Prapanca, even considered him as the father of Indonesian history. While there have been more than a few Bergs in the past several decades, there seem to be many more commentators who could identify with Sutjipto Wirjosuparto's assessment.[35] So, any overly dismissive evaluation of Nugroho as a modern-day Prapanca, or as an intellectual prostitute, reflects only one side in a highly contentious and continuing debate. It may be a case of asserting one's politics against those of others. Such a debate is embedded in, though by no means confined to, the historiographic terrain.

Summing up

This chapter sets out to provide a nuanced examination of the relationship between politics and scholarship, power and knowledge, as evidenced in SNI project. It elucidates how the content and structure of SNI reflected and, at the same time, were influenced by the historiographic development and political contexts in Indonesia in the 1970s. Rather than the static and commonly believed frame of the-powerful-manipulating-knowledge, it demonstrates the dynamic relationship between scholarly and political forces, at times clashing, at other times reinforcing or simply running parallel with one another.

The primacy of the political and historiographic factors had a profound impact on the writing of the various versions of SNI. While the epithet 'official history' was on the whole not unwarranted, it is wrong to suppose that all SNI versions (1975; SNI-SMP and SNI 1984) were coherent and singularly favorable to the interests of the New Order regime. It is rather ironic that the version of SNI that was the most criticized and believed widely to be *the* official history—the original edition, SNI (1975)—was the least propagandistic, whereas the most ignored, SNI-SMP, was among the most virulent. It seems that the perception of the nature of official history needs to be re-calibrated to make it more textured and thus able to accommodate cases like SNI. It also flags the presence of a simulacral aspect of reality, in which public perceptions replace or take precedent over the real. As the public responses to SNI and its other versions show, perceptions could have serious material consequences.

Another important point is that the variations, incoherence, or even contradiction within and across different versions of SNI suggests the multiplicity or power and fluidity of power relations that shape knowledge. It also points to the agency of individual scholar-participants, as well as to the need to acknowledge the power of scholarship, whose established conventions (approaches, theories, practices) helped inadvertently or not in restricting the political interests of the regime. This point goes against the still common, though by no means universal, understanding of the power–knowledge relations, where the role or power of scholars and scholarship tend to swing between the poles of being exaggerated as an antidote to the political (the liberal notion of "speaking truth to power"), on the one hand, and being downplayed, ignored or assumed to be out of the equation, as if scholars and scholarship are neutral and beyond the ambit of power relations, on the other. Just like Tadhana, what the case of SNI shows is that in between these poles lies the intimate, complex, and shifting relationship between the scholarly and the political. The differences between the two cases are mainly on the mechanics of how embodiments of power and knowledge interact. The logic that underpins such interaction appears to be fundamentally the same. It is the task of the next chapter to elucidate further this point.

Notes

1 *Kompas* "Demonstran Bakar Buku Sejarah Nasional," 3 March 2002.
2 For early works, see Anderson and McVey (1971); Nugroho Notosusanto and Saleh (1968); Crouch 1978; Wertheim 1970); Robert Cribb (1990); and Sulistyo (2000, 46–89). For more recent publications, see McGregor, Melvin, and Pohlman (2018); Kammen and McGregor (2012); Melvin (2017, 2018); Robinson (2018); Roosa (2006, 2012). For a comprehensive and detailed review of Sukarno's involvement, see Beisi (2004). For a review that is favorable to Suharto's position, see Elson (2001, 99–119).
3 This episode relates to the attempt by the left-leaning artists and cultural workers to assert the primacy of the 'political' (captured in the slogan "Politics is in Command!" or "Politik adalah Panglima!") in all aspects of life, including art-related matters. It elicited a response from a group of artists who signed the *Manifesto Kebudayaan* (Cultural Manifesto) asserting freedom of artistic expression. For a perceptive, insider's view of the issues, events and personalities surrounding this incident, see Goenawan Mohamad (1988).

SNI: contents and contexts 157

4 It is notable that Ariwiadi's colleague, Moela Marbun, who was assigned to the period of Guided Democracy wrote the paper apparently without much desire to paint an overly negative picture of the period. See Marbun (1972).
5 Interview with an anonymized informant, 23 & 25 June 2005, Yogyakarta.
6 Interview with an anonymized informant, 22 August 2005, Depok.
7 Interview with an anonymized informant, 18 December 2005, Jakarta.
8 Nugroho was quoted as saying, *"Saya tahu itu (SNI-SMP) tidak sempurna karena saya bukan guru SMP, tapi bahan isinya sudah baik dan memenuhi syarat yang dikehendaki Pak Harto* (Sumantri 1982).
9 Interviews with anonymized informants who worked closely with Nugroho, 18 December 2005, Jakarta; 8 August 2005 Depok; 22 August 2005, Depok.
10 Interview with an anonymized informant, 22 August 2005, Depok.
11 Interview with Taufik Abdullah, 8 June 2005, Jakarta.
12 Heryanto (2006) shows that while the regime had a hand in keeping alive communism's supposed 'latent danger,' the discourse has nonetheless assumed a life of its own apart from state manipulation
13 This is clear in a number of newspaper articles written by Nugroho in defense of his work on Pancasila (Nugroho Notosusanto 1981). For an overview of this debate, see Sutrisno (2003, 1–12). For a compilation of articles about the debate, see Yayasan Idayu (1981). A similar effort is evident in Nugroho's foreword of SNI-6 (1975). He took pains to emphasize that because not all facts can be included in the narrative, they did the best they could to examine them carefully "based on the requirements of historical methods." (See "Prakata" SNI, Jilid 6, n.p., 1975).
14 Interview with an anonymized informant, 22 August 2005, Depok.
15 See Drakeley (2000) for a concise and perceptive interpretation of what purportedly transpired in Lubang Buaya and for the importance of the event in the subsequent response to the PKI and the birth of the New Order. This brief article anticipates significant issues raised by Wieringa's important book (Wieringa 2002). See also the unpublished PhD dissertation of Yosef Djakababa (2011).
16 A valuable and detailed treatment of this and other military-sponsored museums in Indonesia can be found in McGregor (2007, Chapters 3 and 6)
17 For a systematic and detailed account of the process by which the military deceived the public, see Saskia Wieringa, *Sexual Politics in Indonesia,* 310–317.
18 The following passages are examples:

> In Lubang Buaya, the officers who were still alive were tortured using sharp weapons and rifle butts. They were then sprayed with bullets and finally were thrown in an old well.
>
> (SNI-6, 1975 p. 122)

> In a gruesome or cruel manner, they were tortured and finally killed by the members of the Pemuda Rakyat, Gerwani and other PKI-affiliated organizations. Satisfied with their cruelty, the bodies of dead officers were afterwards thrown in an old well and covered with garbage and soil.
>
> (SNI-6, 1984 390)

"The doctors' autopsy revealed that the officers suffered severe (berat) torture" (SNI-6 1984 p. 394).

19 Interview with an anonymized informant, 22 August 2005, Depok.
20 The official reason given for Suharto's call focused on the need of the younger generation to know the 'truth' about the periods 1950–1965, as well as the New Order. Considering the detailed treatment of the periods in the SNI 1984 edition, as well the long-standing presence of the SNI-SMP (and its accompanying texts, SNI-SMA), the official reason given by Alamsjah, a high-ranking minister, was unusual. Suharto's call elicited spirited public discussion in the media. See *Kompas* (1987a, 1987b), Abdullah (1987a, 1987b), Moedjanto (1987).

21 For a useful biography of Soedjatmoko, see Nursam (2002). See also Kahin and Barnett (1990).
22 It may have been a stroke of fate that Soedjatmoko spoke at that conference. Originally he was not the intended speaker. It was Hatta. For an undisclosed reason, Hatta could not come, so Soedjatmoko was asked to replace him. See *Panitia Seminar Sedjarah* (1958, 12).
23 Kahin recalled that Soedjatmoko wrote to him sometime in the late 1950s that the latter felt it was his personal responsibility to protect history from the impetuous dictates of the nationalist atmosphere. See Kahin and Barnett (1990).
24 In their introduction to the first set of papers in their book *Pemahaman Sejarah Indonesia* (*Understanding History of Indonesia*), Frederick and Soeroto have noted that while perhaps, Soedjatmoko's views had some influence in the 1950s (and 1960s), by the 1980s, "it does not surprise that these were considered not apt" (Frederick and Soeroto 1982, 28).
25 Soedjatmoko was aware that he was going against very strong currents of the time. In his acutely perceptive essay "The Indonesian Historian and His Time" (1965), he identified the currents as, first, the pervasive ahistorical attitude of the people that emanated from the feudal, agrarian setting of much of Indonesia. The second was the impatient demands of nationalism that tended to subordinate everything to the quest for national strength, pride and unity. So, the lukewarm response must not have surprised Soedjatmoko. In an obituary for Soedjatmoko, written by Hannah Papanek and Goenawan Mohamad (1990), they called him a "voice of reason…in a world too seldom has listened to such voices." (p. 449). They also noted that "his influence at home remained muted" (450). In the review of "Transforming the Humanity: The Visionary Writings of Soedjatmoko," Leslie Palmier (1996, 198) stated that "his country was too blinkered to appreciate him."
26 However, it would be a mistake to regard the Sartono School, despite looming large in most major accounts of historiographic development in Indonesia, as central or dominant in terms of actual influence. The alleged dominance of the School may be a projection of a deep-seated desire rather than a representation of what was actually the case. If we take a look at the general map of historical outputs in Indonesia—be it in academic, popular or instructional terms—the quantity of those following the Sartono approach to historical writing occupy very little space. See Curaming (2003) for a more developed detailed argument along this line.
27 For instance, Kahin and Barnett (1990), Van Klinken (2001), Vickers and McGregor (2005).
28 Mohammad Ali was emphatic about the need for a 'scientific history,' but he was aware that such a kind of history can be realized only within the context of a "new culture suitable to life in the modern world." See Ali (1965, 22–23).
29 Sartono Kartodirdjo, despite being considered by many as a sort of an icon for 'scientific history' in Indonesia, never failed to at least mention in his writings that history-writing can never be divorced from its *Zeitgeist*, and since he deemed national unity and identity to be among the needs of the time, he had no qualms in aligning history to serve those needs. See Kartodirdjo (1982, 2001).
30 Despite being one the most vocal critics of SNI and biggest influences on the politics on history-writing, Abdurrachman Surjomihardjo recognized the 'obligations' of the historians to contribute to nationalist undertakings. See Surjomihardjo (1978), for example.
31 See, for instance, *Sinar Harapan* (1986).
32 See the introductory chapter of Kuntowijoyo (2003).
33 The debates surrounding the philosophy of national history in the 1957 national seminar gave rise to a sharp differentiation between the terms "national" and

"nationalist," the latter being associated with 'chauvinistic' forms of nationalism. That Sartono's articles written as late as the 1990s, contained references to such a differentiation attests to the enduring tension between the two concepts. See Kartodirdjo (1970, 33–34; 1982, 2001).
34 Sutjipto Wirjosuparto wrote in "Prapanca as a Historian (Prapanca Sebagai Penulis Sedjarah)," (1960/1982) a defense against Berg, whose ideas cast doubt on the historical value of Nāgarakṛtāgama, among other babads (Sutjipto Wirjosuparto 1982).
35 Frederick and Soeroto (1982, 176–177), for instance, described Sutjipto Wirjosuparto's piece as his 'best,' offering a new perspective on the early history of Indonesia and demonstrating that, contrary to what many foreign scholars believed, pre-modern Javanese had a historical consciousness, and Prapanca was among the clearest proofs of that.

References

Abdullah, Hamid. 1987a. "Beberapa Kendala Penulisan Sejarah (Some Constraints in Writing History)." *Suara Merdeka*, June 11.
———. 1987b. "Dilema Sejarawan Nasional (Dilemma of National Historians)." *Suara Pembaruan*, July 14.
Abdullah, Taufik. 1975. "The Study of History." In *The Social Sciences in Indonesia*, edited by Koentjaraningrat, 89–166. Jakarta: Indonesian Institute of Sciences (LIPI).
———. 1994. "In Search of a National History: Experiences of a Multi-Ethnic and Multi-Historic Indonesia." In *Constructing a National Past: National History and Historiography in Brunei, Indonesia, Thailand, Singapore, the Philippines, and Vietnam: A Collection of Conference Papers from the International Workshop on National History and Historiography*, edited by Putu Davies, 203–218. Brunei: Department of History, Universiti Brunei Darussalam.
Ali, Mohammad. 1965. "Historiographical Problems." In *Introduction to Indonesian Historiography*, edited by Soedjatmoko, M. Ali, G. J. Resink, and G. Kahin, 1–23. Ithaca, NY: Cornell University Press.
Anderson, Benedict, and Ruth T. McVey. 1971. *A Preliminary Analysis of the October 1, 1965 Coup in Indonesia*. Interim Reports Series. Ithaca, NY: Modern Indonesia Project, Cornell University.
Ave, J. B. 1958. "Pandangan Pendebat J.B. Ave (Views of Reactor J.B. Ave)." In *Seminar Sedjarah: Laporan Lengkap Atjara I dan II Tentang Konsepsi Filsafat Sedjarah Nasional dan Periodisasi Sedjarah Indonesia, Seri II*, 62–63 (History Seminar: Complete Report of Sessions I & II About Philosophy of National History and Historical Periodization). Yogyakarta: Universitas Gadjah Mada.
Beisi, Kerstin. 2004. *Apakah Soekarno Terlibat Peristiwa G30S?* Yogyakarta: Ombak.
Bosch, Frederick. 1956. "C.C. Berg and Ancient Javanese History." *Bijdragen Tot de Taal-, Land- En Volkenkunde*, 112: 1–24.
Budiawan. 2004. *Mematahkan Pewarisan Ingatan: Wacana Anti-komunis dan Politik Rekonsiliasi Pasca-Soeharto* (Breaking the Legacies of Memory: Anti-Communist Discourse and the Post-Soeharto Politics of Reconciliation) Jakarta: Lembaga Studi dan Advokasi Masyarakat.
Cribb, Robert, ed. 1990. *The Indonesian Killings of 1965–1966: Studies from Java and Bali*. Monash Papers on Southeast Asia, no. 21. Clayton: Centre of Southeast Asian Studies Monash University.

Crouch, Harold A. 1978. *The Army and Politics in Indonesia*. Ithaca, NY: Cornell University Press.
Curaming, Rommel. 2003. "Towards Reinventing Indonesian Nationalist Historiography." *Kyoto Review of Southeast Asia*, March. http://kyotoreview.cseas.kyoto-u.ac.jp/issue/issue2/index.html.
Diah, B. M. 1987. *Meluruskan Sejarah* (Straightening History). Jakarta: Pustaka Merdeka.
Djakababa, Yosef. 2011. "The Construction of History under Indonesia's New Order: The Making of the Lubang Buaya Official Narrative." PhD Dissertation, University of Wisconsin, Madison.
Drakeley, Steven. 2000. *Lubang Buaya: Myth, Misogyny and Massacre*. Clayton, VIC: Monash Asia Institute.
Elson, Robert E. 2001. *Suharto: A Political Biography*. Cambridge: Cambridge University Press.
Frederick, William H., and Soeri Soeroto, eds. 1982. *Pemahaman Sejarah Indonesia: Sebelum dan Sesudah Revolusi* (Understanding Indonesian History: Before and After the Revolution). Jakarta: Lembaga Penelitian Pendidikan dan Penerangan Ekonomi dan Sosial.
Goodfellow, Rob. 1995. *Api Dalam Sekam: The New Order and the Ideology of Anti-Communism*. Working Papers (Monash University, Centre of Southeast Asian Studies), 95. Clayton, VIC: Monash Asia Institute.
Heryanto, Ariel. 1999. "Where Communism Never Dies: Violence, Trauma and Narration in the Last Cold War Capitalist Authoritarian State." *International Journal of Cultural Studies* 2 (2): 147–177. doi:10.1177/136787799900200201.
———. 2005. *State Terrorism and Political Identity in Indonesia: Fatally Belonging*. London: Routledge.
Kahin, George, and Milton Barnett. 1990. "In Memoriam: Soedjatmoko, 1922–1989." *Indonesia*, 49: 133–139.
Kammen, Douglas, and Katharine McGregor, eds. 2012. *The Contours of Mass Violence in Indonesia, 1965–1968*. Singapore: NUS Press.
Kartawirana, A. 1958. "Pandangan Pendebat Sdr. Major A. Kartawirana (Views of Reactor Major A. Kartawirana)." In *Seminar Sedjarah: Laporan Lengkap Atjara I dan II Tentang Konsepsi Filsafat Sedjarah Nasional dan Periodisasi Sedjarah Indonesia, Seri II*, 59–61 (History Seminar: Complete Report of Programs I & II, Philosophy of National History and Historical Periodization). Yogyakarta: Universitas Gadjah Mada.
Kartodirdjo, Sartono. 1966. *The Peasants' Revolt of Banten in 1888: Its Conditions, Course and Sequel. A Case Study of Social Movements in Indonesia*. The Hague: Martinus Nijhoff.
———. 1970. "Sekali Lagi Pemikiran Sekitar Sejarah Nasional: Meneruskan Langkah Kearah Dekolonisasi Historiografi Indonesia (Rethinking National History Once Again: Towards Decolonization of Indonesian historiography)." *Lembaran Sejarah* 6: 23–35.
———. 1972. "Merenungkan Kembali Pemikiran Tentang Persoalan Sekitar Rekonstruksi Sejarah Indonesia Sebagai Sejarah Nasional (Revisiting the Ideas of Reconstructing the History of Indonesia as National History)." In *Lokakarya Buku Standar Sejarah Indonesia* (Workshop on the History of Indonesia Standard Text) Vol. 3, n.p. Tugu, Bogor.
———. 1975. "Kata Pengantar Umum (General Introduction)." In *Sejarah Nasional Indonesia* (National History of Indonesia), edited by Sartono Kartodirdjo,

Marwati Djoened Poesponegoro, and Nugroho Notosusanto, Vol. 1, vi–ix. Jakarta: Departemen Pendidikan dan Kebudayaan dan Balai Pustaka.

———. 1982. *Pemikiran dan Perkembangan Historografi Indonesia: Suatu Alternatif* (Ideas and Development of Indonesian Historiography: An Alternative). Jakarta : Gramedia.

———. 1987. *Pengantar sejarah Indonesia baru, 1500–1900* (An Introduction to New History of Indonesia, 1500–1900). Jakarta: Gramedia.

———. 2001. *Indonesian Historiography*. Yogyakarta: Penerbit Kanisius.

Kartodirdjo, Sartono, Marwati Djoened Poesponegoro, and Nugroho Notosusanto, eds. 1975. *Sejarah Nasional Indonesia* (National History of Indonesia) 6 vols. Jakarta: Departemen Pendidikan dan Kebudayaan and Balai Pustaka.

Klooster, H. A. J. 1982. "'Some Remarks on Indonesian Nationalist Historiography." In *Papers of the Dutch-Indonesian Historical Conference*, edited by Schutte, G and Sutherland, H, 47–62. Leiden and Jakarta: Bureau of Indonesian Studies.

Kompas. 1984. "Penulisan Sejarah Indonesia Belum Perhatikan Fakta dan Multidimensional (Indonesian Historiography Has Not Yet Paid Facts and Multi-Dimensional Approach Attention)," December 17.

———. 1985. "Penulisan Sejarah Indonesia (Historical Writing in Indonesia)," September 17.

———. 1987a. "Sejarah Zaman Baru Indonesia Memang Perlu Ditulis Kembali" (History of the Indonesia's New Era Needs to Be Re-Written) May 5.

———. 1987b. "Pemerintah Perlu Menyusun Buku Acuan Sejarah Indonesia, 1950–65" (The Government Needs to Prepare a Reference Guide for the Indonesian History, 1950–65), May 27.

———. 2002. "Demonstran Bakar Buku Sejarah Nasional (Demonstrators Burn National History Books)," May 3.

Kuntowijoyo. 2000. "Indonesian Historiography in Search of Identity." *Humaniora*, 1: 79–85.

———. 2003. *Metodologi Sejarah* (Historical Methodology). Yogyakarta: Jurusan Sejarah, UGM dan Tiara Wacana Yogya].

Leirissa, Richard, and Z. Ghazali, eds. 1993. *Sejarah Nasional Indonesia VII: Lahir dan Berkembangnya Orde Baru* (National History of Indonesia VII: The Birth and Development of the New Order). Vol. VII. Jakarta: Departemen Pendidikan dan Kebudayaan and Balai Pustaka.

Marbun, Moela. 1972. "Djaman Demokrasi Terpimpin (1959–1965) (The Guided Democracy Era (1959–1965))." In *Lokakarya Buku Standar Sejarah Indonesia* (The History of Indonesia Standard Text Workshop). Vol. 3. Tugu, Bogor.

McGregor, Katharine. 2007. *History in Uniform: Military Ideology and the Construction of Indonesia's Past*. Southeast Asia Publications Series. Singapore: NUS Press.

———. 2009. "A Reassessment of the Significance of the 1948 Madiun Uprising to the Cold War in Indonesia." *Kajian Malaysia* 27 (1 & 2): 85–119.

McGregor, Katharine, Jess Melvin, and Annie Pohlman, eds. 2018. *The Indonesian Genocide of 1965*. Cham: Springer International Publishing. doi:10.1007/978-3-319-71455-4.

Melvin, Jess. 2017. "Mechanics of Mass Murder: A Case for Understanding the Indonesian Killings as Genocide." *Journal of Genocide Research* 19 (4): 487–511. doi:10.1080/14623528.2017.1393942.

———. 2018. *The Army and the Indonesian Genocide: Mechanics of Mass Murder*. New York: Routledge.

Miller, Stephen. 2018. "Zombie Anti-Communism? Democratization and the Demons of Suharto-Era Politics in Contemporary Indonesia." In *The Indonesian Genocide of 1965: Causes Dynamics and Legacies*, edited by Katharine McGregor, Jess Melvin, and Annie Pohlman, 287–310. Cham: Springer International Publishing. https://doi.org/10.1007/978-3-319-71455-4_15.

Moedjanto, G. 1987. "Demitologisasi Sejarah (De-mythologizing History)." *Suara Pembaruan* June 15.

Moelyadi. 1992. "Konsep Baru Kronologi Pra-sejarah Indonesia (A New Concept of the Chronology of Indonesia's Pre-history.)" *Berita Buana*, February 12.

Mohamad, Goenawan. 1988. *The "Cultural Manifesto" Affair: Literature and Politics in Indonesia in the 1960s, a Signatory's View*. Working Paper Centre of Southeast Asian Studies 45. Clayton, VIC.: Centre of Southeast Asian Studies Monash University.

Nichterlein, Sue. 1974. "Historicism and Historiography in Indonesia." *History and Theory* 13 (3): 253–72.

Notosusanto, Nugroho. 1964. *Hakekat Sedjarah dan Azas2 Metode Sedjarah* (The Nature of History and Principles of Historical Methods). Jakarta: Mega Bookstore.

———. 1972. "Periode sedjak 1942: Pengantar (The Period since 1942: An Introduction)." In *Lokakarya Buku Standar Sejarah Indonesia* (Workshop on the History of Indonesia Standard Text]. Tugu, Bogor.

———. 1978. *Masalah Penelitian Sejarah Kontemporer: Suatu Pengalaman* (Problems in Contemporary History Research: An Experience). Jakarta: Yayasan Idayu.

———. 1981. *Proses Perumusan Pancasila Dasar Negara* (The Process of Formulating Pancasila as National Ideology). Jakarta: Bali Pustaka.

———. 1981b. "Teori: Ajinomoto Dan Metode Sejarah," *Kompas*, August 30.

———. n.d. *Norma2 Dasar Penelitian dan Penulisan Sejarah* (Foundations of Research and Writing of History). Jakarta: Pusat Sejarah ABRI.

Notosusanto, Nugroho, and Yusmar Basri. 1976. *Sejarah Nasional Indonesia Untuk SMP* (National History of Indonesia for Junior High School) Jakarta: Balai Pustaka.

Notosusanto, Nugroho, and Ismail Saleh. 1968. *The Coup Attempt of the "September 30 Movement" in Indonesia*. Jakarta: Pembimbing Masa.

Nursam, Mohammad. 2002. *Pergumulan Seorang Intelektual: Biografi Soedjatmoko* (Struggles of an Intellectual: A Biography of Soedjatmoko). Jakarta: Gramedia Pustaka Utama.

Oetomo, Bambang. 1961. "Some Remarks on Modern Indonesian Historiography." In *Historians of Southeast Asia*, edited by D. G. Hall, 73–84. London: Oxford University Press.

Panitia Seminar Sedjarah. 1958. *Laporan Seminar Sedjarah* (History Seminar Report). Yogyakarta: UGM & UI.

Poesponegoro, Marwati Djoened, and Nugroho Notosusanto, eds. 1984. *Sejarah Nasional Indonesia* (National History of Indonesia). Jakarta: Balai Pustaka.

Purwanto, Bambang. 2001a. "Mencari Format Baru Historiografi Indonesiasentris: Sebuah Kajian Awal (Search for a New Indonesia-centric Historiography: A Preliminary Analysis)." Paper Presented at the 7th National History Conference, Jakarta, 28–31 October 2001.

―――. 2001b. "From the Real Past to Myth: Some Issues in Writing Contemporary Indonesian History." Paper presented at the Third World Studies Center, University of the Philippines, Diliman, February 11.

Resink, Gertrudes. 1968a. "Fairness and Certainty in Indonesian Historiography." In *Indonesia's History Between the Myths: Essays in Legal History and Historical Theory*, 61–72. The Hague: W. van Hoeve Publishers, Ltd.

―――. 1968b. "Europocentric, Regiocentric, and Indocentric Historiography." In *Indonesia's History Between the Myths: Essays in Legal History and Historical Theory*, 4–12. The Hague: W. van Hoeve Publishers, Ltd.

Robinson, Geoffrey. 2018. *The Killing Season: A History of the Indonesian Massacres, 1965–66*. Princeton: Princeton University Press.

Roosa, John. 2006. *Pretext for Mass Murder: The September 30th Movement and Suharto's Coup D'état in Indonesia*. Madison: University of Wisconsin Press.

―――. 2012. "The September 30th Movement: The Aporias of the Official Narratives." In *The Contours of Mass Violence in Indonesia, 1965–68*, 25–49. Singapore and Copenhagen: NUS Press and NIAS Press.

Setyadi, A., and H. Saptono. 2006. "Mesu Budi vs Ultraliberalisme." *Kompas*, February 16. www2.kompas.com/kompas-cetak/0602/16/utama/.

Sinar Harapan. 1986. "Taufik Abdullah: Kita Harus Berikan Porsi yg Pas Pada Sejarah & Mitos" (Taufik Abdullah: We Must Allot Enough Space for History and for Myth)", January 20.

―――. 1980a. "Sejarah Demi Masa Kini (History for the Sake of the Present)," January 9.

―――. 1980b. "Setuju Konsep Sartono, Kecuali yang 'Hahahaha:' Wawancara dengan Prof. Dr. Nugroho Notosusanto ttg. Sejarah Kontemporer (Agree with Sartono's Ideas Except the Hahaha: Interview with Prof. Dr. Nugroho Notosusanto about Contemporary History)," *Sinar Harapan*, October 1.

Siswadhi, Richard Leirissa, and Atmakusumah. 1976. "Buku Babon Sejarah Nasional: Objektivitas yang Ideal? (National History Standard Text: Objectivity that Was Ideal?)" *Prisma* 5 (Edisi Khusus): 81–90.

Soedjatmoko. 1958. "Merintis Masa Hari Depan (Pioneering the Future)." In *Seminar Sejarah: Laporan Lengkap Atjara I Dan II Tentang Konsepsi Filsafat Sedjarah Nasional Dan Periodisasi Sedjarah Indonesia* (History Seminar: Complete Report of Sessions 1 & 2 on the Philosophy of National History and Historical Periodization of Indonesia), *Seri II*, 35–53. Yogyakarta: Universitas Gadjah Mada.

―――. 1965. "Indonesian Historian and His Time." In *Introduction to Indonesian Historiography*, 405–415. Ithaca, NY: Cornell University Press.

Soeharto. 1989. *Soeharto: Pikiran, Ucapan, dan Tindakan Saya* (Soeharto: My Thoughts, Words and Deeds). Jakarta: Citra Lamtoro Gung Persada.

Soejono. 1972. "Tinjauan Tentang Pengkerangkaan Prasejarah Indonesia (Another Look at the Framing of Indonesian Pre-history)." In *Lokakarya Buku Standar Sejarah Indonesia* (Workshop on the History of Indonesia Standard Text). Vol. 3. Tugu, Bogor

Sulistyo, Hermawan. 2000. *Palu Arit di Ladang Tebu: Sejarah Pembataian Massal yang Terlupakan (1965–1966)* (Hammer and Sickle on Sugar Cane Fields: History of the Forgotten Mass Killings (1965–1966)). Jakarta: Kepustakaan Populer Gramedia.

Sumantri. 1982. "Nugroho: Interpretasi Boleh Bebas tetapi Fakta jangan Diubah" (Nugroho: Interpretations May Vary but Facts Ought Not Be Changed). *Sinar Harapan*, September 29.

Surjomihardjo, Abdurrachman. 1976. "Penulisan Sejarah Mutakhir (Recent Historical Writings)." *Kompas*, November 17.

———. 1978. *Pembinaan Bangsa dan Masalah Historiografi: Kumpulan Esei dan Artikel* (Nation-building and Historiographic Issues: Compilation of Essays and Articles). Jakarta: Lembaga Ekonomi dan Kemasyarakatan Nasional.

———. 1980. "Sejarah Kontemporer dan Kemelut Penulisan Buku Sejarah Nasional Indonesia" (Contemporary History and the Crisis in Writing the Book of National History of Indonesia). *Sinar Harapan*, October 15.

Sutrisno, S. 2003. *Kontroversi dan Rekonstruksi Sejarah* (Controversy and Historical Reconstruction). Yogyakarta: Media Presindo

van der Kroef, Justus. 1958. "On the Writing of Indonesian History." *Pacific Affairs* 31 (4): 352–371.

van Klinken, Gerry. 2001. "The Battle for History after Suharto: Beyond Sacred Dates, Great Men, and Legal Milestones." *Critical Asian Studies* 33 (3): 323–350. https://doi.org/10.1080/14672710122604.

van Leur, Jacob C. 1955. *Indonesian Trade and Society: Essays in Asian Social and Economic History*. The Hague: W. van Hoeve.

Vickers, Adrian, and Katharine E. McGregor. 2005. "Public Debates about History: Comparative Notes from Indonesia." *History Australia* 2 (2): 44.1–44.13.

Wahid, Abdul. 2018. "Counterrevolution in a Revolutionary Campus: How Did the '1965 Event' Affect an Indonesian Public University?" In *The Indonesian Genocide of 1965*, edited by Katharine McGregor, Jess Melvin, and Annie Pohlman, 157–178. Cham: Springer International Publishing. doi:10.1007/978-3-319-71455-4_8.

Wertheim, W.F. 1970. "Suharto and the Untung Coup — the Missing Link." *Journal of Contemporary Asia* 1 (2): 50–57.

Wieringa, Saskia. 2002. *Sexual Politics in Indonesia*. Basingstoke, Hampshire: Palgrave/Macmillan.

Wirjosuparto, Sujipto. 1982. "Prapanca Sebagai Penulis Sedjarah (Prapanca as a Historian)." In *Pemahaman Sejarah Indonesia: Sebelum dan Sesudah Revolusi* (Understanding Indonesian History: Before and After the Revolution), edited by William Frederick and Soeri Soeroto. Jakarta: LP3ES.

Yamin, Mohammad. 1951. *6000 Tahun Sang Merah Putih* (6000 Years of Red and White). Djakarta: Siguntang.

———. 1968. "Tjatur Sila Chalduniah." In *Seminar Sedjarah: Laporan Lengkap Atjara I Dan II Tentang Konsepsi Filsafat Sedjarah Nasional Dan Periodisasi Sedjarah Indonesia, Seri II* (History Seminar: Complete Report of Sessions 1 & 2 on the Philosophy of National History and Historical Periodization of Indonesia), 14–34. Yogyakarta: Universitas Gadjah Mada.

Yayasan Idayu. 1981. *Sekitar Tanggal dan Penggalinya: Guntingan Pers dan Bibliografi Tentang Pancasila* (On Dates and Its Discoverer: Newspaper Clippings and Bibliography on Pancasila). Ed. 2. Jakarta: Yayasan Idayu.

Zain, Umar. 1976. "Penulisan Kembali Karya Standar Sejarah Indonesia," *Sinar Harapan*, March 22.

6 The calculus of power–knowledge relations

The term calculus is used in the title of this chapter as a metaphor for the nature of power relations that enable knowledge production. As a branch of mathematics, calculus refers to the study of continuously changing quantities (or combinations thereof), and it is characterized by infinite processes in the same way that the power–knowledge nexus seems to operate. By that, I mean knowledge and power, and the relationship between them seem to be formed at the confluence of crisscrossing factors whose possible combinations may be theoretically infinite and their interaction is continuous, but on the ground, the resulting permutations are patterned and limited. Any effort to present power as power and a knowledge claim as authoritative knowledge (regardless of whether it is in fact truthful or not) cannot but be an act of 'freezing' artificially the otherwise dynamic process. As such it is definitely propped up by power relations that need to be uncovered.

This chapter compares, highlights, and integrates the key points in the analysis of Tadhana and SNI projects. It underscores the importance of contexts in shaping the contents and features of, as well as the power relations that underpinned, the two projects. While the idea of 'context' is by now so trite that highlighting it here is like flogging a dead horse, the logic of contextuality is seldom applied to the very core of knowledge production and consumption—scholars, scholarship, knowledge and power. This is what I shall attempt to do in this chapter with the hope of extracting some insights which may carry important theoretical and political implications.

Primacy of contexts and the power of scholars

The primacy of context is an idea that has long been axiomatic in human sciences, particularly the disciplines that are dominated by historicist, constructionist, and constructivist approaches, such as history and sociology of knowledge. It is context that decides, so the strongest formulation of this analytic tack goes. A tendency persists, however, to tame or downplay the roles of human knowers and historical contingency in knowledge production.

This tendency is evident in the aspirations among many scholars for universality or objectivity, which amounts to a usurpation of the God's eye or the metaphysical omniscient viewpoint, as well as in the persistent anxiety towards relativism (even among non-positivists) in the social sciences. As if, knowing without a knower and context-free representations in the human sciences are possible.

Conceding the predominance of contexts does not mean upholding structural determinism, which denies the agency or power of individual actors. Rather, the active roles of individual agents form a dialectical relationship with the structural forces to shape the overall contexts. This Hegelian formulation is in line with Bourdieu's idea of habitus and Gidden's structuration. As previous chapters show, scholars involved in the two projects were agents with their own interests to pursue and power to exercise. They were not passive, or merely manipulated or co-opted. The Tadhana scholars had a free rein in designing the project and in writing, except in a chapter that involved the Marcos years. In the case of SNI, the discrepancies and contradictions within and across its various versions point to the active role of scholars.

The ideas behind Tadhana and SNI projects began to germinate at around the same time in the late 1960s. Both were carried out in the following decade. The confluence of political and historiographic factors at that time seemed conducive to the pursuit of these projects, as discussed in Chapters 1, 3, and 5. Nevertheless, their respective prime movers, Ferdinand Marcos and Nugroho Notosusanto, encountered obstacles of contrasting nature in the beginning. Fellow scholars in Indonesia were skeptical of Nugroho's proposal because they knew of the still limited intellectual resources. For their part, Filipino scholars courted by Marcos since 1967 refused to participate on the strength of the shared expectation to uphold ethical and academic or professional standards. When Marcos finally found in 1973–1974 willing participants, they were those imbued with a sense of confidence in their ability and autonomy as scholars.

Given the confidence and relative strength in scholarly terms of the Filipino scholars vis-à-vis their Indonesian counterparts, one might expect that they would be more able to neutralize the political interests of the regime they worked for. Rather ironically, this was not the case as the original edition of SNI (1975) showed comparatively more resilient to political manipulations than Tadhana. The more scholarly approach and contents of the latter notwithstanding, Tadhana proved to be no better shielded from political appropriation. As noted in Chapter 3, the highly scientific exposition of the geological formation of the Philippine archipelago, for instance, assumed an unexpected (by scholars) political meaning when seen against the total structure and aims of Tadhana, as well as Marcos's overall political interests. For the Harvard-trained geologist, Ben Austria, who wrote the relevant volume, it was nothing more than an innocent, matter of fact description and analysis of the origin of the Philippines. However, this scientific analysis fits into Marcos's eschatological claim that the New Society which he intended to build by declaring Martial Law was a destiny waiting to happen as it was anchored in the indigenous Filipino identity, whose sources can be traced to the deepest possible roots—the geological process. This point raises an important question that needs reiterating here: if something as dry and seemingly politically innocuous as a geological process can be politicized, what else cannot? Tadhana scholars like Salazar, Austria and Tan did not seem to have anticipated such appropriation. As far as they were concerned, their main goal was scholarly writing in the most scientific way possible and pushing the frontiers of the Philippine historiography. Regardless of their original intent, however, their scholarly output was used differently, and no amount of disavowal on their part can undo this. Similarly, if Tadhana were undertaken as an independent project by scholars, upon its publication Marcos could have also used its contents to support his political interests.

Noteworthy here is the importance of the context of the actual knowledge use, the pragmatics of knowledge, in defining meaning. Most often, the focus of attention is the content—what is being said and how. The presumption is that some fixed meanings inhere in the content. Supposedly, it is defined by the author's intent, and it corresponds to a reality out there. This point is clear in many debates in the scholarly community, particularly among historians. These debates tend to concentrate on empirical accuracy and the suitability of methodology and theory. This is also the foundation of the confidence of scholars likes Tan and Salazar, who firmly believed that by confining themselves to the Spanish or pre-Spanish periods, periods very far removed from the Marcos years, they were 'safe' from any political or Marcos-related issues. What is often ignored is that the context of knowledge use could alter, even overturn, the meaning and implications of a particular knowledge claim. Within the holistic context of Tadhana's framing, and given Marcos's intended use for it, even the volumes far from the Marcos period, such as those concerning the geological and pre-Spanish eras, were implicated. This was the case as they were necessary constitutive elements of Tadhana's main argument.

Sartono's use of Indonesia-centrism and the multi-dimensional approach also illustrates the paramount role of contexts. At first glance, his scholarship was simply seen as an innocent, sophisticated attempt to reconstruct the process of nation-formation. If seen, however, against the backdrop of a number of separatist efforts that punctuated Indonesia's postcolonial history, it concurrently served the political purpose of validating and naturalizing the state-sponsored nationalism. Without him intending to, focused as he was on his scholarly pursuit, his scholarship helped delegitimize the nationalist aspirations of separatist groups. These groups included those who fought to establish an Islamic State (such as Darul Islam and its successors or splinter groups), the Acehnese (who were fighting for freedom until 2005) and the Papuans (whose separatist struggle persists up to now). The nationalist historiography that underpins the SNI, in other words, constituted a simultaneous encoding of the official and scholarly justifications for the state-sanctioned nationalism.

Without consciously being political, Sartono's scholarly approaches could be appropriated or interpreted as such. In addition, the manner in which they became enmeshed within the nationalist discourses in the country and beyond made them so. Just like the case of Tadhana scholars mentioned above, this case suggests that the political gets constituted at the moment of knowledge consumption—when people actually use it for their own purpose—and not necessarily at the time the scholars produce it. The contexts of actual knowledge use play a determinant role.

Foregrounding context is crucial, both analytically and politically. The refusal of many 'conservative' scholars to acknowledge the role of power relations in knowledge production coincides with their denial of the situatedness or contextuality of the act of knowing. Likewise, the hesitance of many 'progressive' scholars to push the logic of power–knowledge relations to its conclusion, or power/knowledge, goes with selective application, rather than full consummation, of the logic of contextuality. By highlighting the primacy of contexts in shaping the two projects, this study flags the need to include the power of scholars and scholarship or the scholarly among areas to be subjected to full contextual analysis. In other words, the emphasis on contexts and the power of scholars are two sides of the same analytico-political coin. Realizing it is needed to expose and, if one needs, neutralize the uncanny partnership between hidden political interests and denial of the full logic of contextuality.

Responses and dynamics of power relations

The contrasting characteristics of the SNI and Tadhana projects, and the different contexts that gave rise to them set the frame for dissimilar responses. As noted in Chapter 2, Tadhana was never completed and was never widely used. Out of the originally projected 19 volumes, only four were published. Of the two planned abridged volumes, only one came out. All in all, five out of the total twenty-one volumes were published. SNI, on the other hand, was not only completed but even underwent reprints and revisions. It was, at least in theory, also widely used either as a reference text in the university or as the basis for writing textbooks for high school and elementary school. Likewise, while Tadhana project operated under a shroud of mystery, the SNI took shape under the watchful eyes of the media. As a result, the controversial character of the SNI was publicly known, whereas that of Tadhana was mostly confined to a fairly small group within the community of scholars and activists.

Three decades of SNI's more widespread usage and sporadic but intense media coverage set the parameters within which its controversial character had been publicly discussed. The result was a multifaceted, shifting and more ambiguous picture of power relations discernible in the SNI when compared to the case of Tadhana. Whereas the scholars who participated in

Tadhana were depicted in a negative light by those who knew about the project, a perception that has changed only slowly, if at all, only the members of the Vol. 6 team of the SNI (1975 and 1984 editions) have been vilified, at least publicly. Moreover, the SNI saw vicissitudes of fortune depending on a number of factors, including the altered power structure wrought by the fall of the New Order regime in 1998.

The official but largely symbolic withdrawal of the SNI in the early 2000s illustrates this change of fortune (*Kompas* 2004). The government finally responded to the public clamor, occasioned by the proliferation since 1998, even much earlier, of stories of deliberate distortions of history that the media profusely covered. After enjoying the status of the official, standard history text for more than two decades, the SNI was denigrated as a testament to the New Order government's unscrupulous behavior. Right from the very start, there were, of course, people who believed that the SNI (specifically Vol. 6) was no more than government propaganda. But they appeared to be a tiny minority. For many others, especially the younger generations who grew up in the 1970s and 1980s, there was hardly any other history apart from what was inscribed in SNI-SMP and SNI-SMA textbooks, and versions derived from them. With the demise of the regime in 1998, the situation has been reversed. Many were convinced of the 'engineered' (*direkayasa*) character of Indonesian history and thus thought that it needed to be rectified or 'straightened' (*diluruskan*) (Adam 2007; cf. Karsono 2005). However, there were those who remained steadfast in their belief in the truthfulness of the SNI accounts or at least parts of it. This is clearly shown in the vociferous complaints against history textbooks written based on the 2004 curriculum, some of which dropped PKI from the usual term 'G30S/PKI.' The dropping of PKI reflected efforts of some historians to reinterpret the tragic G30S event into something that was not masterminded by PKI. The decision of the Attorney General office in 2007 to withdraw such textbooks due to public clamor clearly shows the resilience of the long-standing interpretation that blamed the PKI for the tragic G30S. At the same time, it underscores the political forces that influenced or shaped historical knowledge in the post-Suharto Indonesia.

Nugroho's reputation is another good illustrative example. His image varied over time, depending largely on the prevailing political atmosphere. While he had his own share of bitter critics during the New Order, he also had admirers who seemed to be much greater in number. As a published historian and an important government official, he enjoyed a degree of power and influence at the national level which lingered even after his death in 1985. His standing within the community of historians, however, paled in comparison with, say, Sartono, who was deeply respected and admired by both local and foreign scholars. Under the atmosphere of *reformasi* that prevailed soon after the collapse of the New Order, a far greater number of people seem to have viewed Nugroho and his legacy in a very

170 *The calculus of power–knowledge relations*

negative light. The re-alignment of power relations in the post-Suharto period considerably diminished whatever was left of Nugroho's lingering power or influence. However, the resilience of the New Order official interpretation of events surrounding the G30S and the supposedly enduring threat of communism suggest the persistence of the New Order's and Nugroho's influence.

In the case of Tadhana, the unpopularity of Marcos among intellectuals and the large segment of the public since the 1970s overshadowed its scholarly value and whatever academic credentials held by those who created it. One can assume that so long as anti-Marcos sentiments remain rife in the Philippines, Tadhana is not likely to be viewed favorably. The past three decades witnessed a gradual revival of the rosy memories of the Marcos years, often labeled as 'authoritarian nostalgia' (Chang, Chu, and Park 2007). With the near victory in 2016 in the Vice-Presidential elections of the son of the former dictator—Ferdinand 'Bongbong' Marcos Jr.—the tide appears to be turning. I have heard about the more serious efforts, including scholarly ones, to take another look at the body of published works attributed to Marcos, including Tadhana. Time will tell what happens in the future.

Politics and/as scholarship

The cases of Tadhana and SNI show that relations between 'good' scholarship and politics are not necessarily oppositional. There are instances when they clash, as was the case of the role played by the multi-dimensional approach in limiting Nugroho's intent. But they could, and often do, also work together. In fact, what Marcos wanted was precisely the highest possible quality of available scholarship as this was the kind of scholarship that he might have believed would serve his political interest. It appears that regardless of the quality of scholarship, it may be utilized for contrarian or supportive political purposes, so long as its content, approach, or assumption affirms or opposes a particular political position.

As I have noted in the Prologue, the impetus for this study derived from my initial wonderment why this relationship is often viewed as oppositional and anomalous. From this viewpoint, scholarship is equated to the pursuit of truth, neutral, empowering and liberating, whereas politics is deemed self-serving, constricting, and inherently biased. A well-known Indonesian intellectual, Soedjatmoko (1960, 18), expressed this view clearly:

> (W)e should realize that history, as a scholarly discipline is not and cannot be made the handmaiden of a particular ideology – cannot that is, as long as it is true to its scholarly character.

The critics of both SNI and Tadhana operated to a varying extent within this premise. The distinct contexts and the varied features of the two projects resulted in different ways in or degrees by which this dichotomy was deployed. In the case of Tadhana, critics chided the participant-scholars mainly for allowing themselves to be co-opted or manipulated by Marcos, the 'infamous' dictator. As noted in Chapter 2, their criticisms carried a moral subtext as if saying, had scholars-participants been resilient enough, as any scholar worthy of the name should be, they could have resisted the temptation of 'selling' their 'soul' to Marcos. That Agoncillo and de la Costa successfully deflected Marcos's efforts to enlist them in his project foregrounds the incontrovertible availability of choice Filipino scholars had had during that time. In the case of SNI, on the other hand, only Nugroho and, to a lesser degree, the members of his team were faulted for promoting the New Order regime's political agenda. Other participants were called out, if at all, for other reasons, such as the weaker foundation of academic training and lack of experience.

The moral high-ground assumed similarly by critics of Nugroho and Tadhana scholars was often couched in terms of avowed duty to preserve the integrity and nobility of the scholarly community. One should not commit the "treason of the intellectuals," so Julian Benda (1969) admonished. This line of thought has a long lineage. Well-intentioned, it is meant to protect individuals and the society in general from the abusive tendencies of the powerful entities, such as the oppressive state. It also seeks to prevent danger which might ensue from the collusion between the powerful and the knowledgeable, or the politicians and the scholars. By occupying a position above or outside of politics, the scholars are supposed to act as guardians of conscience, as critics of abusive power, and as protectors and promoters of the common good. As I have earlier noted in the Introduction, Rubio and Baert (2012, 2) call it the "liberal view" of politics-knowledge relations. This view coincides with the separation and hierarchy between the facts and values, reason and emotion, and pure knowledge and ideology, which, even if acknowledged to be unattainable in day-to-day practice, is nevertheless set as an aspirational goal to measure the success of a scholarly endeavor.

In the scheme of things, the scholars' championing of impartiality or objectivity, is hardly an innocent or an apolitical position. Borrowing the idea from Bourdieu (1989a, 22), the "consecration of symbolic capital", which arguably scholarship does in functionally similar way as the legal system to which Bourdieu refers, "confers upon a perspective an absolute, universal value, thus snatching it from a relativity that is by definition inherent in every point of view, as a view taken from a particular point in social space." The idea of impartiality is at once a weapon and a repository of the scholars' intellectual capital and symbolic power. It is the anchor to which the whole institution of scholarship is tied. Also, it is a 'corporate' responsibility of each member of the intellectual class to contribute towards the protection and growth of their investment (Bourdieu 1989b). It is to their advantage as a class to maintain autonomy as the gatekeepers of knowledge production, and the notion of objectivity or impartiality is key to preserving this privilege. Any challenge to the status—a transgression—would be met by symbolic violence, perhaps in the form of marginalization, if not expulsion from the scholarly community (Schubert 1995, 1009).

In the case of Indonesia, it was not always clear cut who were the transgressors and who were the defenders of the privileged historiographic position. When Abdurrachman Surjomihardjo confidently castigated Nugroho on various occasions from the mid-1970s for relativism and its moral implications, he did so against a strong current of a long-standing tradition of historicist or relativist history-making in Indonesia (Nichterlein 1974). Abdurrachman's critique presupposed the ascendancy of an established set of standard or scientific historical methodology as the basis for assessing knowledge claims. His self-assurance in rebuking Nugroho rested, among other things, on belief that the supposedly scientific or impartial methodology he invoked was the right one, and every historian worthy of this name should abide by it. Abdurrachman was in effect echoing Soedjatmoko's arguments in the 1950s–1960s for openness and an impartial approach to history-writing. One problem for him and others who subscribed to this approach, however, was that it was a minority view in Indonesia at the time (Frederick and Soeroto 1982, 28). There were certainly other historians in Indonesia who agreed with such critiques, but he had few comrades in his public crusade against Nugroho and his relativism. By openly positing his preferred historical methods as a given, Abdurrachman had put under erasure the long history of struggle to install this as the 'standard' historical methodology. I refer to such struggle not only in the context of the development of Western historiography from Herodotus and Thucydides all the way to Vico, Ranke Collingwood, White, Rorty, and beyond but also in that of Indonesian historiography from the days of Prapanca (Wirjosuparto 1982) and Mohammad Yamin (1951) up to the time of Resink (1968), Soedjatmoko (1958, 1960, 1965), Nichterlien (1974), Frederick and Soeroto (1982), and Sartono (Kartodirdjo 2001). By doing so, Abdurrachman seemed to be trying to offset what he lacked in number by invoking the power of a modern, established scholarly tradition in which the scientific approach was a keystone.

Within this frame, one may argue that upholding historical or scientific methodology is the basis of the scholars' hidden politics. When scholars like Nugroho and Salazar joined a state-sponsored project, their decision to work for or with the powers-that-be rendered obvious which political side they were on. From the standpoint of the public consumers of knowledge, this transparency deserves to be applauded as it helps them decide whether to believe in and use the knowledge they offer. After all, even if scholars do not explicitly work for politicians, on a daily basis, the knowledge they produce—accurate or not, scientific, humanistic, or whatever—circulates in social spaces, and it is interpreted, repackaged and used by different groups or individuals depending mainly on their ideological proclivities or personal interests. In short, the logic of partnership between embodiments of power and knowledge is always operative on the ground. It is just a question of which knowledge claims that are available in the marketplace of ideas may be compatible with the whatever ideological or personal interests of political power holders, or anyone for that matter. What SNI and Tadhana scholars did was merely formalize what may be happening informally every day. But this formalization is precisely what transgresses the ethos of impartiality, objectivity, or apoliticality upon which the collective interests of the scholarly class hinge. From the scholarly community's standpoint, therefore, it is dangerous for their interests. As a self-protective measure, the most vocal in the community are quick to expel, at least symbolically, the likes of Nugrohos, Tans and Salazars by calling them names such as 'intellectual prostitutes' or 'academic mercenaries.' With such names, they are rendered excluded from the category of 'true scholar.' This is a move either supported or opposed by politicians, depending on the compatibility of the scholar's knowledge claims with their ideological or short-term political interests. The vicissitudes of fortune SNI underwent in line with the change in political dynamics in Indonesia from the New Order to Reformasi period and beyond exemplified this point.

Things, however, are not so straightforward on the ground. For every critic of Nugroho during the New Order period, there seemed to be more who either defended him, silently concurred with him, just stayed neutral, or regarded the whole question as a non-issue. For Salazar and his fellow Tadhana authors, the ratio may not be as favorable. The point here, though, is not the number, though in itself, that is important, but the often ignored deeply political terrain within which labels, criticisms, and counter-criticisms were exchanged. The moral framing of labeling and criticisms appears to be a rhetorical and strategic device employed by critics who were trying to take the issue outside of scholarship or politics, where they may feel at a disadvantage. By invoking moral absolutes, critics moved the debate into the moral sphere, whose deeply political nature was concealed and where they might have believed they had the upper hand. Who can argue against morality or ethics that supposedly uphold the common or public good? Besides, allowing these critical exchanges to be seen as 'merely' an academic, social, or political conflict contravenes the image of scholarship as above the fray. Of course, there may be other reasons, but this is a possibility that is often ignored, and which is what this study seeks to underscore.

I should quickly add that this tendency is often not a conscious or a calculating move on the part of scholar-critics. Scholars and society at large have long internalized the moral imperatives attributed to scholarship as a supposedly neutral instrument. The moralist rhetoric, therefore, could have already become a knee-jerk or natural response by scholars to those who supposedly violate the established scholarly norms of conduct.

On a related note, it is not just how the public (including fellow scholars) reacted to the projects that were instructive of the dynamics of power relations. The interaction between scholars and the political sponsor (or its representative), as well as between members of the team, can likewise offer important insights. Chapter 2 noted that the members of Tadhana team were treated very well by Marcos. Not only were they given ample provisions—good pay, access to scholarly materials, clerical assistance—but they were also shown the utmost respect. Whether or not such an expression of respect was genuine is beside the point. What seems to weigh heavier was that Marcos could not afford to be less than respectful, at least in appearance, to these scholars. Considering that earlier on, he encountered difficulties in persuading historians to enter into a partnership with him, he seemed to have understood well the risks entailed if he treated them otherwise. The slightest offence, or sign of willful manipulation, could lead the scholars to resign, and thus jeopardize the success of the project. The picture that emerges here is not that of the dictator as all-powerful and the scholars as helpless, co-opted, or manipulated. Instead, one side had the power that the other did not have. They needed each other.

Nugroho's attitude towards some members of the team stood in stark contrast. His treatment of Abdurrachman and Taufik, his printing of their volume without allowing it to be completed, was bad enough. It was, however, his removal of Sartono from the project on account of the latter's valid wish to have the main editors' names printed on an inner page rather than on the cover of the books that was downright cruel. Sartono, who kept quiet about this for so long, endured in silence the ignominy of being treated so badly. These incidents display how much more restricted a space the Indonesian scholars had in the face of the regime's representative, especially when compared to the treatment that their counterparts in Tadhana enjoyed.

Nugroho's power or influence, however, must not be exaggerated. That there were passages in SNI (1975, 1984) and SNI-SMP that do not support, or even contradict, Nugroho's interpretation indicated that he had no full control of the younger historians under his direct supervision. Also, as discussed in the previous chapter, the contents of SNI-6 (1975) reflected the extent to which Nugroho and his team were restricted by Sartono's multidimensional approach. Nugroho and his team could not but abide by it, albeit half-heartedly. The contents of the history textbook SNI-SMP reveal the kind of history Nugroho would have written without the constraints set by Sartono and other scholars. It seems possible that the former was removed precisely because his presence in the project made it difficult for Nugroho to have his way. Sartono may have been more respected and influential than Nugroho within the scholarly community, and he seemed to recognize that, but that he could eject Sartono from the project in such a blatant manner indicated a different type of power play in which Nugroho proved more dominant. What stands out here is the contextual and relational nature of power play. That is, power as a capacity or ability to make a difference at least partially rests on the configuration of contending or mutually reinforcing social and individual forces, interests, and beliefs in a particular context, both temporal and spatial. As contexts change, the configuration of power may also change.

Contents and the power of scholarship

Tadhana and SNI (1975) similarly shunned the approach to history-writing that focused primarily on politics. Both adopted a multi-dimensional approach in the sense that all aspects—social, economic, cultural, and political—were given due considerations in narrative and analysis. Both were also organized chronologically and thematically wherein different aspects were discussed under each period. There was an important difference, though. Whereas the SNI allotted a particular section in each volume to aspects like economy or culture, Tadhana tried to weave these various aspects together to form a coherent narrative analysis within a section or a chapter. Simply put, the approach used for Tadhana was not only multi-dimensional; it could also be considered interdisciplinary. SNI (1975) also aspired to be interdisciplinary, but the output proved to be confined to being multi-disciplinary.

If the multi-dimensional approach was able to restrain the political intent of SNI-6 (1975) despite the uneven and rather problematic application of this approach, why was it not the case for the more cohesive Tadhana? The reason seems to be that, as already discussed, Marcos's political interest lay precisely in the coherence of Tadhana's design. Taking each volume separately, what Tadhana scholars had written were scholarly treatises unconcerned with whatever political interests Marcos had. Put together, however, they present an integrated, indigenously rooted narrative that coincided perfectly with the justificatory requirement of Marcos's vision for the New Society. Among other things, this point reinforces the idea that, regardless of the quality of scholarship, it may or may not support a particular political interest. More importantly, it suggests that the meaning of each part could be altered by the meaning of the whole, which has significant implications on how various knowledge claims may be put together to support a claim that runs contrary to their original meaning or intent.

In the case of SNI, Nugroho's political intent focused on a specific personality (Sukarno), groups (PKI, military), periods (Old and New Order), and events (G30S). The piecemeal nature of their agenda made Nugroho and his team's effort susceptible to the limits imposed by the multi-dimensional approach. To enhance the efficacy of the propaganda message, the authors of SNI-6 (1975) needed a less restricted space to characterize with ample details, their target personalities, groups or events. Towards this purpose, the narrative or story-telling approach to writing, rather than the analytic, multi-dimensional approach, was deemed more appropriate. In short, for both SNI and Tadhana, the intent and the way things were framed or organized had a bearing on whether the approach would make a politically efficacious impact or not.

Both projects elicited varying judgments from different sectors, depending partly on power differential. For Nugroho and for Tadhana scholars, such as Salazar and Tan, the output of their respective projects was scholarly, not political. However, their assessment needed concurrence from others in society. Without such support, it was like a shout in the wilderness. With the New Order regime's endorsement of the SNI as official or standard history, it stood against the contrarian assessment of scholars such as Sartono, Taufik, and Abdurrachman, who categorically declared that it failed to meet the standard of respectable scholarship. Because the regime had enormous power and control over apparatuses such as the school and the media, the SNI came to be regarded by many Indonesians as a legitimate history, not a propaganda. More discerning observers, such as scholars and informed activists, were no doubt able to identify which parts qualified as state propaganda and which ones did not. As they appeared to be a minority, however, their assessment tended to carry much less weight, at least during the New Order period. For the larger segment of the public, popular perceptions of SNI as a legitimate standard and official history defined how the project would be classified during the New Order.

It seems that one fundamental way in which power relations are constituted lies in the formation of a 'coalition of forces' that carry out the act of definition. A person's definition of things, accurate as it may be, might not coincide with that of coalesced forces. The difference reflects the power differential coming from various sources that produce the disjunction between the two. When Salazar, for instance, implied that the task of a 'good' Filipino historian was to contribute towards the efforts at writing a 'truly' nationalist history, and his participation in Tadhana project exemplified such effort, his definition of a Filipino historian's task and the meaning he attached to his participation may have been an attempt to cushion the impact of unfavorable social perception. This proposition might have held, provided, of course, that there were enough people who agreed with such a formulation. Apparently, however, not enough scholars concurred with Salazar. Most Filipino historians would readily agree that it is their task to help develop nationalist historiography, but only a handful may concede that doing it in partnership with Marcos was a legitimate way of doing so. It was the differing level of support for a contrasting definition of how things are, or should be done—the unwritten code of ethics that forbids consorting with politicians, for example—that put Salazar and other members of the Tadhana team, in unfavorable power relations vis-à-vis their critics and other observers.

Likewise, it was the government's definition of a 'standard' history text that put the SNI in a privileged position during the New Order. Being officially proclaimed as the standard, it readily assumed that authority manifested in the fact that the history textbooks used in public and even private schools, not to mention the examination questions given at the national level, were based on the SNI, at least in theory, if not exactly in practice. So long as the New Order regime was in power, it managed to form a 'coalition of forces' that made the SNI accepted by the majority. With the sharp turn of events in 1998, what used to be a minority definition of what SNI was—not an acceptable history—gained more and more adherents, raising a public clamor for its withdrawal. The battle for the definition of what standard history is, or what history should be, was a primary fixture in public discourse in the early years of post-Suharto Indonesia (van Klinken 2001).

Considering the centrality of definition in scholarly practice— defining words, terms and concepts, the relationship between variables, the mode of analysis, the standard of scholarship itself—it appears that scholarship is an essential mechanism for configuring power relations. Considering as well that history is the record of what supposedly really happened in the past, among the branches of human knowledge, history, along with science, contributes perhaps the most in the act of definition and constituting power relations. That there have been fiercely contested 'science wars' (Ashman and Barringer 2014; Ross 1996) and 'history wars' (Linenthal and Engelhardt 1996; Macintyre and Clark 2003; Nash, Crabtree, and Dunn 1997) in various countries but no 'political science wars' or 'sociology wars' seems indicative of the fundamental importance that science and history enjoy in the public sphere.

Marcos's need for and intended use of a scholarly history points to this possibility. Simply put, he wanted to establish the rightfulness of his own definition of the Philippine history. As noted in Chapter 2, he hoped for vindication and even adulation. Aware that many of his contemporaries were bitterly critical of him, he was deeply worried that the hostile responses to his initiatives would jeopardize his desired position in history. Through Tadhana, he cast his hope that the unfavorable power relations he had with his contemporaries would be reversed in the future. Marcos's case demonstrates how historical knowledge's power to define seems to serve as a fundamental constituting element in power relation, which hints at why he had a keen interest in history. Whether power relation would indeed be reversed in the future in favor of Marcos would depend largely on the shift in public perception of him as well as in the compatibility of his and of the future generation's definition of what history is and what history should be.

The idea of the power of scholars emanating from power to define seems incongruous with the common lament among scholars as to how often their scholarship is ignored and that they are not being listened to or are even being dismissed outright, as is starkly shown, for instance, in Trump's and Republicans' attitude toward scientific evidences of climate change. The upswing in the trajectory of anti-intellectualism in the United States, Europe, and Australia validates the idea of scholars' powerlessness. That said, even the most powerful nations or corporations or individuals in the world cannot dispense with the services (both actual and symbolic) of scholars or intellectuals and the institutions of learning and research that they represent. This does not mean that their definitions of things, concepts, and phenomena always take precedence over other definitions. No one has the monopoly over the power to define, particularly in the post-truth era of fake news and anti-intellectualism. Nevertheless, given the scholars' grasp of the scholarly methods, their access to empirical data, and the level of esteem that built-up through the centuries for them, it is difficult to view the scholarly community as having no power. It seems that the narrow conception of what power is effectively excludes scholarship from the domain of power relations. But beyond conceptual blindness, scholars did, and still do, have a decided advantage over non-scholars, particularly in Asia and other parts of the world, where the respect for learned persons remains firm.

In a nutshell, the existence of the academic community, the tradition of scholarship, and the institution of universities and research centers serve as potent signifiers of the 'knowability' or 'definability' of things. Despite the continuing rise of anti-intellectualism in the West, the very presence of these institutions validates and enables the act of definition to serve as a potent device for constituting power relations. The side that falls within a definition is upheld, and those who use or favor it may be empowered. Whatever is on the other side is denied or delegitimized. The definition of reality lends knowledge, especially history, enormous power, and this makes the contest for definition among competing interests expected and understandable.

The extent to which historical knowledge may have power over an individual is partly contingent on how an individual deals with history. Reacting to or negotiating with various forces in a specific environment, there are those to whom history and historical judgment matter because they believe in it of their own volition. A good example was Marcos, over whom history had power because he believed in and aspired for its favorable judgment. His dialectical relationship with history enabled it to have power over him, but it also afforded him agency, by writing (or sponsoring) history, to influence its judgment or, so he hoped. Whether, in fact, his efforts would yield positive results is beside the point. There are others, on the other hand, who were conditioned or forced to believe by pressures from the state or society, more broadly. The Indonesian public under the New Order, as well as those associated with the PKI and their families, who were marginalized, ostracized, and repressed during this era, belong to this category. However, even among the PKI-associated groups or individuals, there were those who, by sheer force of their personal convictions, refused to be cowed down (for example,

Proletariyati 2002). They believed in what they knew had happened, notwithstanding the publicly accepted history during the New Order. In other words, the power of knowledge (and the scholars who embody it) rests, on the one hand, on the constellation of social forces that come together to empower it and, on the other hand, the individual knower's position in the power-differential scale. An individual who agrees, or is conditioned to agree, with socially defined knowledge, in effect further empowers it. On the other hand, those who assert their personal power and cling to their contrarian beliefs are likely to have their 'truths' dismissed by the rest of society under various names: propaganda, apostasy, personal memory, gossip, idle talk, lies, etc. The lack of power of individuals or small groups made their 'truth' not credible or acceptable. As noted earlier, the change in power relations during the reformasi era endowed a certain level of respectability or believability to what used to be easily dismissed by the New Order regime as lies, propaganda, or gossip. The movement of *pelurusan sejarah* (straightening history) during the post-New Order helped make this shift possible (Adam 2007; Cf. Karsono 2005).

While the flight of trust has indeed occurred away from the New Order brand of history, it appears that a sizable number of Indonesians remain faithful to at least some crucial parts of it. The strong public backlash against changing the long-held interpretation of PKI-related historical events and the failure of the Truth and Reconciliation Commission on the mass killings of 1965–66 may indicate, to an extent, this faithfulness (Sulistiyanto and Setyasiswanto 2016). For Indonesians, who have, for one reason or another, deeply internalized demonic images of the PKI and its supposedly enduring 'latent danger' (*bahaya laten*), neither the heightened conditioning by the media nor legislation by the Parliament, nor even rigorous historical methodology, may be able to change their view of the New Order version of history. From the viewpoint of those across the political divide, such as the *reformasi* activists, the 'truths' the government upholds are plain lies or propaganda. The pro-New Order groups, on the other hand, view the 'truths' of the reformasi activists in the same way: as distortions of history. This is not to reiterate the old question of objectivity vs. relativism but to highlight the complex and shifting power relations that define the shape and status of knowledge. Also, this does not mean that good or rigorous scholarship does not matter. This remains the scholars' Holy Grail and a source of their power. What needs to be underlined is that scholars and scholarship—rigorous or not—are among the various sources of power that compete or converge to define what may be regarded in society as acceptable knowledge, history or otherwise.

The scholars' ability to make a difference, or their power, comes from two primary sources: their expertise and their standing in society. The first emanates from the power that the entire scholarly community has accumulated through the ages, and whoever becomes a scholar partakes in that. In Bourdieu's parlance, it is the symbolic power from intellectual expertise or academic credentials (Brubaker 1985, 755–758). The second is derived from the alignment of social powers, one indicator of which is the level of esteem received from the people. In the case of Marcos, it was largely on account of the first that he sought the service of the scholars. The New Order, on the other hand, seemed interested in both. Herein probably lies the reason for the difference in the reception of the two projects. Marcos and Tadhana authors overlooked the fact that, to maximize the influence of scholarship, the two sources of its power should be tapped. Expertise was not enough; favorable social perception of such expertise was also required. That Tadhana was rejected offhand despite its scholarly contents indicate instances in which perception precedes expertise. Favorable perception is an outcome of social alignment that enjoins the scholars to fit into socially defined expectations, which include upholding objectivity or impartiality. Whenever scholars are seen violating this injunction—by consorting, for instance, with the politically powerful—negative perceptions may be generated, and the power of the scholars may be diminished. The extent of the diminution of power depends on the depth of expertise as well as on the perception of the gravity of the social offence committed. The contrasting fates of Salazar, Sartono, and Nugroho illustrate this point.

Salazar's involvement in Tadhana project adversely affected, to an extent, his reputation within the community of Filipino scholars. Despite his creditable contribution, which made Tadhana a notable contribution to Philippine historiography, for fellow scholars, his ideas appeared suspicious and insignificant within the community so long as they were within Tadhana's confine. The Marcos signature ensured that Tadhana would be dismissed by many as mere propaganda. However, upon leaving the project and returning full time to the university, Salazar further developed similar ideas and approaches, and they flourished in the succeeding decades to become the bedrock of the *Pantayo school*, one the most dominant schools in Philippine historiography, perhaps since the 1990s (Reyes 2002, 2008). His impeccable academic credentials; his remarkable intelligence that even his detractors acknowledged, if sometimes grudgingly; and his very strong personality enabled him to rise above the political fallout from his participation in Tadhana. He remained bitterly criticized by some, but he exemplified nonetheless the case of a scholar who had a huge reservoir of power accruing from expertise (intellectual capital, in Bourdieu's term) that was huge enough to offset the hitherto unfavorable socio-political alignment.

Sartono shared with Salazar a deep wellspring of power that derives from expertise. In terms of personality, however, they are very different. Sartono was gentle, soft-spoken, well-liked, and respected by fellow Indonesian historians. This perception contributes enormously to his favorable social standing. Whatever criticisms the SNI project received hardly affected his reputation. The widespread information about his supposed withdrawal from the project could also have been a factor as it heightened public perception of his desire to protect his integrity as a scholar. Yet, even if he had not withdrawn, his stature in the community seemed secure, not just because of his academic credentials but also because of his personality and integrity that perhaps almost everyone recognized. His power as a scholar, in short, was strengthened both by expertise and by favorable social perceptions.

Nugroho was a different story. He attracted diverse opinions, and his actions were quite ambiguous. Critics often pointed to the mediocrity of his scholarly outputs, but for many of his admirers, including former students and colleagues, he was a scholar of respectable standing. For them, he was decent, intelligent and patriotic. In the wider society during the New Order, it was difficult to approximate his overall social standing, but I hazard a guess that admirers seemed to outnumber critics by a perceptible margin. In the post-Suharto period, with the changed political atmosphere, critics significantly increased, but admirers by no means disappeared. The contrasting social alignment for and against Nugroho, as well as the temporariness and temporality of such alignments, renders it difficult to pin down the configuration of his power as a scholar.

Nugroho, thus, stands as a metaphor for the complexity, mutuality, or inseparability, and inscrutability, of power-knowledge relations. Often skating between two seemingly contradictory things, he cruises through the boundaries between scholarship and politics, self and national interest, the credible and the suspicious, the moral and the immoral, mere gossips and valid knowledge claims. He defies straightforward characterization. Any effort to paint him in black or white, or to define exactly what constitutes the power-knowledge nexus, is bound to yield uncertainties or tentative results. If there is anyone among those involved in the two projects who could personify most clearly the calculus of power-knowledge relations, it appeared to be Nugroho.

References

Adam, Asvi Warman. 2007. *Pelurusan Sejarah Indonesia* (Straightening Indonesian History) Ed. Rev. Yogyakarta: Ombak.
Ashman, Keith, and Phillip Barringer, eds. 2014. *After the Science Wars: Science and the Study of Science*. Florence: Routledge.
Bourdieu, Pierre. 1989a. "Social Space and Symbolic Power." *Sociological Theory* 7 (1): 14–25.
———. 1989b. "The Corporatism of the Universal: The Role of Intellectuals in the Modern World." *Telos* (81): 99–110.
Brubaker, Rogers. 1985. "Rethinking Classical Theory: The Sociological Vision of Pierre Bourdieu." *Theory and Society* 14 (6): 745–775.
Chang, Yu-tzung, Yunhan Chu, and Chong-min Park. 2007. "Authoritarian Nostalgia in Asia." *Journal of Democracy* 18 (3): 66–80. doi:10.1353/jod.2007.0043.

Frederick, William, and Soeri Soeroto, eds. 1982. *Pemahaman Sejarah Indonesia: Sebelum Dan Sesudah Revolusi*. Jakarta: Lembaga Penelitian Pendidikan dan Penerangan Ekonomi dan Sosial.
Karsono, Sony. 2005. "Setting History Straight? Indonesian Historiography in the New Order." MA Thesis, Ohio University.
Kartodirdjo, Sartono. 2001. *Indonesian Historiography*. Yogyakarta: Penerbit Kanisius.
Kompas. 2004. "Penulisan Sejarah Indonesia Masih Menunggu Berbagai Masukan Baru (Indonesian Historiography Still Awaits for New Contributions)." September 6.
Linenthal, Edward, and Tom Engelhardt, eds. 1996. *History Wars: The Enola Gay and Other Battles for the American Past*. 1st ed. New York: Metropolitan Books.
MacIntyre, Stuart, and Anna Clark. 2003. *The History Wars*. Carlton, VIC: Melbourne University Press.
Nash, Gary, Charlotte Crabtree, and Ross Dunn. 1997. *History on Trial: Culture Wars and the Teaching of the Past*. 1st ed. New York: A.A. Knopf.
Nichterlein, Sue. 1974. "Historicism and Historiography in Indonesia." *History and Theory* 13 (3): 253–272.
Proletariyati, Ribka Tjiptaning. 2002. *Aku bangga jadi anak PKI* (I am Proud of Being a Child of PKI). Jakarta: Cipta Lestari.
Resink, G. 1968. "Between the Myths: From Colonial to National Historiography." In *Indonesia's History between the Myths: Essays in Legal History and Historical Theory*, 15–25. The Hague: W. van Hoeve Publishers, Ltd.
Reyes, Portia. 2002. "Pantayong Pananaw and Bagong Kasaysayan in the New Filipino Historiography: A History of Filipino Historiography as an History of Ideas." PhD diss., University of Bremen.
———. 2008. "Fighting Over a Nation: Theorizing a Filipino Historiography." *Postcolonial Studies*, 11 (3): 241–258.
Ross, Andrew, ed. 1996. *Science Wars*. Durham: Duke University Press.
Rubio, Fernando Domínguez, and Patrick Baert. 2012. "Politics of Knowledge: An Introduction." In *The Politics of Knowledge*, edited by Fernando Domínguez Rubio and Patrick Baert, 1–10. London and New York: Routledge.
Soedjatmoko. 1958. "Merintis Masa Hari Depan (Pioneering the future)." In Seminar Sejarah: Laporan Lengkap Atjara I Dan II Tentang Konsepsi Filsafat Sedjarah Nasional dan Periodisasi Sedjarah Indonesia (History Seminar: Complete Report of Sessions 1 & 2 about Conceptualizing Philosophy of National History and Periodization of Indonesian History), Seri II, 35–53. Yogyakarta: Universitas Gadjah Mada.
———. 1960. An Approach to Indonesian History: Towards an Open Future. Ithaca, NY: Modern Indonesia Project, Cornell University.
———. 1965. "Indonesian Historian and His Time." In *Introduction to Indonesian Historiography*, 405–415. Ithaca, NY: Cornell University Press.
Sulistiyanto, Priyambudi, and Sentot Setyasiswanto. 2016. "Still Seeking Truth and Reconciliation for the 1965 Victims: Is It Possible?" In *Asia-Pacific between Conflict and Reconciliation*, edited by Dong-Choon Kim, Maria Palme, and Phillip Tolliday, 69–86. Göttingen: Vandenhoeck & Ruprecht. doi:10.13109/9783666560255.69.
van Klinken, Gerry. 2001. "The Battle for History After Suharto: Beyond Sacred Dates, Great Men, and Legal Milestones." *Critical Asian Studies* 33 (3): 323–350. doi:10.1080/14672710122604.

Wirjosuparto, Sutjipto. 1982. "Prapanca Sebagai Penulis Sedjarah" (Prapanca as a Historian). In *Pemahaman sejarah Indonesia: Sebelum dan Sesudah Revolusi* (Understanding Indonesian History: Before and After the Revolution), edited by William Frederick and Soeri Soeroto. Jakarta: LP3ES.

Yamin, Mohammad. 1951. *6000 Tahun Sang Merah Putih* (6000 Years of Red and White). Djakarta: Siguntang.

Conclusion

The PhD thesis upon which this book is based was originally titled "When Clio Meets the Titans: State-Scholar Relations in Indonesia and the Philippines." In Greek mythology, Clio is the muse of history. The muses signify the lofty aspirations of the arts and intellect. They represent dignity, refinement, gentleness, knowledge, wisdom, eloquence, and service. They stand for what is good, truthful and beautiful. The Titans, on the other hand, are a race of gods who ruled the cosmos for a long time. They personify many forms of power: natural, political, and personal, among others. Their reign ended when the group led by Zeus defeated them. The Titans were very powerful, yet not omnipotent.

What happens when truth and goodness interact with supreme power and self-interest? It is one of those ancient philosophical questions whose fundamental import lies beyond the abstract, forged as it is in the empirical complexity of everyday life. As common reactions to SNI and Tadhana projects indicate, the encounters between actors who embody these abstractions tend to be simplified into an idea of one side manipulating or co-opting the other. The notion of 'official history' encapsulates this tendency. What tags along with the label 'official' is the comfort of knowing whose interests this type of history reflects or represents. It misleads for the same reason. This comforting presumption effaces whatever ambiguity or complexity there might be in official histories. It also denies or downplays the agency of scholars in knowledge production. The stale and imbalanced picture of otherwise dynamic relationships leads to a missed opportunity for examining what makes it dynamic and what such dynamism implies. After all, to pursue the metaphor further, Clio's mother was a Titan. Titans' blood ran through her veins. So, the separation or opposition between the two—politics and scholarship, power and knowledge—appears contrived. Be that as it may, the popularity in the academic community, and society at large, of the "liberal view" which posits this oppositional relationship is persistent. What has been elided or concealed by it, and what price have we been paying for holding onto this dichotomy? Who benefit and who are disempowered by such conceptualization? More importantly, how might power–knowledge relations be reconceptualized to be politically and ethically more efficacious for the interest of the truly marginalized? These are big and potentially inconvenient questions. Given its limited scope, this study cannot fully address them. What it hopes to do is offer some important insights generated through comparative analysis of the cases examined here. At the same time, it seeks to keep those key questions in view as areas for further exploration.

The emphasis on the primacy of contexts, as well as the agency or power of scholars and scholarship in this study, go hand in hand with its call to push the logic of power/knowledge to its conclusion. The premise behind this call rests on the need for full transparency of all the sources of power that make knowledge production possible. As I explain in the Preface, this is a way to help minimize the possibility of well-intentioned scholarship being used for unscrupulous purposes. Foucault (1980) and many other scholars have long emphasized power/knowledge, and the idea proved to be very influential in critical humanities and social sciences. But, as discussed in Introduction, even some of those who did the most to advance power/knowledge analytics proved hesitant to push the logic of this relationship to its conclusion. Why this hesitation and what can be done to overcome it?

The lack of adequate understanding of the nature of power and its relationship to knowledge production is, in my view, a major factor. Scholars in general and those involved in Tadhana and SNI in particular are not oblivious to their power. In themselves, they know power intuitively as something they 'possess,' and they act it out in their daily life. They enjoy the privileges and perks that go with it. Despite the mounting anti-intellectualism in the 'West' that became pronounced even before the Trump era, the intellectual bedrock that holds the very foundation of civilizations across the world renders it likely that scholars and other knowledge workers will remain important and, in a particular sense, powerful. However, scholars and the public in general have not been conditioned to view scholars or scholarship as powerful. Including those who took part in Tadhana and SNI, scholars tend to hesitate to label what they do or what they have as a form of power. Some of them may admit to being influential or prominent but coy to admit they are powerful. More than semantics, it seems the connotative difference is symptomatic of how people have grown accustomed to the restricted definition of power and the political, which effectively excludes knowledge production within the scope where the idea of power operates. It may also be a testament to how deep-seated scholars' anxiety toward the notion of power in general and state power in particular has become, perhaps due to the morally adverse connotations that gather around the notion of power. Bourdieu's use of the term 'capital' to refer to various enabling mechanisms, which in some sense may also be rightly called power, is, in my view, an exemplary illustration of this anxiety. I invoked in the Introduction Foucault's broad-based and capillary-like conception of power as dispersed and both coercive and creative or enabling. The reason for this lies precisely in my desire to address this concern.

Conclusion

So, what we have is a situation in which scholars may in fact be powerful, yet they refuse to acknowledge it openly. If we follow the dictum that those who have power must also bear responsibility, scholars who are mindless of their power can hardly care to be accountable. The public, who do not regard scholars as powerful, would not demand accountability. This lack of a sense of responsibility leaves scholars and scholarship liable to causing harm in their desire to do good, by lending inadvertent support to unscrupulous political interests, even if, or because, they mean well. It also means that they may end up being more easily appropriated for purposes they expressly oppose. The naiveté of some of the Tadhana scholars in thinking that the farther away from the Marcos years they worked, the more politically 'safe' they were illustrates this point. Had they been forthright about the power of the scholarly class to which they belong, they would have understood better that it was such power that Marcos was desirous of, and that their mere participation in the project, highly credentialed scholars as they were, lent it at least a patina of scholarly validation. This was the case, regardless of which period in history they wrote about. Also, in aspiring to be rigorous and accurate, many scholars, like those who took part in SNI and Tadhana, believe that they were being non-, anti-, or apolitical, that they were merely doing their jobs as scholars. They seem unaware, possibly not blissfully but 'knowingly,' that what makes knowledge useful and liable to politically motivated appropriations, such as what Marcos had in mind for the use of Tadhana, was the semblance or aura of truth enabled by perception of rigor and impartiality.

The scholars' disavowal of power and their anxiety towards relativism and its concomitant push for objectivity or impartiality are well-meaning. Such disavowal has deep roots in the centuries of struggle to overcome obscurantism, superstition, oppression, inequality, and injustice. It is meant to uphold and help realize the full potentials of the supposedly free-willed human beings. Part of the Enlightenment traditions nurtured the liberal scholarly ethos that assumes the ability of humans to know reality in its truest essence. Also presupposed is the fundamental goodness of knowing and that knowledge is key to a continuous progress both in material and moral senses. By drawing dichotomies between scholarship, ethical responsibility, objectivity, reason, and knowledge, on the one side, and politics, subjectivity, emotion, and power, on the other, the liberal tradition sought to enhance, promote, and protect human welfare and freedom against any form of tyranny by absolutizing one side (supposedly the 'good' side) against the other (Fuller 2018, 25–37; Rubio and Baert 2012). As the absolutist entities, like God upon whom everything used to be anchored, were exiled to the periphery, if not to oblivion, they were replaced by a secular absolutism of liberal assumptions of the ability, rights, and freedom of individuals. Herein lies the crux of contradictions in liberal scholarly tradition. The optimistic visions of human nature and the future of humanity cannot but contend with the finite and unequally distributed resources, including power, on the ground. This optimistic vision stands in tension as well with the inherently ambiguous and possibly zero-sum aspects of the exercise of individual freedom.

These contradictions bedevil power-knowledge analytics on various levels. At the most basic, many scholars refuse to see knowledge as power-driven because they define knowledge as simply what is true, and what is true supposedly does not depend on who has a greater power, who because of presumed negative attributes of power is believed to manipulate things in their favor, and thus produce false claims. Also, having taken knowing as a fundamental good, they treat knowledge offhand as among the key solutions to inequality and many other problems in society. Again with the supposed negative or manipulative nature of power, they find it difficult to imagine knowledge being defined by power. The reason why I opt in Introduction for a broadly-encompassing and (hopefully) more morally-neutral definitions of power and knowledge is precisely to address the problems emanating from the use of biased and restricted formulation of the key concepts.

Another reason lies in fear that it could destabilize the very fabric of the moral and social order. Power/knowledge supposedly risks plunging society into anarchy or nihilism by depriving any scholarly or political effort a solid platform to stand on. The supposed 'fascination with fascism' of intellectuals identified with poststructuralism, such as Heidegger, Paul de Man, and Nietzsche, is often used to exemplify the danger as well as the moral and political bankruptcy of the anti-foundational philosophies which inform the power-knowledge analytics (Wolin 2006). In the same vein, critics claim that it tends to disarm well-meaning individuals in their struggle against social inequality and injustice (Moore and Muller 1999). How can 'relativism-minded' sociologists, Brown rhetorically asks, fight social ills by saying, "Yes, all theories are equally good; they merely serve different social interests"? In Brown's view, "relativism...tend(s) to produce quietism and inaction rooted in a sense of hopelessness and pointlessness" (Brown 1989, vii). Given these apprehensions, one may argue that less, not more power–knowledge relations, and retreat from, rather than a push to its logical conclusion, is the solution.

In my view, the fear of anarchy that is supposed to emanate from pushing the power-knowledge analytics to its conclusion is unfounded. The reason is simple: existential reality demands that various sources of powers will always align in accordance to an equilibrium compatible with the convergence of unequal, ever-changing, and competing interests. The process of alignment and re-alignment will be driven by differentiated access (depending on the structure of society) to the social, economic, political, and cultural capitals. This situation precludes a perfectly fluid or anarchic environment and rules out, for instance, Brown's concern that all theories would appear 'equally good.' A particular arrangement or network of power relations (including those within the scholarly field) will emerge more dominant than others, lending particular theories at least the appearance of greater acceptability than other theories, for the given context.

188 Conclusion

More important from the ethical standpoint, the fear of plunging into anarchy appears to have long served as a bogeyman that conveniently conceals the self-interests of the scholarly class. It is by drumbeating the fear of anarchy, among other means, that the scholars have rationalized and, at the same time, covered up their power and privileged position in the scheme of things. The *raison d'être* for this study precisely lies on shedding light on this analytic black spot. Rather than weakening the moral and political standpoint from which to address inequality, injustice, and poverty, as commonly believed, pushing the logic of knowledge/power, so I contend, can instead help strengthen efforts along this line. This may be achieved by rendering transparent the insidious partnership between scholars (and all other knowledge workers) and political power holders that enable, sustain, or intensify inequality, injustice, and poverty. With the matrix of the power-knowledge nexus laid bare before the public, an informed public sphere will be in a better position to decide which and whose knowledge claims deserve to be upheld. In the end, not only would the scholars be spared from doing inadvertent harm in their desire to do good; much more importantly, the public would also be rescued from the adverse consequences.

There is a need to rethink seriously the liberal imperatives that informed much of the progressive or critical scholarship in social sciences and the humanities. The situation in the previous centuries, when it was clear who or what liberal aspirations were up against, no longer holds today, when power relations is so much more multi-layered, crisscrossing, and shifting, determined as it is by specificities of contexts, as this study highlights. Serious rethinking of the liberal ethos in scholarship has long been mooted, but the rise of US President Donald Trump and Philippine President Rodrigo Duterte offers an excellent opportunity to revisit this issue. Trump and Duterte are known for flaunting fake news as alternative facts. They tend to brand claims they do not agree with as fake news. Situations like these are often viewed as constituting a new height in the supposedly *posties*-induced (such as poststructuralism, postmodernism, and postcolonialism) relativization and bastardization of knowledge. What is often missed is that the potency of the Trump-Duterte 'lies' resides, among other sources, in the widely shared liberal assumption about the nature of knowledge, which posits that it is a container of truth, not dependent on power relations, as the *posties* have long insisted. For Trump and Duterte supporters, their idols' claims are not lies but facts denied or subjugated by the 'errant' media or the liberal establishments, including scholars. Trump and Duterte are lionized for their supposed courage to say the 'suppressed truths.' Responses have focused on criticizing and fact-checking Trump and Duterte, continually painting them as inveterate liars and morally flawed. Given the strong support they still enjoy, one wonders what it is with their supporters, or what it is with critics, that makes things challenging to comprehend. It seems the claim to intellectual and moral ascendancy of liberal scholarly tradition, upon which fact-checking is premised, has already been exposed as yet another political standpoint, as one of those 'power games,' to use Steve Fuller's (2018) apt terminology.

It must be noted, however, that not all scholarship is regarded by Trump and Duterte and their supporters as untrustworthy. Trump, for instance, has conveniently used or misused scholarly work—such as that produced by Massachusetts Institute of Technology (MIT) on climate change—that includes details or ideas supportive of his position on, say, the United States' withdrawal from the Paris climate agreement (Temple 2017). For many, Trump's declaration that there are 'fine scholars' on 'both sides' of the climate change debates ominously flagged his intent to justify his selective use of evidence in support of his preferred position. I do not wish to invalidate the critics' concerns over this matter, as I personally share them, but what needs highlighting here are the often-missed implications of Trump's and Duterte's behavior.

Just like Nugroho and Tadhana scholars who were labeled as 'intellectual prostitutes' or 'academic mercenaries' and expelled by fellow scholars and other critics from their moral universe, it is easy to dismiss Trump and Duterte and their supporters as morally depraved and stupid. For the purpose of this study, I intend not to do so for the simple reason that it is analytically unproductive. For the record, as a liberal myself, I personally do not agree with much of Trump's and Duterte's demeanor and many of their declarations. However, I believe I understand the roots in liberal traditions of the frustrations that made so many people supportive of leaders like them. It is not my intent to morally or politically defend Trump and Duterte, nor do I wish to undermine their critics, whose right to castigate them I uphold and respect. I am aware though that despite my intentions, I end up sounding as though I defend and side with them against their critics. This is collateral consequence of my analytic choice. I believe that the stakes in this whole analytic exercise are far more significant than scoring points against Trump, Duterte, and their supporters. Convinced of the need to re-orient and revitalize progressive scholarship to make it truly empowering for the people it seeks to help, I believe that my analytic decision is a carefully calculated risk. Whatever unintended adverse consequences it brings about drives home the point that any analytic decision may have a corresponding political consequence. Analysis is double-edged, and its impact could be inherently ambiguous. By stating thus, I wish not to naturalize it and absolve myself of accountability. The idea is to highlight the need for scholars to pay more attention to, and embrace, this nature of knowledge and analysis. In opting for this analytic tack, I am fully aware of my analytico-political interests in the whole exercise, and I bear full personal responsibility for whatever collateral consequences my decision brings.

My analytic position is that judging Trump and Duterte in the usual manner of underscoring how bereft of rationality, integrity, and morality they are will merely affirm one side of morals and politics over another, leftist over rightist or centrist, or liberals over conservatives, to put things in overly simplified terms. One politics is merely replaced by another politics, leading to a political stalemate. Stuck in the liberal view of the opposition of scholarship–politics relations, the analysis is paralyzed. The Trump/Duterte phenomenon seems to me an exemplary opportunity to break this impasse by taking a close look at how knowledge is in fact being produced and used on a daily basis and what role power has in the process. Trump's brazen use of his power to define what is to be considered valid knowledge, particularly on climate change, can only shock many people, particularly scientists and scholars. But rather than taking it as idiosyncratic or exceptional to leaders like Trump, I take it as illustration of the logic of what happens on a day-to-day basis as we—liberals, leftists, rightists, centrists, or whatever—'shop' in the marketplace of circulating ideas for knowledge which is supportive of our interests or positions. Others that we do not like or do not agree with, we ignore or dismiss as untrue. What the likes of Trump and Duterte do is make this day-to-day, subtle process of producing/consuming knowledge formal and explicit. Doing so lays bare, in all honesty, the process and actors that install a particular network of power, following Latour (1986), to define what gets to be considered as valid knowledge. Trump is not a scholar, but what he does parallels in functional terms, if in a short-circuited manner, what the scholarly community studiously undergoes in producing knowledge. Despite the long, intricate process, it may not necessarily be the (real) 'truth' that is upheld as knowledge but what scholars regard as true or accurate based on acceptable procedures. In short, at the end of the day, it is the power of the scholars or collectively the scholarly community that decides. The logistics of power relations are different in the two cases, Trump's power vs. scholars' power, but the logic is essentially the same. This fundamental similarity in the logic of knowledge production is one that is often missed. Among other things, figures like Trump, Duterte, Nugroho, and Tadhana scholars embody the logic which the liberal view of scholarship–politics relations has blindsided us from.

What are the possible implications? First, there is a need to re-calibrate scholars' preoccupations, which conventionally focus on getting things empirically accurate, conceptually clear, theoretically relevant, methodologically adequate, and analytically logical. These things will remain important as mainstays of what scholars do. But for scholars who deliberately seek to pursue progressive aspirations of empowering the marginalized, more attention needs to be given to the pragmatics of knowledge: how is knowledge actually produced and used in various contexts, by whom, for what purpose, and with what effects, both actual and potential? A cartography of the types and sources of power that enable a particular body of knowledge to be produced and consumed by different groups in various context and for whatever purposes, needs to be carried out. Various streams of progressive scholarships, such as postcolonialism, cultural studies, and critical discourse analysis, have already been doing this in one way or another. As creditable as their efforts are, they can be made more efficacious via a more comprehensive and systematic approach. Certainly, it is a huge undertaking, which unfortunately I cannot explicate here. I would just like to note that in this undertaking, Bruno Latour's (2005) ideas and approaches, including the Actor-Network Theory (ANT), may prove to be very useful. Whatever forms this effort takes, pushing the logic of power/knowledge to its conclusion is essential. This would allow us to deal with the contradictions that inhere in many progressivist approaches such as postcolonial theory, rendering them vulnerable to charges of hypocrisy or critiquing others for the sins they are also guilty of. They would also cease to reinforce the myth that it takes only the 'right' kind of scholarship to neutralize power/knowledge. As Foucault and others remind us, power/knowledge may be a natural property of knowledge production and power relations. We can only deal with it, not transcend it, and one good way to do so is to lay it bare for everyone to see. Continual mapping is crucial as knowledge may be reconstituted, not merely transmitted, at every moment of actual use. It is in these moments, rather than at the time of original conception by scholars (or any knowledge producer), that interpretations with a material impact on the lives of common people get formed. What is entailed in this cartography of power/knowledge is a project worth pursuing in the future.

Second, what goes with the emphasis on the agency and power of scholars and scholarship is the accompanying demand for full accountability. Currently, accountability is confined within the community of scholars. The main concern is the extent to which one observes the acceptable protocols for data gathering, analysis, and reporting, and whether the corresponding ethical procedures were carried out properly. This is what gets satisfied by the common demand for self-reflexivity among critical scholars in the humanities and social sciences. But being self-reflexive in this manner may not be enough. Full accountability demands awareness of the position of the scholarly community in the scheme of things and of what roles and impact it has had on individual scholars and the community at large. It requires mindfulness of the types or forms of power that the scholars as a class enjoy. This power needs to be factored into analysis and eschew the tendency to treat scholarly practices as neutral or beyond power relations. This carries profound implications, not just on analytic practices but also on the ethics of doing scholarship. This subject matter requires a lengthy explanation, and thus I reserve it for another paper. Suffice to note that once we acknowledge the power or the fundamentally political character of scholarship, we may have to rethink practically everything we do as scholars.

Finally, a full accounting of the power/knowledge nexus entails acknowledging the scholarly viewpoint as one among many possible political standpoints. It must be included among those that need to be mapped out. If progressive scholarship wishes to be true to its vision to serve the interests of the truly marginalized, it must be honest about its own politics and assume a meta-analytic position. Doing so will allow it to serve as a monitoring device that renders transparent the various ways in which knowledge and powers from all ideological standpoints—rightist, centrist (including scholarship), leftist—interact with and affect people on the ground. This way, there is a greater chance to create a transparent and informed public sphere that is conducive to a more peaceful, equal, compassionate, and prosperous life.

References

Brown, James Robert. 1989. *The Rational and the Social*. Philosophical Issues in Science. London: Routledge.

Foucault, Michel. 1980. *Power/Knowledge: Selected Interviews and Other Writings, 1972–1977.* Edited by Colin Gordon. New York: Pantheon Books.

Fuller, Steve. 2018. *Post-Truth: Knowledge as a Power Game*. New York: Anthem Press.

Latour, Bruno. 1986. "The Powers of Association." In *Power, Action and Belief: A New Sociology of Knowledge?*, edited by John Law. London: Routledge & Kegan Paul.

———. 2005. *Reassembling the Social: An Introduction to Actor-Network Theory*. Clarendon Lectures in Management Studies. Oxford and New York: Oxford University Press.

Moore, R, and J. Muller. 1999. "The Discourse of 'Voice' and the Problem of Knowledge and Identity in the Sociology of Education." *British Journal of Sociology of Education* 20 (2): 189–206.

Rubio, Fernando Domínguez, and Patrick Baert. 2012. "Politics of Knowledge: An Introduction." In *The Politics of Knowledge*, 1–10. London and New York: Routledge.

Temple, James. 2017. "Trump Misused MIT Research in Reasons for Ditching Climate Deal." *MIT Technology Review*, June 1.

Wolin, Richard. 2006. *The Seduction of Unreason: The Intellectual Romance with Fascism from Nietzsche to Postmodernism*. Princeton, NJ: Princeton University Press.

Glossary

Abangan   Nominal Muslims who follow a form of Islam that is mixed with Hindu-Buddhist and animistic influences.

Asal bapak senang   Indonesian for 'so long as the boss is happy'; attitude or mentality that predisposes one to value form over substance to please the boss.

Bagong Kasaysaysan   Tagalog term for 'New History'; a movement that sought to employ new approaches and perspectives in historical writing.

Barangay   Tagalog word which means a village or a settlement consisting of dozens or a hundred families; social, economic and political unit during the pre-Hispanic and Spanish Periods.

Biro Khusus   Indonesian for 'special bureau'; a clandestine group tasked with infiltrating the military and propagating communist teachings.

Buku babon   Indonesian for 'master or original text'; a book that serves as the basis of another book or whose importance makes it a fundamental reference.

Caciquism   Spanish-derived term for the rule of the local chiefs or bosses.

Compadre   A word of Spanish origin. In the Philippines, it refers to the person (male) who served as the sponsor, or godfather, in the baptism of one's child.

Doktorandus   Dutch-influenced post-Bachelor's degree in the old educational system in Indonesia.

EDSA Revolution   The uprising that toppled Marcos in 1986.

Ethical Policy   An ambitious program promulgated by the Dutch colonial government in Indonesia starting in the early 1900s.

Filipinization   The program to replace with Filipinos the American officials in colonial government.

Filipino Heritage   A ten-volume encyclopedia of the Philippines, a project that was almost contemporary with Tadhana.

Frailocracy   A term often used to refer to the rule of the friars in the Philippines during the Spanish Period; another term is friarocracy.

Hamlyn Group   An Australian publishing company that financed the Filipino Heritage Project.

194 Glossary

Ilustrados Educated Filipinos during the Spanish Period in Philippine history.

Indonesiasentrisme Indonesian for an Indonesia-centric perspective in historiography.

Istruktural In Indonesian historiography, it refers to the structural or multi-dimensional approach.

Katipunan Secret revolutionary society founded in 1892 in Manila, which led the revolution in 1896.

La Liga Filipina Spanish term which meant 'The Philippine League,' a short-lived organization founded by Rizal in 1892.

Lubang Buaya Indonesian for 'crocodile hole.' It is a village south of Halim Airbase in Jakarta; it became famous as the place (a well) where the bodies of abducted generals were dumped.

Malacañang The President's official residence in the Philippines.

Manila Times One of the national daily newspapers in the Philippines.

Martial Law Marcos proclaimed martial law in September 1972 to prolong his stay in power.

Nasakom A doctrine developed by Sukarno who attempted to synthesize nationalism, religion, and communism.

Pancasila State ideology in Indonesia; literally Five Principles.

Pantayong Pananaw Tagalog term for 'From-us-for-us Perspective,' one of the dominant schools of Philippine historiography.

Pemuda Rakyat People's Youth, one of the organizations affiliated with the Communist Party of Indonesia.

Pre-Hispanic Period In Philippine history, it refers to the time before the Spaniards arrived in 1521 or 1565.

Propagandists Group of young educated Filipinos in Spain and the Philippines who campaigned in the 1880s for reforms in the Philippines.

Prosesuil In Indonesian historiography, it refers to the narrative, processual or chronological approach to writing history.

Reform Movement Another term for the movement created by the Propagandists (see above).

Santri Devout Muslims, following forms of Islam that are fairly strictly based on the Koran.

Sejarah Indonesian word for 'history.'

Sejarah Nasional Indonesia (SNI) Title of book; National History of Indonesia

Sejarawan murni Indonesian for 'pure historian'; a rhetorical term that sets a marker of qualitative difference between historians who were well trained in methods and those who were not.

Serangan Umum Indonesian for 'General Offensive,' a landmark event in the struggle against the Dutch (1 March 1949) whereby the Republican forces carried out a concerted attack on Dutch-controlled Yogyakarta and held it for six hours

Sikolohiyang Pilipino Tagalog for 'Filipino Psychology,' a school of thoughts in Psychology that upholds indigenous perspectives.

Syariah Islamic law.

Sumpah Pemuda Youth Oath or pledge for unity and national identity made by the participants in the youth congress in Indonesia in 1928.

Tadhana Tagalog word which means 'fate' or 'destiny'.

Tripartite view In Philippine historiography, it refers to the condition during and division between the period before, during, and after colonization.

1896 Revolution A landmark event in Philippine history; the revolution against Spain.

Index

Abercrombie, Nicholas 5
Academia/academic 11, 79, 105; community 178, 184; credentials 62, 170, 180, 181; history/historian 2, 101, 108; mercenaries 173, 189
accountability 13, 18, 109, 113, 186, 189, 191
Aceh, Acehnese 26, 28, 130, 167
Achmad Djajadiningrat 32, 33
Actor-Network Theory 191
ADHIKA 36, 37
Adrian Lapian 34, 35, 109–111, 164
Africa 4, 25, 53, 101, 104
Agoncillo, Teodoro 4, 26, 32–35, 44, 45, 48, 49, 61, 63, 73–77, 79, 80, 82, 83, 90, 91, 93, 94, 96, 97, 171
Aguinaldo, Emilio 83, 90
ahistorical 152, 158
aksi sepihak or unilateral action 134
Alamsjah 157
Alexander Robertson 57
Alfonso, Oscar 44, 93
Alip, Eufronio 34, 75
Almonte, Jose 50
Althusser, Louis 5
Alzona, Encarnacion 34, 35
America 4, 9, 25–29, 31, 33, 35, 70, 75, 79, 84, 85, 154, 193
Amsterdam 33, 34, 39, 100, 101
analytical constipation xiii, xiv
Angkor 70, 72
anti-colonial 4, 25, 26, 28, 29, 44, 55, 77, 84, 91
anti-foundational 187
anti-intellectualism 178, 185
antiquarian 109
Anwas 135
Apilado, Digna 33, 35

apolitical 3, 12, 18, 171, 173, 186
apologist 101
archaeology 35, 69, 93
archives 56, 57, 78
Aria Hoesein Djajadiningrat 99
Ariel Heryanto 30, 31
Ariwiadi 105, 135, 140, 157
art 28, 40, 44, 47, 53, 54, 54, 134, 147, 156, 184
asal bapak senang 116, 193
Asia and Southeast Asia 4, 5, 7, 8, 16, 32, 70–72, 94, 101, 104, 122, 161, 178, 181
Asmar 105
ASPENSI 36
Asvi Warman Adam 19, 181
Ateneo de Manila University 34, 45
Atmakusumah 111, 113–115, 117, 127, 131, 132
Atmodjo 105, 135
Australia 7, 46, 57, 68, 178
Austria, Ben 56
Austronesian 47, 71, 73, 74, 80, 88
Authoritarian and authoritarianism 4, 8, 9, 16, 29, 30, 38, 85, 89, 170

Burhanuddin M. Diah 114, 115, 117, 118, 131
babad 159
Bagong Kasaysayan 36, 98, 193
Bagong Kasaysaysan 193
Bailey, Thomas 51
Bali and Balinese 6, 8, 128, 132
Bambang Oetomo 152, 154
Bambang Purwanto 131
Bambang Sumadio 105
Banjar 130
Banten 32, 101
barangay 72, 73, 87, 89, 193

Index

Barnes, Barry 14, 15
Barnett, Milton 154, 157, 158
Barringer, Phillip 177
Barrows, David 85
base-culture 80
Batavia 24
Bauman, Zygmunt 1, 10, 12, 19
Bauzon, Leslie 36
bayi yang cacat 115
Benda, Harry 29, 30, 72, 101, 171
Benda, Julien 2, 171
Benitez, Conrado 34, 35, 68, 73, 75, 85
Berg, Cornelis Christiaan 126, 155, 159
Berger, Peter 13
Berita Buana 162
Berita Yudha 150
Berkeley, University of California 106, 107, 113
Bevernage, Berber 4
Beyer, Otley 70, 71
Biro Khusus, Special Bureau 134, 135, 139, 146, 193
Bogor 107, 135, 141
Boquiren, Rowena 64
Bosch, Frederick 128, 155
Boudreau, Vincent 29–31
Bourchier, David 6, 30
Bourdieu, Pierre 11, 13, 166, 171, 179, 180, 185
Britain and British 4, 25, 192
Brown, Colin 26, 192
Brown, James 187, 192
Brubaker, Roger 13, 180
Buchori 105, 107
buku babon 115, 116, 193

caciques 93, 193
Cagayan Valley 69
calculus 165, 181
Calderon, Felipe 36
capital and capitalism 87, 171, 180, 185
Cardinal Sin 59
cartography 190, 191
caste system 128
Catholic 23, 45, 59, 94
Cavite 76, 90
Cebuano 28
centrists 190, 192
Christianity 25, 52, 73, 75, 80
Churchill, Bernardita 94
Churchill, Winston 43, 50
civilization 1, 69, 70, 72, 87, 185
class 1, 5–7, 18, 23, 27, 31, 32, 77, 80, 83, 84, 90, 93, 94, 154, 171, 173, 186, 188, 191

Clio 6, 85, 89, 92, 184
Code of Kalantiao 70
Coedes, George 128
colonial 4, 16, 24–30, 32, 33, 37, 38, 53, 58, 69–77, 79, 81, 83, 85, 88–91, 103, 104, 126, 132, 138, 152, 153, 193, 195
Columbia University 33–35, 39, 47
communism 4, 7, 24, 26, 27, 31, 87, 133–135, 138, 139, 146–148, 157, 170, 193, 194
conservative 1, 83, 168, 190
Constantino, Letizia 6
Constantino, Renato 5, 26, 73, 77–80, 83, 90, 98
constructionist 165
constructivist 165
contemporary history 141, 144
context and contextuality 2, 3, 5, 8, 10, 13–17, 23, 24, 39, 52, 55, 59, 62, 67, 70, 74, 78, 80, 90, 99, 114, 125, 129, 133, 142, 152, 155, 158, 165–168, 170, 172, 174, 175, 185, 187, 188, 190
contingency 15, 165, 178
contradictions 10, 60, 84, 115, 137, 147–149, 166, 170, 176, 179, 181, 186, 187, 191
Cook, Tim 6
Cornell University 33, 34, 39, 56, 100, 106, 107, 134, 148
Crabtree, Charlotte 7, 177
Craig, Austin xx, 33
Cribb, Robert 26, 156
Cristobal, Adrian 64
Cubitt, Geoffrey 8
Curaming, Rommel 3, 34, 85, 93, 101, 132, 158

Daniel Dhakidae 6
decolonization 4, 29, 103, 104
de Joevenel, Bertrand 14
de la Costa, Horacio 34, 44, 45, 48, 49, 61, 171
de los Reyes, Isabelo 32, 41
de Man, Paul 20–22, 187, 192
de Morga, Antonio 32
de Ocampo, Esteban 37
Dery, Luis 54, 57, 63, 64
dictatorship 4, 29–31, 38, 62
Diliman 2, 45, 79
discourse 65, 77, 79, 82, 84, 87, 93, 99, 102, 129, 150, 157, 168, 177, 190
Djoko Suryo 34, 105, 108, 110, 111, 120
Djokosuyono 138
Doktorandus 34, 101, 119, 193
Doronila, Luisa 5, 6

Dutch 4, 24, 25, 29, 30, 99, 119, 125, 126, 138, 151, 193, 194
Duterte, Rodrigo 188–190

Edi Sedyawati 105
Edmonds, Sir Edward 6, 7
EDSA 29, 60, 193
Eka Darmaputera 27
elite and elitism 5, 7–10, 14, 26, 27, 29, 45, 77, 78, 82–84, 90, 93, 126
Elson, Robert 28, 156, 160
Emilia Wiesmar 105
empirical 1, 3, 6, 9, 24, 107, 152, 153, 167, 178, 184, 190
emplotment 107
epistemology 1, 12
ethics and ethical responsibility 10, 13, 18, 112, 115, 166, 173, 176, 184, 186, 188, 191
Ethical Policy 25, 193
ethos 173, 186, 188
Euro-American 4
Europe, European, Euro-centric 1, 33, 46, 47, 57, 71, 73, 105, 127, 152, 178
expert and expertise 46, 47, 50, 56, 88, 100, 108, 113, 137, 179–181

fact-checking 188, 189
fake news 149, 178, 188
Fascism 187
fatalism 23, 89
Feith, Herbert 27
feminists 1, 15
Fernandez, Leandro 34, 35, 73, 75, 85
feudalism 28, 30, 82, 84, 158
field 9, 11, 12, 14, 15, 134, 152, 163, 187
Filipinization 29, 193
Filipino 2, 5, 6, 23, 25–29, 32–35, 38, 43, 44, 46, 47, 49–51, 53, 61, 62, 68–89, 93, 94, 166, 167, 171, 176, 180, 193–195
Filipino Heritage 46, 68, 74, 193
Filipino historian 33–35, 38, 75, 76, 176
Filipino identity 69, 73, 88, 89, 167
Filipino ideology 61, 88
Filipino nationalism 25, 27, 28, 53, 72, 80, 82, 86, 93
Filipino psychology 79, 94
Filipino viewpoint 75–77, 79
foreign and foreigners 2, 5, 25, 47, 67, 72, 73, 76, 77, 80. 83, 87, 88, 113, 117, 125, 134, 140, 144, 146, 153, 154, 159, 169
foreign scholars 2, 32, 35, 131, 140, 159, 169

Foronda, Marcelino 34
Foucault 9–11, 14–16, 185, 191
Foulcher, Keith 27, 40
Friars, frailocracy, friarocracy 82, 84, 90 193
France 1, 27
Francisco, Adrianne 26
Frederick, William 154, 158, 172
French 7, 20, 55, 76
French, David 55, 76
Fuad Hasan 117

G30S, Gerakan 30 September 133
Gealogo, Francis 37, 93
geography 4, 23, 68, 69, 81, 126, 130
geology and geological period 53, 56, 69, 88, 166, 167
Gerwani or Gerakan Wanita Indonesia 136, 146, 150, 151, 157
Germany 25, 27
Goenawan Mohamad 156, 158
Gomburza 76
Gomez, Mariano 76
Goodfellow, Rob 133
gossip 12, 43, 99, 102, 179, 181
Green, Andrew 7, 182
Guerrero, Amado (aka Jose Maria Sison) 91
Guerrero. Milagros 83, 93
Guillermo, Alice 78
Guillermo, Ramon 31, 94

habitus 166
Hadimulmuno 105
Hadimulyo 105
Hamid Abdullah 122, 159
Hamlyn Group 46, 193
Harsja W. Bachtiar 102, 103, 119, 120
Harvard University 33, 34, 39, 45, 47, 53, 54, 56, 166
Hasan Djafar 105
Hassan Ambarry 105, 117
Hawaii 34, 71
Hedman, Eva-Lotta 28, 30
Hegelian 166
Hegemony 16, 24, 38
Heidegger 187
Heller, Agnes 15
Hidalgo, Cesar 47
Hindess, Barry 14
historians 2, 3, 6, 26, 32–36, 38, 43–45, 47, 48, 50, 51, 61, 71, 73, 75–78, 80, 100, 101, 104–106, 108, 111, 120, 129, 131, 133, 137, 139, 141, 142, 148–152, 154, 158, 167, 169, 172, 174, 176, 180, 194

historicist 154, 165, 172
historiography 3, 16, 17, 24, 32, 33, 38, 44, 48, 52, 53, 62, 63, 67, 68, 70, 73, 75–81, 85, 86, 90, 91, 93, 96, 114, 116, 125, 126, 128, 130, 131, 150, 152, 154, 155, 158, 166, 167, 172, 176, 180, 194, 195; Philippine historiography 48, 67, 73–76, 91, 167, 180; Indonesian historiography 38, 116, 130–132, 154, 172
history-writing project 2–4, 10, 16, 31, 33, 35, 38, 43–45, 48, 49, 55, 61, 87, 99–101, 104, 106, 108, 109, 116, 122, 158, 172, 175
Homo Academicus 11
homogenizing politics 90
homonization 69
Hufana, Alex 47, 56
humanization 53
hyper-inflation 140, 145
hyper-reality 31

Ibrahim Alfian 34, 39
ideology 1, 5, 6, 12, 27, 58, 61, 82–84, 87, 88, 170, 171, 194
Ileto, Reynaldo 9–11, 44, 45, 54, 56, 64, 65, 69–71, 78, 82, 87, 88, 94
ilustrados 27, 82–84, 93, 194
impartiality 1, 7, 11–13, 18, 23, 149, 150, 166, 171–173, 180, 186
India and Indians 4, 71, 72, 79, 127, 128, 132
indigenous 25, 26, 31, 49, 73–75, 79–81, 86–89, 91, 125, 128, 131, 167, 175, 195; politics of indigenism 86, 91
Indonesia 2–4, 6–9, 16, 23–39, 70–72, 92, 99–109, 113–116, 118–122, 125–133, 135–137, 140, 141, 143, 144, 146, 147, 150–155, 157–159, 166, 167, 169, 170, 172–174, 176–180, 184, 193–195
Indonesia-centrism 125–128, 130, 131, 167, 194
intellectual prostitutes 45, 155, 173, 189
intellectuals 1–3, 18, 23, 31, 32, 36, 43, 44, 48, 51, 55, 61, 64, 72, 78, 80, 103, 106, 108, 109, 132, 153, 155, 166, 170, 171, 173, 178–180, 185, 187–189; capital 171, 180; prostitute 155, 173, 189
Irma Notosusanto 119
Islam 3, 7, 26, 27, 52, 104, 105, 167, 193–195
Ismael Saleh 147
Istruktural 194

Japan 4, 5, 7, 27, 29, 33, 104, 118, 141, 144
Java and Javanese 24, 69, 126, 128, 132, 134, 135, 138, 147
Jesuits in the Philippines 45
Joaquin, Nick 76

Kahin, George 27, 154, 157, 158
Kalaw, Teodoro 85
Kammen, Douglas 156, 160
Kartawirana, A. 153
Kasaysayan 36, 193
Katipunan 64, 83, 84, 90, 94
Kemp-Welch, Tony 2, 20
keterbukaan 117
Klooster, H. A. J. 32, 116, 117, 121, 154
knowledge 1, 3, 5–18, 49, 50, 58, 62, 77, 88, 92, 93, 107, 114, 117, 139, 149, 155, 156, 165, 167–169, 171–173, 175, 177–179, 181, 184–186, 188–192; definition 12–14; expert knowledge 88; politics of knowledge 1, 171
Kompas 36, 100, 103, 111–116, 121, 122, 130, 143, 156, 157, 169
Konfrontasi 134, 136
Koonz, Claudia 62
Kumar, Ann 33, 41
Kuntowijoyo 33, 34, 155, 158
Kutai 128

Larkin, John 87
Latour, Bruno 14, 190, 191
leftist 2, 24, 36, 77, 85, 88, 90, 136, 137, 146, 147, 156, 189–192
legitimacy 2, 11, 13, 30, 82, 86, 104, 134, 142, 145
Leigh, Barbara 6
LEKRA 147
Leninism 87
liberal 1, 3, 18, 23, 84, 86, 87, 90, 130, 132, 144, 156, 171, 184, 186, 188–190; assumption 186, 188; democracy 87, 144; ethos 188; intellectuals 132; view 1, 171, 190
Lie Tek Tjeng 33, 34, 39
Linenthal, Edward 7, 177
local 28, 33, 35, 36, 53, 57, 67, 72, 87, 100, 101, 125–127, 131, 169, 193
logic 4, 13, 17, 18, 73, 78, 91, 93, 144, 155, 156, 165, 168, 172, 185, 188, 190, 191; of contemporaneity 144; of contextuality 165, 168; of geography 4; of nationalism 155; of power/knowledge 17, 168, 185, 188, 191

Index

Longino, Helen 12, 13, 21
Lubang Buaya 135, 138, 139, 150, 151, 157, 194
Luckmann, Thomas 13
Lukes, Steven 14, 21
lumads 80
Luzon 83

M. D. Sagimun 105–107, 123
Macalanang 58
Macdonald, Charles 25, 41
Macintyre, Stuart 7, 177
Madiun Affair 104, 134, 137–139, 161
Magdalena Manus 120
Majapahit 70, 128, 132, 155
Malacañang 46, 57, 58, 60, 61, 87, 194
Malay and Malaysia 4, 80, 134, 136, 147
Malayo-Polynesian 4, 71, 73
Malolos 44, 64
Maluku 24
Mangahas, Fe 58, 60, 64
Mannheim, Karl 13
Maoism 87
Maragtas 70
Marcos, Ferdinand 'Bongbong' Jr. 170
Marcos, Ferdinand 2, 5, 16, 17, 27, 29–31, 38, 39, 43–53, 55–64, 69–74, 81, 83–90, 92, 94, 166, 167, 170, 171, 174–178, 180, 186, 193, 194
Marcos, Imelda 44, 45, 63
Marcos diaries 39, 45, 51, 58, 61–63, 69, 88
Mark, Ethan 4
martial law 30, 38, 40, 46, 49–51, 55, 62, 65, 85, 87, 94, 167, 194
Marwati Djoened Poesponegoro 33, 34, 105, 111
Marxism 5, 31, 32, 78, 80, 87, 95
Masduki Baidlawi 103, 117, 122
Mashuri 100
massacre 133, 160
Mataram 130, 132, 155
McCoy, Alfred 25, 27, 29, 61, 96
McGregor, Katharine 2, 3, 5, 30, 37, 103, 104, 113, 120, 123, 138, 148, 156–158, 164
Melanesians 71
Meluruskan Sejarah 118
memory 8, 12, 50, 108, 150, 179
mestizos 26
meta-analytic 192
metaphor 30, 89, 115, 165, 181, 184
metaphysical 89, 166

methodology and methodological issues 1, 10, 13, 14, 59, 76–79, 106, 108, 114, 149, 150, 152, 167, 172, 179, 190; holism 14; individualism 14
metropole 27
Micronesians 71
middle-class 23
military 2, 6, 17, 21, 29, 31, 51, 55, 61, 78, 103, 104, 108–110, 112, 120, 133–136, 138, 139, 145–151, 157, 175, 193; historians 6, 61, 139, 148, 150
Mindanao 4, 31, 39, 72
Miseducation of Filipinos 5, 95
Moedjanto 157
Moela Marbun 105, 135, 157
Mohammad Nursam 123
Mohammad Ali 154, 158
Mohammad Hatta 138, 158
Mohammad Yamin 32, 153, 172
Mojares, Resil 32, 82
Mollucas 76
moral, morality, moral issues 18, 30, 53, 62, 75, 76, 109, 133, 141, 171–173, 181, 185–189
MSI, Masyarakat Sejarawan Indonesia 36, 37, 105, 194
Muller, J. 187
multi-dimensional 17, 47, 107–109, 117, 125, 126, 129, 131, 132, 137, 141, 143, 144, 154, 167, 170, 175, 176, 194
Murba 136
museums 2, 150, 157
Muslims 27, 31, 52, 73, 80, 90, 126, 138, 193, 194
mutualism 9

Nāgarakṛtāgama 155, 159
Nakpil, Carmen 65
narrative 4, 8, 24, 30, 47, 52, 53, 73, 76, 77, 91, 93, 109, 125, 129, 132, 135, 137, 140, 141, 144, 147, 148, 150, 151, 157, 160, 163, 175, 176, 194
narrative-chronological approach 130, 141, 143, 145
nation and national 2, 4–6, 8, 16, 25–28, 30, 36, 37, 40–42, 46, 48, 49, 56, 57, 60, 67, 69, 70, 72–77, 80–85, 89–91, 96–99, 100, 103–108, 113–116, 118–126, 128–130, 134, 138, 144, 153–155, 158–164, 169, 177, 181, 194, 195; community 27, 74, 75, 83, 84; historians 122, 159; historiography 42, 182; history 2, 41, 48, 65, 97, 99, 100, 103, 104, 106, 107, 113, 115, 116, 119,

120, 122–125, 130, 153, 158–164, 182, 194; identity 5, 20, 69, 81, 85, 126, 195; ideology 27, 162; integration 66, 80, 98, 129; nationalism 4, 6, 16, 19, 21, 23–28, 38, 39, 41, 42, 44, 52, 53, 55, 74, 76, 82, 85, 86, 90, 91, 93–95, 97, 133, 153, 155, 158, 159, 167, 194; nationalist 4, 7, 16, 19, 24, 26–29, 32, 33, 38, 41, 45, 48, 52, 53, 69, 71–73, 75, 78–80, 89, 91, 93, 95, 99, 103, 104, 122, 133, 153–155, 158–161, 167, 168, 176; nation-building 23, 72–75, 79, 80, 164, 167; nations-of-intent 26, 40, 42; revolution 25, 95, 96; unity 72, 90, 138, 153, 158
National Historical Commission 37
Navarro, Atoy 93
Negritos 70
neo-colonial 29
Nietzsche 187
nihilism 187
Nugroho Notosusanto 2, 17, 18, 32–36, 100, 101, 105, 113, 127–129, 132–137, 139–143, 145, 147–151, 155–157, 161–163, 166, 169–176, 180, 181, 189, 190

objectivity 1, 12, 18, 61, 103, 115, 116, 122, 141, 142, 145, 149, 150, 152, 163, 166, 171, 173, 179, 180, 186
Ocampo, Ambeth 32, 45, 63
official historian 2, 45, 100, 101, 103, 113, 115, 119, 120, 124, 131, 132, 158, 163, 164, 169, 172, 176, 182, 183, 194
official history 2, 3, 6, 17, 20, 22, 114, 135, 137, 139, 147–149, 151, 155, 156, 176, 184
oligarchic 85, 86, 90
Onghokham 34, 39
Ong Hok Ham 33
opposition 1, 3, 11, 18, 27, 31, 38, 79, 84, 125, 132, 136, 153, 170, 184, 190
Orientalism 9, 27

Pagan 70
Pakistan 50
Palaeolithic 127
Pancasila 27, 30, 100, 157
pang-kami 93
Pantayong Pananaw, From-Us-For-Us Perspective 36, 78–80, 93, 94, 96–98, 180, 182, 194
Papanek, Hannah 158
Paras-Perez, Rodolfo 47, 53, 56, 63, 64
parliamentary 29, 30, 134–136

parliamentary democracy 29, 134, 136
Paschalis Maria Laksono 6, 20
PCGG, Presidential Commission on Good Governance 63, 96
pelurusan sejarah 179
Pe-Pua, Rogelia 94, 97
periodization 58, 67, 73–75, 93, 106, 127, 160
personalism 8, 10
philosophy and philosophers 12, 16, 78, 100, 101, 153, 158, 160, 163, 164, 182, 184, 187, 192
Philpott, Simon 9
PKI, Partai Komunis Indonesia 104, 133–136, 138, 139, 145–148, 150, 151, 157, 169, 175, 178, 179
PKP, Partido Komunista ng Pilipinas 31
pluralism 7, 10
Poerbatjaraka 99
political 1–18, 23, 24, 26–31, 38, 43, 45, 46, 50–52, 55, 58, 59, 61, 62, 67, 68, 70, 73, 74, 78, 80–82, 85–93, 99, 103, 104, 108, 109, 114, 117, 119, 121, 125–127, 130–140, 143–145, 147–150, 152, 153, 155–158, 165–177, 179–181, 184–191, 193; politicians 30, 50, 81, 90, 117, 171–173, 176; politicization 15; politicized 15, 101, 134, 167; politics-scholarship 130; politics of knowledge 1, 171
postcolonialism, postcolonial theory 1, 4, 9, 10, 22, 28, 38, 79, 91, 167, 182, 188, 190
postmodernism 85, 188, 192
poststructuralism 1, 10, 187, 188
power, definition 14–16
power/knowledge 5, 6, 9–14, 20, 44, 92, 156, 165, 168, 181, 184, 185, 187, 188, 191, 192
powerful and powerless 3, 6, 8, 10, 14, 26, 38, 51, 62, 77, 92, 128, 149, 171, 178, 180, 184–186
power-knowledge analytics 1, 5–12, 14–16, 92, 155, 156, 165, 168, 173, 181, 184, 187, 188
power of scholars and scholarship 3, 10–13, 18, 38, 49, 86, 132, 152, 156, 165–170, 171–173, 175–181, 184–186, 188, 189, 191, 192
power relations 1, 7, 9–12, 14, 15, 17, 18, 30, 38, 43, 44, 92, 99, 102, 149, 156, 165, 168, 170, 173, 176–179, 181, 187, 188, 190, 191
Priyambudi Sulistiyanto 182

Index   203

processual-narrative 129, 194
professional 6, 24, 30, 32, 33, 35, 36, 38, 44, 50, 55, 59, 61, 73, 101, 102, 149, 150, 166
progressive 1, 3, 29, 168, 188–191
propaganda 6, 49, 61, 75, 83, 84, 89, 92, 103, 118, 119, 134, 137, 139, 141–143, 146, 150–152, 156, 169, 175, 176, 179, 180; self-propaganda 90; history-as-propaganda 150
proto-Filipino 72
PSPB 30
PSSC 36
pujangga 152, 155

Quiason, Serafin 46, 47, 53–56, 58–60, 63, 64
Quibuyen, Floro 25, 26, 32, 42, 96, 97
Quiros, Conrado 49, 50, 61, 64, 65

Rafael, Vicente 42, 89, 97
rebellion 28, 39, 138
relativism 166, 171, 172, 179, 186–188
Rempel, William 61, 63, 87
Resink, Gertrudes 99
revolt and revolution 25–29, 39, 41, 44, 55, 61, 64, 65, 67, 69–71, 77, 78, 82–85, 87, 88, 90, 91, 95–99, 101, 123, 129, 130, 137, 138, 160, 164, 183, 193–195
rhetoric and rhetorical 5, 29, 50, 89, 135, 173, 194
Richard Leirissa 131
rightist 85, 88, 190, 192
Roces, Alfredo 46, 47, 63, 68
Rochmani Santoso 105
Rockefeller Fellowship 101
Rodriguez-Tatel, Mary Jane 93, 97
Romanticism 1

Saburo Ienaga 20
Said, Edward 2, 9, 10
Salazar, Zeus 18, 34, 47, 48, 52–56, 58, 59, 63, 64, 69, 71, 72, 75, 79, 80, 85, 87, 91, 93, 167, 172, 173, 176, 180
Saleh As'ad Djamhari 105, 140
Sammut, Jeremy 7, 22
Sanusi Pane 32
Sartono 17, 33–36, 100–114, 116, 119–124, 126, 127, 129–132, 141–144, 154, 158, 159, 167–169, 172, 174, 176, 180

Sartono Kartodirdjo 17, 33–36, 39, 99–101, 105–107, 110, 113, 116, 120, 126–129, 132, 154, 158, 159, 172
Schmitt, Carl 15
scholarly community 92, 110, 167, 171–174, 178, 179, 190, 191
scholarly practice 3, 10, 18, 177, 191
scholarship and politics 1, 3, 152, 170, 181, 190
Schumacher 32, 78, 82, 93
scientific history 1, 11–13, 18, 35, 38, 101, 150, 153–155, 158, 166, 167, 172, 178
secessionism 28, 31, 72, 90
Sedijono 109
sejarawan murni 101, 194
Sentot Setyasiswanto 179, 182
Setyadi 131, 163
Shalom, Stephen 29
Sikolohiyang Pilipino, Filipino Psychology 79, 94, 195
simulacrum 149, 156
Singhasari 132
Siswadhi 103, 115, 121, 127, 131, 132
Smail, John 72
SNI, Sejarah Nasional Indonesia 2–4, 17, 18, 33, 92, 99, 100, 102–105, 111, 113–122, 125–127, 129, 130, 132, 133, 135–137, 141–144, 146–152, 155–158, 165–171, 173–177, 180, 184–186, 194; comparison with other versions 143–148; historiographic contexts 125–132; implementation and dynamics 105–113; inception and driving forces 100–105; political contexts 133–143, 149–155; reactions 113–118
SNI-SMA 137, 143, 157, 169
SNI-SMP 119, 136–143, 146, 147, 150, 151, 156, 157, 162, 169, 174
Sobral, Carlos 36
sociology of knowledge 1, 5, 13, 20, 21, 35, 102, 119, 165, 177, 192
Soedjatmoko 106, 152–154, 158, 170, 172
Soedjatmoko-Yamin debate 153
Soeharto 151, 163
Soejatmi Satari 105
Soekarto 105
Soeroto 111, 124, 154, 158–160, 164, 172, 182, 183
Sony Karsono 169, 179
Sorbonne 33 34, 47
Spaniards 4, 24, 25, 27, 68, 70–76, 80, 82, 84, 88, 89, 93, 167, 193, 194

Index

Srivijaya 70, 72, 128
state-formation 24, 28, 72, 75, 81
state–intellectual relations 3, 5, 6, 18
state-sponsored project 4, 10, 16, 19, 167, 172
statism 5–7, 10
Steinberg, David Joel 26
Suara Merdeka 122, 159, 162
Suara Pembaruan 122, 159, 162
subjectivity 114, 133, 152, 153, 186
subject-position 23
Suharto 2, 5, 31, 111, 113, 114, 116, 122, 133, 135, 145, 146, 151, 152, 156–158
Sukarno 27, 30–32, 107, 108, 113, 114, 120, 133–136, 138–140, 145, 146, 149–151, 175, 194
Sultan Hamengku Buwono IX 151
Sumadio 105
Sumantri 133, 140, 157
Sumatra 4, 24, 132
Sumpah Permuda 27, 40, 195
Sunardi 135
Surjomihardjo, Abdurrachman 105, 107, 110–116, 119–122, 124, 130, 154, 158, 164, 172, 174, 176
Suryanegara 103, 124
Sutjipto Wirjosuparto 105, 131, 155, 159, 164, 183
Sutrisno 157, 164
Suzuki, Mary 26
Syamdani 111, 124
Syam Kamaruzaman 146
Syariah 27, 195
Syarif Thayeb 113

Tadhana 2–4, 16–18, 29, 31, 43, 44, 47–49, 51, 53, 54, 57–63, 65–69, 71–75, 79–92, 94, 96–98, 103, 118, 125, 156, 165–168, 170, 171, 173–177, 180, 184–186, 189, 190, 193, 195; dynamics 56–62; historiographic contexts 67–84; Iginuhit ng Tadhana 89; motivations 43–45, 49–56, 121; political contexts 85–92
Tagalog 23, 28, 83, 89, 93, 193–195
Tan, Samuel 47, 53, 55, 57, 60, 63, 64, 80, 98
Taufik Abdullah 26, 33–35, 37, 39, 99, 100, 103, 105, 107, 110–112, 116, 117, 119–122, 126, 133, 154, 157–159, 163
textbooks 2, 3, 5–7, 44, 45, 70, 77, 85, 93, 99, 100, 104, 118, 119, 125, 136, 137, 141–143, 168, 169, 174, 177
Thaveeporn Vasavakul 7

theory and theorizing 1, 9–11, 14, 15, 58, 70, 71, 79, 91, 93, 106, 115, 129, 152, 156, 165, 167, 168, 177, 187, 190, 191
Thomas, Megan 27
Thucydides 172
Timor-Leste 26
Titans 184
TNI, Tentara Nasional Indonesia 138
transparency 6, 18, 23, 89, 137, 172, 185, 188, 192
TRD, Today's Revolution: Democracy 61, 69, 87
tripartite view of history 75, 76, 97, 195
tri-sectoral comunities 80
Tri Wahyuning Irsyam 120
Trump, Donald 178, 185, 188–190, 192
truth, truth-making 1, 2, 11–13, 17, 20, 22, 44, 52, 59, 61, 85, 88–90, 102, 111, 149, 156, 157, 165, 169, 170, 179, 182, 184, 186, 188, 190
Truth and Reconcilliation Commission 48, 179
Tugu, Bogor 107, 113, 123, 124, 135, 141, 160–163

UGM, Universitas Gadjah Mada 33, 34, 39, 100, 102, 105, 120, 123, 129–131, 154, 161, 162
UI, Universitas Indonesia 33, 34, 39, 100–103, 119, 120, 123, 129, 162
Umar Zain 99, 100, 104, 109, 113, 124, 133, 164
Uka Tjandrasasmita 103, 105, 106, 113, 124, 131
UP, University of the Philippines 2, 33–36, 45
UST, University of Santo Tomas 32, 33, 94
Untung Syamsuri 135, 139, 146, 164

Vandenberghe, Frederic 11, 12
van Leur, Jacob Cornelis 72
Veneracion, Jaime 49, 66, 73, 82, 98
Vickers, Adrian 101, 158
Vico, Giambattista 172
Villan, Vic 93

Wartenberg, Thomas 14
Weekley, Kathleen 4, 31
Weldon, Kevin 46, 48
Wertheim, W. F. 101, 156, 164
west, western 2, 4, 14, 20, 24, 69, 70, 77, 79, 87, 94, 114, 172, 178, 185

William Howard Taft Paper 57, 182
Wolin, Richard 187
women 146, 150, 151
Wood, Michael 2, 3, 5
Wouters, Nico 4
Wuryantoro 105

Yale University 33, 34, 100, 106
Yosef Djakababa 157

Yusmar Basri 105, 111, 113, 120, 136, 137, 140

Zafra, Nicolas 26, 34, 35, 68, 73, 75, 79, 83, 93, 94, 98
Zaide, Gregorio 26, 33–35, 68, 73–79
Zamora, Jacinto 76
Zamora, Mario 70
zeitgeist 4, 152, 158
Zurbuchen, Mary 22

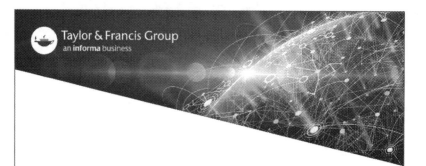

Printed in the United States
by Baker & Taylor Publisher Services